PRINCE OF PUBLISHERS

PRINCE OF PUBLISHERS

A BIOGRAPHY OF GEORGE SMITH

Jenifer Glynn

Allison & Busby
LONDON · NEW YORK

First published in Great Britain 1986 by
Allison and Busby Limited
6a Noel Street, London W1V 3RB
and distributed in the USA by
Schocken Books Inc.
62 Cooper Square, New York 10003

Copyright © 1986 by Jenifer Glynn

British Library Cataloguing in Publication Data:
Glynn, Jenifer
Prince of publishers: a biography of
George Smith
1. Smith, George, *1824–1901*   2. Publishers
and publishing —— Great Britain ——
Biography
I. Title
070.5′092′4   Z325.S65/

ISBN 0-85031-697-9

Set in 11/12pt Sabon by
AKM Associates (UK) Ltd, Ajmal House, Hayes Road, Southall, London
Printed and bound in Great Britain by
Billings and Sons Ltd, Hylton Road, Worcester

To Ian

Contents

Preface

George Smith was a dominating figure in literary life throughout Queen Victoria's reign. He appears – as publisher and friend – so often in literary memoirs that it is surprising to find that he himself has had no biography. The material is there, in his own manuscript *Recollections of a Long and Busy Life*, in Sidney Lee's *Memoir* written as a preface for the second supplement of the *Dictionary of National Biography*, and in many letters from his authors.

Parts of the *Recollections* were used by Leonard Huxley in his privately printed *History of the House of Smith Elder* in 1923, and parts by Robertson Scott in *The Story of the Pall Mall Gazette* in 1950; the rest has never been used, and I am very grateful to George Smith's granddaughter, the late Mrs Seton Gordon, for allowing me to make use of it now.

I should like to thank Messrs John Murray for their great kindness in allowing me to search through and quote from many letters in their archives; the National Library of Scotland for access to the Smith Elder archives and for permission to quote from many letters there; the Brontë Society for allowing me to quote from letters and manuscripts in the Parsonage Museum at Haworth and in the Brontë Society *Transactions*; Mrs Belinda Norman-Butler for permission to quote letters from her grandmother Anne Thackeray Ritchie; Manchester University Press for permission to quote extensively from *The Letters of Mrs Gaskell* (edited by J.A.V. Chapple and Arthur Pollard); Harvard University Press for permission to quote from *The Letters and Private Papers of W.M. Thackeray* (edited by Gordon Ray); Oxford University Press for permission to quote from the Pilgrim Edition of the *Letters of Charles Dickens*; Mrs Gordon Haight for permission to quote from her late husband's biography of George Eliot; Messrs John Murray for permission to quote two letters

[vii]

from *Browning to his American Friends* (edited by Gertrude Reese Hudson).

For the photograph of George Smith I am indebted to the Brontë Society.

Jenifer Glynn
Cambridge, September 1986.

Chronology

1861	Firm's turnover £405,000
1862	Thackeray resigns from *Cornhill*; Publication of *Romola*
1865	First number of *Pall Mall Gazette*
1866	Firm's turnover £627,000
1867	Browning leaves Chapman for Smith Elder
1868	Firm splits, King taking the Indian agency and leaving Smith the publishing
1869	Attempt at morning edition of *Pall Mall Gazette*
1870–9	Shipping Agency
1871	Leslie Stephen becomes editor of *Cornhill*
1872	Start of Apollinaris deal
1872	Firm buys up medical publications
1873	Marriage of daughter Dolly to Henry Yates Thompson; Death of George Smith's mother
1873	Quarrel with Ruskin
1880	Yates Thompson takes over *Pall Mall Gazette*
1882	James Payn becomes editor of *Cornhill*
1885	Publication of first volume of *Dictionary of National Biography*
1888	Publication of *Robert Elsmere*
1892	*Pall Mall Gazette* sold to W.W. Astor

I

Beginnings

George Smith, "Prince of Publishers", was the ideal Victorian business-man. Born in 1824 above the shop in Fenchurch Street where his father and Alexander Elder were selling their stationery and books, he built up a successful publishing and export firm and died, in the same year as the Queen, a millionaire with a mansion in Park Lane. He had launched Charlotte Brontë and published almost every important Victorian novelist except Dickens, he had founded the *Cornhill Magazine* and the *Pall Mall Gazette*, and he had started and financed the *Dictionary of National Biography*.

This Publisher's Progress, where hard work, skill and generosity brought their due rewards, could itself have been the outline for one of the novels of his day; it is the story of a boy who left school turbulently at fourteen but who was ambitious, and lucky enough to be given the opportunity of working in a field that completely suited him. Publishing brought him a happy combination of personal friendship, literary heroes and business challenge. He became wealthy from a variety of business activities, and he used that wealth to back his publishing and to live comfortably and hospitably, at a time when comfort and hospitality were respected and well-understood virtues.

One of his authors, who arrived in England from Australia in the last years of George Smith's life and became a close friend, persuaded him to start his memoirs. This was Dr W.H. Fitchett, the writer of a series of patriotic stories that appeared in the *Cornhill Magazine* at the time of the Boer War. Smith's *Recollections of a Long and Busy Life* were dictated to Fitchett, and four chapters of them, with some revisions, were printed in the *Cornhill* in 1900 and 1901. The rest have never been revised, and ramble as such reminiscences might; but the *Recollections* are the main source of information about Smith, and have been used extensively in this biography. They give a contented, slightly self-satisfied picture, looking back over a life that had been interesting, enjoyable, and well-spent.

The first George Smith, father of the Prince of Publishers, was born in Scotland in the year of the French Revolution. He should have inherited a small farm, but it had been "managed with ill-fortune" before he was old enough to take it over; instead of becoming a farmer he was apprenticed to Isaac Forsyth, a bookseller and banker in Elgin.

The younger George Smith remembered Mr Forsyth:

> Although he was stone deaf when I knew him he took a keen interest in everything passing in the world. I stayed with him for some time when I was about sixteen. He was very hospitable, and I should have enjoyed his constant dinner parties more if he had not insisted on my sitting beside him and writing down on his slate anything that seemed to excite amusement at the table. "What are they laughing at, Geordie – write it down."

Smith senior left Scotland for London when his apprenticeship was over, but Isaac Forsyth remained a friend.

Arriving in London by boat, Smith set out from the docks with his bundle of belongings to look for lodgings. He was quick-tempered, and not amused by the sailors who taunted him, calling: "Any old clothes to sell?" In no time he became involved in a fight, and although he was triumphant it was a tough start to life in London.

His first job was with Rivington's, the publishers. Mr Rivington, wrote George Smith in his *Recollections*,

> was an energetic and clever man of business, but he was eccentric and blunt, and employed methods towards his staff which in these days would be regarded as extraordinary. If a clerk applied for an increase of salary old Mr Rivington would ask, with an air of astonishment, if he had not enough to live on, and, if

so, why he wanted more? "How many rolls do you eat for breakfast?" he demanded of one such candidate. "Two, sir," was the humble reply. "Why," the head of the firm exclaimed indignantly, "I never eat more than one myself! Surely if one is enough for me it is enough for you?"

From Rivington, Smith moved on to work for John Murray – Byron's John Murray – and got on extremely well with him. Long after, at Murray's Coffee-house Sale Dinners, his son remembers, "he would, when he became genial after dinner, bawl out to me, 'Come and sit beside me, young Smith,' and he would talk to me about my father. Mr Murray was sometimes more than genial on these occasions and used to make the most atrocious jokes."

John Murray's shop, according to the advertisement first put out in 1768,

> Sells all new Books and Publications, Fits up Public or Private Libraries in the neatest manner with Books of the choicest Editions, the best Print, and the richest Bindings, Also, Executes East India or Foreign Commissions by an assortment of Books and Stationery suited to the Market or Purpose for which it is destined: all at the most reasonable rates.

This same mixture of publishing and East India commissions later reappeared with Smith & Elder.

The partnership with Alexander Elder started in 1816, when he and Smith took a small bookselling and stationery shop in Fenchurch Street. For the first year or so Elder worked there full-time, and Smith only joined him in the evenings after he had finished at Murray's. But Smith soon became the dominant partner. In 1818, when he married, he and his wife lived over the shop and there, on 19 March 1824, his second child George was born. George seems sensitive about this, and is anxious to point out that in those days it was highly respectable for merchants and bankers to live over their places of work: "still in the old buildings in some parts of the City you can see the carved ceilings and the handsome decorations, showing that what to-day are mere offices, a generation ago were comfortable, if not handsome and stately, dwelling places." Not that the apartment over the Fenchurch Street shop was likely to have been stately, and George himself described the shop as small. Soon after George was born, the family moved to live over the firm's new and grander premises at

[15]

65 Cornhill; in 1841 they took a house in Denmark Hill, but had been there only three years when George Smith senior had to retire through ill-health. He moved to a smallholding at Box Hill, where he died in 1846.

George Smith's father had even more than a normal share of nineteenth-century seriousness and worthiness. He worried over his business, and lacked his son's liveliness and flair. For him "punctuality, a good hand-writing, and a sober demeanour" were the important virtues. The first entry in his ledger was an earnest and rather touching prayer that "in the transactions recorded in its pages there might be nothing dishonourable".

It must have been George's mother who gave George his enterprise and his strength of character. He greatly admired his mother, and describes her as brave, shrewd, strong-minded and calm. She is shown in her fifties as the Mrs Bretton of *Villette*, both in her own character and in her close relationship with an able and energetic son. George gave her maiden name, Murray, as a middle name to all his children, and from 1873 added it to his own signature. She was the daughter of a successful and somewhat eccentric glassware manufacturer, who had retired to the coast between Margate and Ramsgate.

My mother told us that kegs of brandy and other smuggled goods were often hidden in the woods of their grounds, and that my grandfather prudently abstained from noticing them when he took his early walks. He was no doubt watched, for on several occasions kegs of brandy were sent to the house with Captain's compliments. I gathered from what my mother said that the presents were accepted without much scruple. I have a portrait of my grandfather done in pastel. He has a shrewd expression and a good head, not handsome, but rather good-looking. He had a strong dash of eccentricity. He had given my grandmother an unusually costly engagement ring. When they were on their honeymoon this ring was suddenly missed. Great was the excitement in the Hotel in which they were staying! A Bow Street runner was sent for, every search was made, a handsome reward was offered; but no trace of the ring could be found and the youthful bride's honeymoon was quite overcast by the tragedy of this loss. Many years after, when my grandfather died, the ring was found carefully packed away amongst his deeds, with a little piece of paper round it. On the paper was written, "Ladies who leave rings on wash-stands don't deserve to have rings."

Mrs Smith has been accused of spoiling her son. He had a severe illness, "a brain-fever", at the age of six, which made her perhaps over-protective

[16]

and over-anxious to avoid upsetting him when he was small. It did not, however, stop her from sending him to boarding school, and she hoped this would lead to university and the Bar. When he was sent home from school in disgrace at the age of fourteen these ambitions had to be abandoned, but his parents do not seem to have been too shocked. George felt that the fault lay with the school rather than with himself – that he suffered from an excess of high spirits and a lack of sympathetic teachers.

Academically, he had not done too badly. Always first or second in class, he had worked hard, had a good memory, had learnt his classics and his French, and had had a real pleasure in studying Euclid. But his school memories seem dominated by fights, by practical jokes, and by a "Row Society" which the boys organized, with George as its secretary, to keep the school in a state of disobedience and chaos. George says that he had a reputation for fighting:

> The fact was I was exceedingly tall for my age and I was as thin and lanky as I was tall – I was nearly six feet high by the time I was sixteen years of age, and was so thin that literally I could make the middle fingers and thumbs of my two hands meet round my waist. Now in our schoolboy code a boy had to be prepared to fight one of his own height, irrespective of other dimensions or of age . . . . I had no real love for fighting yet I found myself engaged in incessant combats; and, as the physical odds were badly against me, I was more often than not beaten but never without a stubborn fight.

At a time when Tom Hughes was at Rugby, and Thackeray's nose was suffering at Charterhouse, fights were a standard part of the school scene. All the same, George's fighting was so excessive that his parents were summoned to the school. His tolerant mother was relieved that the complaint was so trivial. "Is *that* all," she said to the master. "I am sorry if he is a quarrelsome boy, but I thought from your sending for us that he had been guilty of something very disgraceful."

It was the Row Society that ended George's school career. "The breaking-up was near", he wrote,

> and the Row Society determined to contribute to the proceedings some highly original features. Their plans, duly recorded in formal "minutes", and in my handwriting, were discovered by the master, who, uneasy as to our intentions, examined my desk. He determined that the breaking-up should not have the

[17]

advantage of my presence and assistance, and he wrote to my parents asking that I should be withdrawn before the breaking-up arrived. He added that the best thing they could do with me was to send me to sea; on the whole, a foolish counsel, as I venture to think that I have been of greater service to the world – in spite of all my faults – than if I had become "food for fishes".

II

Early Days with Smith & Elder

So in 1838, at the age of fourteen, George Smith was taken into the family firm as an apprentice to a new partner, Patrick Stewart.

Stewart, a Scot like the other two partners, was the son of an Edinburgh clergyman and the ward of Aeneas Mackintosh, the head of the firm of Mackintosh & Co. of Calcutta. This connection with Mackintosh changed the whole future of Smith & Elder. Under Stewart's influence the export of books and stationery, which they had already started for Peter Milne's firm at Calcutta, expanded enormously; goods of every possible sort were dealt with, a banking business was established, and Smith & Elder became one of the main Indian agencies. This financial success gave a background which encouraged enterprising publishing, and the dual nature of the business continued until the publishing and the foreign agency work were separated in 1868.

Fifteen years older than George, Patrick Stewart combined business ability, charm and social success in a way that the younger man admired and envied. As his pupil, George looked up to him and "almost worshipped him".

George Smith's father, with his belief in thoroughness, made his son learn every detail of the running of the business. He was taught how to do up parcels, how to make and mend quills, how to bind books. Since it was before the days of copying-presses he also had the job of copying all foreign letters, and he began to model his business style and his handwriting on those of Stewart. Even so, he had not enough work to fill his long hours – 7.30 in the morning till 8 o'clock at night, with half-hour breaks for breakfast and tea, and an hour for dinner.

George used his spare time well. In the office, particularly in the slack period before breakfast, he would read the Bible from end to end, and in the dinner hour he would join some friends for riding lessons. Being young, and with a good memory, his biblical knowledge stuck. "Many years afterwards", he wrote,

> I was at a dinner party, the Dean of Westminster being one of the guests. Someone quoted the phrase about being "saved by the skin of his teeth", whereupon one of the guests remarked, "What wonderful phrases these Americans do invent!" In that gathering nobody but the Dean and myself, it turned out, knew that the phrase came from the Book of Job. There is, no doubt, a touch of modern, and very American, exaggeration in the words. The Dean was so pleased with my scriptural knowledge – a knowledge entirely due to the tedium of the too long hours of my apprenticeship – that he sent me next day, as a present, his commentary on Job.

Riding, George considered, helped to keep him fit and energetic, and it gave him lifelong pleasure:

> I have always accustomed myself, even when most pressed by business, to a certain amount of horse exercise [he wrote] and am now the oldest rider in Rotten Row, that is to say, I have been in the habit of riding there for more years than anyone else among its habitués. It is more than fifty years since I used first to take my ride in the Park before breakfast. I am not the only business man who has learnt by experience the tonic a morning ride is for a busy brain-worker. My sister rode with me at one period, and every morning the late Mr W.H. Smith, who was afterwards Leader of the House of Commons, fell in by my side. He usually went off saying, "Now I must go off to lunch." "Lunch" at 8 a.m. sounds sufficiently odd, and my sister said to me at last, "How strange it is that that gentleman mistakes lunch for breakfast so persistently! He means he must go home to breakfast." "No", I said, "he means lunch. He breakfasts every morning at four o'clock, and is in the Strand at his business by half past four; lunches at nine, and dines at three." Mr Smith was then building up his great newspaper-distributing business.

[20]

George's other recreation, in apprentice days, was theatre-going. He seems to remember the actresses rather than the plays; enthusiasm for Helen Faucit (who later, as Theodore Martin's wife, became one of his circle of friends) would even attract him to the theatre four times in a week. Years later, in 1878, Helen Martin and George Smith were to be the godparents for Thackeray's granddaughter, Hester Ritchie.

One of George's most vivid early memories in the firm was of Lieutenant Waghorn,[1] "a sailor-like man, short and broad, excitable in a high degree and of tremendous energy", who was famous for opening the overland route to India. Smith & Elder became involved in Waghorn's undertakings. They were his London agents, they came to his rescue when money was short, and they paid his wife's allowance when he was away. All this was when George was young, but it was so very much the sort of enterprise that appealed to him and inspired him that it is worth saying more about Waghorn, and the business atmosphere that George was brought up in.

Thomas Waghorn was born in 1800, the son of a butcher in Chatham, and joined the navy as a midshipman at the age of twelve. Before he was forty he had managed to transform the whole system of communication between England and India – not an easy achievement for a sailor without money or influential friends.

In the navy, Waghorn had seen a well-run mail service to the West Indies, and when he later joined the Bengal Pilot Service the slowness and inefficiency of communications with the East led him to bombard his superiors with reforming ideas. He campaigned for steamships, linking with an overland route across Egypt, to cut out the long journey round the Cape. Both the Post Office and the East India Company directors clearly found him pushing and tiresome; they obstructed his plans, and complained that he would not take no for an answer. This was certainly true.

In 1829, after two years of unpaid leave when he was endlessly churning out schemes and pestering his superiors, he was at last given his chance. He was sent by the East India Company to travel through Egypt to Bombay, in order to deliver despatches and to report on the practicability of navigating the Red Sea. Determined to prove his point, he set off at four days' notice and by a mixture of exotic boats, donkeys and camels, and with no prearranged connections, reached Bombay in under five months, including a six-week delay with fever at Jeddah.

After this remarkable journey, Waghorn produced a pamphlet to campaign for the overland route. "The feeling in India is most ardent for it. I have convened large public meetings all over the Peninsula. Lord William Bentinck was enthusiastic, and has done me the honour to predict that if ever the object should be accomplished, it would be by the man who had navigated the Red Sea in an open boat." But the chairman of the East India Company did not share his enthusiasm, and told him that

> the Governor-General of India and the people of India had nothing to do with the East India House, and that if I did not go back and join their Pilot Service, to which I belonged, I should receive "such a communication from that House as would be by no means agreeable to me". On the instant I penned my resignation, and, placing it in his hands, then gave utterance to the sentiment which activated me from that moment . . . that I would establish the Overland Route, in spite of the India House.

Having failed to get official backing, Waghorn then went to Egypt to see how he could manage without it, financed by a few businessmen who believed in him. This is where Smith & Elder came in. The scheme involved establishing agencies at every port – Gibraltar, Marseilles, Malta – across Egypt, and in English cities, with headquarters at 65 Cornhill. In 1835 he offered to race the regular mail, taking letters at 5s 6d. He won the race by ten days, and then started advertising his services. Smith & Elder printed his circulars and pamphlets. George Smith and an office boy stamped "Care of Mr Waghorn" on the letters, and registered them on Waghorn's system so that they could be traced. Smith writes that he himself "was eager – boy-like – to take part in this contest with time and space. My ambition was to ride in one of the expresses between Paris and Marseilles, and I remember a fit of sulks which lasted for more than a week because my father refused his consent to this performance."

Return letters, disinfected in Malta and pricked to "let out pestilential airs", were sometimes alarmingly expensive. "The cost of his trip", wrote Smith, "was distributed over the number of letters he carried, and charged as 'postage' . . . . I can even now remember my father's face when he opened a letter brought by Waghorn and containing a duplicate draft for three or

four pounds, the 'postage' for which was assessed at something like £25!"
But speed was becoming important.

Something of the spirit of modern trade, of its haste and keenness, its eagerness
to outrace not only all competitors but time itself, was already visible in the
operations of the firm. It seemed a great matter to them to get periodicals and
parcels off to India up to the latest moment, and I can remember seeing a
postchaise standing at the door of the shop in Cornhill to take parcels of the
"Quarterly" or "Edinburgh Review", I forget which, off to Deal to catch a fast
ship there. It must, I suppose, have contained some article of special interest to
the Indian public, but it was an expensive way of sending a magazine, and
could only "pay" in the sense that getting the Review to India before any other
agent won for the firm a reputation for energy and enterprise.

For a few years Waghorn flourished, and he kept traffic flowing freely in
spite of political troubles between Turkey and Egypt. He used his surplus
energy to organize tourism in Egypt, building or buying hotels and
resthouses, running river steamboats, and coming into contact with many
distinguished travellers. David Roberts drew him in Cairo in 1838.
Thackeray, in A Journey from Cornhill to Cairo, gave a lively description
of staying in one of his hotels,

a fine new white building with HOTEL D'ORIENT written up in huge French
characters, and which, indeed, is an establishment as large and comfortable as
most of the best inns of the South of France. As a hundred Christian people, or
more, come from England and from India every fortnight, this inn has been
built to accommodate a large proportion of them; and twice a month, at least,
its sixty rooms are full. The gardens from the windows give a very pleasant and
animated view: the hotel-gate is besieged by crews of donkey-drivers; the noble
stately Arab women, with tawny skins and large black eyes, come to the well
hard by for water: camels are perpetually arriving and setting down their loads:
the court is full of bustling dragomans, ayahs, and children from India; and
poor old venerable he-nurses with grey beards and crimson turbans, tending
little white-faced babies that have seen the light at Dumdum or Futtyghur: a
copper-coloured barber, seated on his hams, is shaving a camel-driver at the
great inn-gate . . . . The bells are ringing prodigiously; and Lieutenant Waghorn
is bouncing in and out of the Courtyard full of business. He only left Bombay
yesterday morning, was seen in the Red Sea on Tuesday, is engaged to dinner
this afternoon in the Regent's Park, and (as it is about two minutes since I saw

him in the courtyard) I make no doubt he is by this time at Alexandria, or at Malta, say, perhaps at both.

He lived at the same pace on his visits home. Smith has a story that the chemist who sold the tea Waghorn liked had to toss a packet of it into his chaise at the moment that he invariably passed; there was no time to stop.

More than once, Waghorn arrived at 65 Cornhill in the early morning, when I was the only member of the staff present. I remember his arriving travel-stained and dirty. He had just landed from India, and, without a word of greeting, he shouted, "Have you anyone here who can *run*?" I called in a ticket-porter from the street; Waghorn enquired "if he could run". "Yes, sir," said the porter, "if I am paid for it!" Waghorn handed him a packet and told him to run with it to the Foreign Office. The ticket-porter was stout and scant of breath; running for him was a lost art. Waghorn watched the man waddling down Cornhill; he burst out with a sea-going expletive not to be repeated here, ran after the porter, seized him by the coat-tails which he rent half-way up his back, grasped the packet, rolled the unfortunate porter into the gutter, and ran off himself with the despatches to the Foreign Office! I had to pick the astonished porter from the gutter, and pay him handsomely for his damaged coat and outraged feelings in order to save Waghorn from a charge of assault.

But Waghorn's time of glory was short. Success brought a greater flow of mail and passengers than he could cope with, and the mail was taken over by the Post Office. "When nothing more remained to be learnt from us," he wrote bitterly, "we were forthwith superseded." New transport was soon to replace camels – in 1858 Trollope went to Egypt for the Post Office to negotiate with the Pasha for the use of Egyptian railways for the English mail. New operators joined the tourist trade, though Waghorn managed to keep a good deal of this side of the business, establishing the Globe Travel Agency, with travel guides published by Smith & Elder. He was sufficiently well known for the Christmas show at the Lyceum in 1849 to have a chorus:

> To England we came by the Overland Mail
> Waghornly, quickly done.

The Times continued to use Waghorn's services, and their news from India would start with some such boastful sentence as "We have received, by courier from Marseilles, our own overland dispatch in anticipation of the Indian mail." A leader in *The Times* in November 1845 praised him:

> It cannot be too often repeated that Lieutenant Waghorn has been the pioneer of one of the most remarkable improvements of the time, since to him we are indebted for the overland route itself between the mother country and its richest colony . . . . Before Mr Waghorn stepped forth to devote himself to a task of such magnitude, no part of India could be reached in less than four months. The mails from Bombay now reach England in about 34 days.

There is a statue of Waghorn in Chatham, but the memorial put up in Egypt by De Lesseps was destroyed in the Suez Crisis in 1956. For Smith, Waghorn was a hero, the embodiment of everything exciting in commercial life.

III

Publishing under Alexander Elder

George Smith writes rather disparagingly of the publishing side of the business under Elder, which was, he says, conducted with only "spasms of energy". All the same, it was a small firm, and there does seem to have been a distinguished list of books, of more than passing interest.

The fashion for elegant illustrated books appealed to Elder. He produced *Twenty Four Views of Calcutta*, *Scenery Costume and Architecture of the West Side of India*, *Chronicles of London Bridge*, *The Byron Gallery* with thirty-six engravings to illustrate Byron's poems, a series of drawings of Scotland by Clark, and Clarkson Stanfield's *Coast Scenery* – a fine collection of drawings of both sides of the English Channel, dedicated appropriately to William IV, the sailor king.

The Annual *Friendship's Offering*, first published in 1823, was taken over by Smith & Elder five years later and published by them for fourteen years – "a type of literature", writes Smith,

upon which much ridicule has been expended . . . it had a circulation of from eight to ten thousand copies, and was sold at the price of 12s 0d. The firm offered a prize of £5.5.0d for some lines to serve as a motto for the title page. The prize was won by a Mr Thompson, who pursued the unpoetical trade of a seedsman in Fenchurch Street. His lines were:

> This is affection's tribute, friendship's offering,
> Whose silent eloquence, more rich than words,
> Tells of the giver's faith, and truth in absence,
> And says – "forget me not".

... The firm may thus claim to have been the first publishers in literary history who paid for poetry a higher rate than £1.1.0d per line! The actual publishing of *Friendship's Offering* was a notable event. For two or three days before the day of its appearance everybody remained after the shop had closed. Tables were set out, and we sealed up each copy in a wrapper. When the work was all over we were regaled with wine and cake, and sang songs.

Friendship's Offering may have been ridiculed – Thackeray had fun with the *Spring Annual* in *Pendennis* – but it was one of the books that found its way to Haworth, and it contained, among much turgid poetry and descriptive prose, contributions from Southey, John Clare, Miss Mitford, Coleridge and Tennyson. The volumes were small and beautifully produced, with fine engravings by, among others, William Daniell and John Martin.

In 1833 Elder made a premature attempt to bring out a cheap series of novels, the *Library of Romance*, at six shillings each. But the book trade was dominated by three-volume novels, which sold at a satisfactory profit for 10s 6d each, and after fifteen volumes, which included a Victor Hugo and a John Galt, the Library was abandoned as a business failure. This type of publishing flourished only with the much wider markets of railway bookstalls and more general literacy fifty years later.

"One of the Publishing successes of the firm at that period", Smith wrote,

was Grant's *Random Recollections of the House of Commons*. Grant was a Scotsman, a reporter for the *Morning Advertiser*, who had contemplated for years the doings of the House of Commons from the press gallery. He had an eye for the picturesque, an extra touch of gall in his ink, and his book had an extraordinary sale. Some members of the House of Commons, upon whom Grant had shed his humorous ink, made their indignant appearance at the shop in Cornhill. The book brought Grant some fame and social recognition; but literature in those days hardly filled a man's pockets as generously as it does now. Grant made his appearance in some London drawing-rooms but his own domestic arrangements remained of a primitive character, and this led to one

[28]

somewhat absurd incident. He still had to discharge some humble domestic offices in person, and one Sunday he set out to fetch the shoulder of mutton and potatoes which formed the Sunday dinner of the household, from the local bake-house where it had been cooked. At that moment the congregation was pouring out from a fashionable church at hand, and Grant, with the tin containing the Sunday joint in his hands, came face to face with a distinguished lady whose acquaintance he had made the night before in a fashionable drawing-room.

Smith's amused snobbery is reminiscent of *Cranford*. Captain Brown, Mrs Gaskell tells us, took

a poor old woman's dinner out of her hands one very slippery Sunday. He had met her returning from the bake-house as he came from church, and noticed her precarious footing; and with the grave dignity with which he did everything, he relieved her of her burden, and steered along the street by her side, carrying her baked mutton and potatoes safely home. This was thought very eccentric; and it was rather expected that he would pay a round of calls, on the Monday morning, to explain and apologize to the Cranford sense of propriety.

Of more importance were the scientific books – nine volumes of Humphry Davy's works; Sir John Herschel's *Astronomical observations at the Cape of Good Hope*, with plates done by "the best engraver possible, a Mr Le Queux"; and the *Zoology of South Africa* by Andrew Smith, who used to amuse George Smith with his traveller's tales.

Most important of all, Smith & Elder published the five large quarto volumes of the *Zoology of the Beagle Expedition*, and also Darwin's books on *Coral Reefs*, *Volcanic Islands*, and *Geological Observations on South America*. George Smith had happy memories of meeting Darwin:

Of all the famous men with whom I have had relations there were very few at all comparable with Darwin in charm of manner. Its characteristic was suavity, gentleness: a consideration for others which was the expression of a genuine kindliness of nature. I was very young at the time, and could not, perhaps, realize Darwin's greatness as a scientist: but the natural sweetness of his temper and manner quite took my heart captive.

It was under Elder, too, that the publication of Ruskin's *Modern Painters* was begun. The connection with Ruskin had started when Ruskin was a boy. His elder cousin, Charles Richardson, who was apprenticed to Smith Elder & Co., used to bring him books and also introduced him to Pringle, the editor of *Friendship's Offering*. Ruskin's first verses appeared in *Friendship's Offering* in 1835, when he was only sixteen; there were more, and he became a fashionable success. W.L. Harrison, who took over *Friendship's Offering* two years later, asked for first call on Ruskin's poems and considered them "the eagle's feather of his editorship".

Mr Ruskin senior first offered his son's major work, the book on "Turner and the Ancients", to the more famous firm of John Murray. "Murray", wrote Mr Ruskin, "said the public cared little about Turner, but strongly urged my son's writing on the German School, which the public was calling for works on"; so Mr Ruskin would not show the manuscript to Murray because "I thought if I sent a sheet, and the work was refused, I should be offering my old friend P. Stewart a rejected book. I therefore declined submitting any sheet, and carried the work at once to Smith & Co."[1] George Smith senior courteously offered to induce Murray to take the book, but when Mr Ruskin refused this he accepted it himself. The change of title to *Modern Painters* was suggested by the publishers, and the first volume came out, with impressive reviews but not impressive sales, in 1843.

The previous year the Ruskins had moved to Denmark Hill, becoming near neighbours and good friends of the Smiths. The friendship, and the business connection, continued when the younger George Smith took over the firm, and will come later in his story.

In spite of this fine collection of books there was not great commercial success, and George became increasingly critical of Elder's inadequacy. Two attempts were made at bringing in managers, but by the age of nineteen George was impatient for responsibility himself. He persuaded his father to let him try what he could do with a capital of £1,500:

> I stipulated that I was not to be questioned, or interfered with, in any way as to its use; and with this sum I was to make what publishing ventures I pleased. Behold me, then, a youth of not yet twenty, searching the horizon for authors whose literary bantlings I might introduce to an admiring – and, as I fondly hoped, purchasing world!

He was ambitious – "I remember that I was very indignant that the firm would not allow me to add the profits of my ventures to the original sum which formed my publishing capital. I had reckoned on increasing that capital by profits I made until I could undertake really large transactions." Perhaps if he had not had the enormous luck to have Charlotte Brontë's manuscript sent him less than four years later, he would not have managed so spectacularly well. But during those four years he did not do badly, and certainly learnt about books and publishing, so that he was able to make proper use of the manuscript when it did come.

Looking back, Smith gives a fair assessment of the qualities that helped him to succeed.

> I was precocious. I had a certain faculty for reading men. I was keenly interested in business affairs and quick to see everything that could affect business, and I think I may say that I had at least one useful business faculty, a capacity for clear and quick decision. But I was yet afflicted with great shyness. I often suffered greatly from what is vulgarly called "a blue funk" before making a speech or doing anything important. Then,too, I was essentially practical. My first question in any crisis was "what can we do". Regrets are idle. Speculation is a waste of energy. The sole question for a sensible man is "what is to be done"! It was this characteristic which made Charlotte Brontë describe me as a "practical-minded man"; and practicality of this sort is certainly an essential part of an equipment for business.

A publisher, Smith considered, also needs a judgement of literature, an instinct for gauging popular taste, the courage and inclination to speculate, and a good measure of tact and sympathy. He himself did not claim to have literary knowledge but he had the habit of reading in bed, and read widely in "history, biography, and the literature of action". He always enjoyed speculation, though he was careful to keep well within his means, and the success he later had in other branches of business enabled him to experiment and be generous in publishing. "Oh Father," his eldest son once said to him when discussing a risky proposal, "you will never be as old as I am." He did not seem very old in his account of financial discussions with Trollope in *Cornhill Magazine* days:

> Trollope came to me in Pall Mall, where we now had a branch office, to arrange for a new serial. I told him my terms, but he demurred to my offer of

£2,000, and said that he had hoped for £3,000. I shook my head. "Well," he replied, "let us toss for that other £1,000." I asked him if he wished to ruin me, and said that if my banker heard of my tossing authors for their copyrights he would certainly close my account; and what about my clerks? How I should demoralize them if they suspected me of tossing with an author for his manuscript! We ultimately came to an agreement on my terms, which were sufficiently liberal. But I felt uncomfortable – I felt mean – I had refused a challenge. To relieve my mind I said, "Now that is settled, if you will come over the way to my club, where we can have a little room to ourselves for five minutes, I will toss you for £1,000 with pleasure." Mr Trollope did not accept the offer.

Plenty of Smith's authors pay tribute to his tact and sympathy. He saw himself as a middleman between the "man of genius" and his readers. He had tremendous admiration for the men of genius, and pleasure and pride in their friendship.

So Smith felt he was well equipped for business generally, and publishing in particular. He remembers

the eager audacity – to a large extent unqualified by knowledge – with which I plunged into the great world of business. I tried many experiments. All of them were more or less original, some were ingenious, and some succeeded.

I took an old schoolfellow – to go back to one of my earliest business experiments – whose father had a large Manchester warehouse, into my confidence. I asked him to get me a sheet or two of the various brown papers used in packing, in his father's warehouse; the price paid for it and the time when their accounts were paid. He got me the information I wanted and I found the accounts were paid quarterly. I next took the samples to a paper-maker and asked what he could supply such a paper at, for payment in cash. I had now got all my data; I added a small percentage by way of profit to my paper-maker's prices, walked round the leading Manchester warehouses equipped with my sheets of paper, and in the course of a few days picked up orders for a good deal of paper on my terms, and with the arrangement that the accounts were to be paid monthly. This was, I think, my maiden business effort, and naturally I was exceedingly proud of it. My mother, who was always in my confidence, was – just as naturally – more proud of it than even I was. Whenever I took up any fresh enterprise she used to say "another brown paper scheme". The phrase, indeed, "George's brown paper schemes" – has in my domestic circle, pursued me all my life.

After I became a partner in the firm, I tried a business experiment which now seems easy and commonplace, but which, at the time, was quite unknown, and as far as I was concerned, was entirely original. With our great variety of shipments we naturally had to expend a large sum in insurance. It occurred to me that we ought to do our own insurances, or at least, to confine the insurances we effected in the various offices to the more risky ports alone. I had a list made out of all the ports to which we had shipped goods during twelve months, and took the list to my friend, Mr William Ellis, then the best authority on insurance business in London. Ellis agreed. "You can do your own insurance," he said, "for example, between London and Hong Kong, but not between Hong Kong and Shanghai. Between those two ports the risk is much higher." He took my list of the ports with which we traded, struck out half a dozen, and said, "If you stick to the rest you will be safe." The insurance account thus adjusted brought a considerable annual balance of profit.

IV

George Smith Takes Over the Publishing

Smith's first publishing venture was R.H. Horne's *New Spirit of the Age*. This was a rash book for a beginner. It was a collection of essays on contemporary writers, often strongly critical, that seems calculated to make enemies. There was an attack on the *Ingoldsby Legends* for brutality; Ainsworth was dismissed in four hostile pages – *Old St Paul's* is "generally dull except where it is revolting"; Mrs Trollope "belongs to a class which is, fortunately, very small; but it will always be recruited from the ranks of the unscrupulous, so long as a corrupt taste is likely to yield a trifling profit." Horne, who edited the book but did not write all of it, put an anxious footnote here: "We think Mrs Trollope *is* clever, shrewd, and strong."

But it was not these articles that worried Smith. "The book included an article on Colonel Perronet Thompson," he wrote,

a leading and very advanced politician of the day. Horne's study of Thompson was enthusiastic, and his views were not in the least likely to commend themselves to the book-buying public of that day. I felt very much as I imagine the editor of *The Quarterly Review* would feel if invited to accept an eulogium say on Mr Tom Mann by Mr Keir Hardie. I remonstrated with Horne, who replied that Thompson was a man of sufficient distinction to find a place in the volume, and was a man with a future. A long correspondence followed, dreadfully in earnest on my side; but Horne was firm. At length I went to Horne's residence at Kentish Town to endeavour to settle the matter in person. I have still a vivid remembrance of the interview which followed, and had a sufficient sense of humour to appreciate its absurdity even in my anxious condition of mind. I argued the matter with great earnestness, employing all the eloquent phrases I had invented during my ride to Kentish Town on the outside of an omnibus.

Horne at last said, "My dear young friend, you are rather excited. Let us have a little music." He fetched his guitar and played and sang to me for half an hour; he then asked if my views were still the same? He found they had resisted even the strains of his guitar. Then Horne's good nature came to my aid. He opened his bookcase, and beckoned to me with the gesture of a tragic actor to approach. He took up the offending manuscript, written on brief paper, held one corner in his hand and motioned to me with the utmost solemnity to take the other corner. We then proceeded in funereal silence, keeping step as in a stage procession, to the fireplace, when Horne looked at me in the face with a tragic expression and said "Throw!" We threw. The offending manuscript dropped into the flames; Horne heaved a deep sigh and I shook him warmly by the hand and departed much relieved. Anyone who remembers the quaint and picturesque personality of the author of "Orion" will be able to appreciate this scene.

Horne certainly had a picturesque personality, and this story of Smith's seems entirely characteristic. The guitar-playing, which Horne resorted to in times of stress or of cheerfulness all his life, dated from a youthful excursion to the Mexican Wars in 1825. He achieved fame but not fortune in 1843 with the eccentric publicity for his 137-page epic poem *Orion*, put on sale at ¼d a copy. As he wrote to Leigh Hunt:

I *thought* the price would amuse you, and it has. You are aware that it is no hoax, no joke? Anybody who *ought* to have the poem can buy it for a farthing. The proof that he "ought" which I have directed the Publisher to require, is that the applicant should have a good face and proper accent. A man with a horse-nose and boar's mouth who asked for "Horion" would certainly not obtain it. And very rightly not, I think. The book is refused, in numbers, to the "trade" and to "unlikely" messengers; and no friend can obtain two copies for his halfpenny. Other things I have "ordained" as check to rapacity. You see, this was necessary, for as the poem is published at less than the price of waste paper I had to protect myself from people sending five shillings and a sack.[1]

It was an enormous success, selling six editions by the end of the year, even though the price had gone up to half a crown.

So it was with the fame of *Orion* behind him that Smith published *A New Spirit of the Age* the following year. For Smith it turned out successful enough, and a second edition soon followed. For Horne it was a disaster, bringing terrible reviews from everyone he had upset in the literary world.

"His tragedies have not been acted and his epic has been sold for a farthing," said the *Westminster Review*. "Such a man is not in harmony and cannot be expected to sit in judgement on the spirits of the age."[2] Elizabeth Barrett, who had collaborated anonymously in writing the book, tried to console him: "The slaying fault, we may both be very sure, is by no means in the book, but in the envy, malice, and all uncharitableness on every side of us."[3] Horne still had friends and admirers among those who had escaped his attacks, but no one found him easy. Miss Mitford, who invited him to stay, complained to Elizabeth Barrett about her difficult guest, who asked to be called at four in the morning, took three baths a day, and outstayed his welcome.[4]

For the next eight years Horne wrote poems, plays and children's stories, and worked for Dickens, first on the *Daily News*, then as sub-editor of *Household Words*. But he was restless, adventurous, and in need of money. In 1852 he joined the Australian Gold Rush, hoping that in a year he would return with a fortune. In fact he did not return for seventeen years, after a strange career which often brought him great dangers or left him unemployed in great poverty. He had written admiringly in *Household Words* about Waghorn's travels; he himself became an adventurous traveller. Among other jobs, he was commander of Melbourne's Private Gold Escort Company – a sort of primitive Securicor that brought gold through an unruly country of marshes and swamps to the ports – he was a Gold Commissioner collecting licence fees and keeping order in the Goldfields, a Commissioner for Water and Sewage in Melbourne, a Mining Registrar in the Blue Mountain Goldfields. There were many other sidelines: he continued to write poems and plays, he was twice an unsuccessful Australian parliamentary candidate, he started a vineyard company, he gave lectures, folk-song recitals and swimming displays (he was always an enthusiastic swimmer, even going into the January sea at Margate on his eightieth birthday). Occasionally he reappears from the other side of the world, writing for *Household Words* or for Smith Elder. In 1859 Smith Elder rejected a proposal for reprinting Horne's collected articles from *Household Words*, but they did publish his *Australian Facts and Prospects*, prefixed by his Australian autobiography, with a second edition the following year. In 1862 he sent the *Cornhill* an account of an Australian election.

When he returned in 1869 he had not made a fortune, and the rest of his life was a struggle to get bits and pieces published and a pension to live on. Gosse gives a sad description of him in old age at a wedding:

> Then entered "Orion" Horne, a tiny old gentleman, who all uninvited began to sit on the floor and sing, in a funny little cracked voice, Spanish songs to his own accompaniment on the guitar. The guests grew restless and impatient, but Browning, throwing a protecting arm over the guitarist, exclaimed, "That was charming, Horne! It quite took us back to the sunny warm South," and tactfully put an end to the incident.[5]

Smith's second book was *The Queen of the Stage* by Mrs Baron Wilson; a work of no special merit but not financially unsuccessful. He published a small volume of poems for Mrs Wilson's daughter. Her mother paid for publication because, as she confided to Smith, "I want my daughter to marry and it is a good thing for a girl to have a literary reputation."

A publishing embarrassment inherited by Smith was the large output of G.P.R. James. James, an author of considerable but transient popularity, seems to have had a rather vague contract with Smith Elder & Co. They had undertaken to publish his novels but this undertaking, Smith felt, should have some limit. With three or four of James's manuscripts queuing in the firm's safe, Smith managed to make a compromise, and extricate himself after publishing nine of James's novels between 1845 and 1848. The public had tired of him. G.H. Lewes attributed the fall to the fact that the doctors had ceased to recommend his books, with a milk diet, as unexciting reading for patients recovering from a fever.

A more important contact soon followed.

> My next publishing venture brought me into relations with Leigh Hunt and did this in rather a strange way. I went to Peckham to dine with a Mr Thomas Powell, and while I waited in his little drawing-room for a few minutes before

dinner I took up a neatly written manuscript which was lying on the table, and was reading it when Powell entered the room. "Ah!" he said, "that doesn't look worth £40, does it? I advanced £40 to Leigh Hunt on the security of that manuscript and I shall never see my money again."

When I was leaving I asked Powell to let me take the manuscript with me. I finished reading it before I went to sleep that night and next day I asked Powell if he would let me have the manuscript if I paid him the £40. He readily assented; and, having got from him Leigh Hunt's address, I went off to him at Kensington, explained the circumstances under which the manuscript had come into my possession, and asked whether, if I paid him an additional £60, I might have the copyright. "You young prince!" cried Leigh Hunt in a tone of something like rapture, and the transaction was promptly concluded. The work was *Imagination and Fancy*.

It was succeeded by *Wit and Humour* and other books, all of which were successful, and the introduction was the foundation of a friendship with Leigh Hunt, and with the members of his family, which was very delightful to me. I particularly enjoyed the simple, old-fashioned suppers to which he frequently invited me. His daughter played and sang to us and Leigh Hunt told us the most delightful stories of his Italian travels, and of Shelley and Byron (whom he always called "Birron").

In the preface to the first edition of his autobiography, in 1850, Hunt gives a tribute to Smith. He would not have written at all, he said, "but Mr Smith's favourable opinion of me, and his own kindly feeling, led him to think it would be so much the reverse of a disadvantage to me in the end, that he took the handsomest means of making the task as easy to me as he could, through a long period of engagements overdue, and of interruptions from ill health."

"Business was by no means Leigh Hunt's strong point," Smith wrote;

I once had to pay him a sum of money – either £100 or £200 – and I wrote him a cheque for the amount. "Well", he said, "what am I to do with this little bit of paper?" I told him that if he presented it at the Bank they would pay him cash for it, but I added, "I will save you that trouble." I went to the Bank and cashed the cheque for him. He took the notes away carefully enclosed in an envelope. Two days afterwards Leigh Hunt came in a state of great agitation to tell me his wife had burnt the envelope containing the bank-notes. He had thrown the envelope carelessly down, and his wife had flung it into the fire. Leigh Hunt's agitation while on his way to bring this news had not prevented him from purchasing on the road a little statuette of Psyche, which he carried, without

[39]

any paper round it, in his hand. I told him I thought something might be done in the matter. I sent to the bankers and got the number of the notes, and then, in company with Leigh Hunt, went off to the Bank of England. I explained our business and we were shown into a room where three old gentlemen were sitting at writing tables. They kept us waiting some time, and Leigh Hunt, who had meanwhile been staring all round the room, at last got up, walked up to one of these staid officials, and addressing him said, in wondering tones, "And *this* is the Bank of England! And do you sit here all day and never see the green woods, and the trees and flowers and the charming country?" Then, in tones of remonstrance he demanded, "Are you contented with such a life?" All this time he was holding the little naked Psyche in one hand and with his long hair and flashing eyes made a surprising figure. I fancy I can still see the astonished faces of the three officials; they would have made a most delightful picture. I said, "Come away, Mr Hunt! These gentlemen are very busy." I succeeded in carrying Leigh Hunt off, and, after entering into some formalities, we were told that the value of the notes would be paid in 12 months. I gave Leigh Hunt the money at once and he went away rejoicing.

Thomas Powell, a clerk in the office of the city merchants Chapman Brothers and one of the proprietors of the new *Quarterly Review*, introduced many other literary men to Smith, as well as Leigh Hunt. Smith used often to meet Browning at Powell's house, and through Powell too he joined the Museum Club, a small literary gathering which included some of the writers who later became important for the *Cornhill Magazine*. Smith remembered the Museum Club with the nostalgia of an old man looking back on his undergraduate days:

Never before or since have I been present at such amusing parties. The wit was brilliant, the jokes abundant, the laughter uproarious. I was much the youngest member of the party; but I had a gift of easy listening, and a ready laughter which qualified me for a place at the table; and often I came away from the meeting of the club with sides that were literally sore with laughter. We had one or two lords and members of parliament in the club, but I forget their names. Their contribution consisted chiefly of appreciative silence. The best talkers of the club were Douglas Jerrold, Father Prout and G.H. Lewes. Leigh Hunt's spirit was too mild and unaggressive to enable him to shine in such a gathering. Lewes had a wonderful gift for dramatic representation, and could tell a story, reproducing the dialect and gestures of each actor in it, with life-like effect. Jerrold's flow of wit was unfailing, his repartee was of

[40]

lightning-like swiftness. Father Prout's humour was more subtle and refined, but certainly not less brilliant.

But the Museum Club soon ended with money troubles, and Thomas Powell's hospitality ended more dramatically when he was accused of widespread fraud. Smith was in good company in failing to see through him; he had been trusted by Thomas Chapman, Chairman of Lloyd's Register of Shipping, and he had a wide circle of distinguished friends.

As a minor writer himself, Powell enjoyed entertaining major writers and used to send them, according to Horne, "edible presents" and "private letters of admiration". But both his writing and his entertaining were basically dishonest. In 1842 he published as his own a volume which included several poems he had bought from Leigh Hunt and from Horne. Four years later it was found that he had financed himself by embezzlement and by forging cheques, defrauding Chapman Brothers of a total of around £10,000. Dickens, whose younger brother Augustus worked for Chapman, was appalled.

> I have been perfectly horrified by the whole story, [he wrote to Chapman] I could hardly name a man in London whom I should have thought less likely to stand so committed, than he. Not that I had any intimate knowledge of his pursuits, or any close acquaintance with himself or his usual mode of thinking and proceeding – but I had an idea of his great steadiness and reliability, and a conviction of his great respect and regard for you. God help him, I believe, even now, that he was sincere in the latter feeling, and was overcome and swept away by the tide of circumstances on which he had madly cast himself.[6]

Chapman did not prosecute. He dismissed Powell, who went to live obscurely in Croydon but, after two years, emerged in further trouble. In 1848 Croydon magistrates issued a warrant for his arrest for forgeries, and a very strange episode followed. *The Times* reported that when Powell should have appeared at Croydon,

> his solicitor attended on his behalf, and put in a certificate signed by Dr Southwood Smith, testifying that the defendant was in a dangerous state of illness; in fact, that he was insane, and utterly unfit to appear and undergo an examination; and the magistrate upon this consented to allow the case to stand over a fortnight. During this interval it was ascertained that there were several

[41]

other cases in which the person accused had obtained money by means of forged checks, and from the information obtained by the police there also appeared very good reason for believing that, although the defendant was no doubt very ill, and that his brain was to some extent affected, yet that this state had been produced by artificial means – by the excessive use of opium, and resorting to the expedient of igniting charcoal in his bedroom, the object being to produce a temporary state of delirium, in the expectation by that means to evade justice.[7]

Owing to Southwood Smith's help (whose "good offices are always at the disposal of his friends", as Powell later wrote), Powell did avoid prison and fled to America.

In America Powell once more set himself up as a man of letters, and wrote malicious gossip about English literary men. With rash over-confidence he wrote insultingly about Dickens. Dickens's sympathy for Powell gave way to fury, and he wrote to English and American newspaper editors telling the whole story. The *New York Tribune* printed the letter; Dickens called Powell's article "from beginning to end, one intact and complete lie", and went on to say that Powell himself was "a forger and a thief" who had arrived in New York

with a forged letter of recommendation to credit purporting to come from a partner in the very house he had robbed and drew two bills upon that gentleman (cashed in New York) which of course have been protested and returned. The very same house, to whose moderation he is indebted for not working in chains in Norfolk Island at this instant, is of course the subject of his blackest ingratitude and is libelled in all sorts of ways in his aforesaid life of me. Before his character was discovered he wrote some plays – one dedicated to me – by pushing which he got into the house of certain literary men, and among others into mine, where he once dined, I am sorry to say. I know his late employers well, and tell you this story with the full and complete personal knowledge of its truth, and think your American readers will do well to consider whom they trust sometimes.[8]

Powell's reaction to this letter was to have the publisher sent to prison, and to claim £2,000 libel damages from Dickens. Dickens retaliated by publishing a pamphlet with proof of his claims – a letter from Chapman Brothers saying it was "too painfully true", confirmation from Southwood Smith that Powell had been certified insane, the *Times* report of the Croydon case, and correspondence showing Powell's fraud in New

York. There was no libel action, but nothing is recorded about the poor imprisoned publisher.

Browning, who had been a constant visitor at Powell's house in the days when Powell and Smith were friends, wrote of Powell's literary forgeries and the way he would produce books with signatures and inscriptions from famous authors. Browning called him "a consummate rascal",[9] "an unparalleled forger",[10] and considered he "affected to forge, in sport, the signatures of his acquaintance in order to subsequently induce the belief, when his serious forgeries should be discovered, that he was simply a monomaniac on the matter of an irresistible itch at imitating other folks' writing".[11]

Powell committed suicide in 1887. His full story can be found only through Browning's and Dickens's letters. The *Dictionary of American Biography*, in an article written by the American journalist E.F. Edgett, lists Powell's writings and calls him "one of the liveliest and best-liked of the coterie of New York journalists and literary men". George Smith says nothing more about him; perhaps he deliberately suppressed the scandal. Thomas Powell is not mentioned in the *Dictionary of National Biography*.

V

A Crisis in the Firm

George Smith had proved himself well capable of using his £1,500; it was not long before further responsibility had to follow. In 1846 his father died, leaving George, still only twenty-two, in sole charge of the publishing, with Patrick Stewart running the foreign agency. The Smith household was established back in London with a solid middle-class house in Westbourne Place, and both sides of the firm were flourishing. The following year the wonderful success of *Jane Eyre*, which brought fame to publisher as well as author, made continued prosperity seem certain. Then suddenly, in 1848, a crisis broke, bringing troubles which were a deeply worrying background to Smith's life and work for at least the next five years.

Puzzled by the firm's poor bank balance, in spite of good trading and high turnover, Smith had asked a banking friend to see whether money was coming through as it should. The banker found that correct amounts of money had been sent, but not all had been paid in. Further investigation showed that this had been going on for some time. When Smith also found, on looking at the firm's books, that personal debits in Stewart's name had been altered, it became disturbingly clear that Stewart, his senior partner and one-time hero, had been tampering with the accounts. Smith prided himself, generally with reason, on his ability to judge character. But he had been taken in by Thomas Powell, and now he was faced with the discovery of fraud in a close friend. A more thorough examination showed that the firm had been cheated over the years of at least £30,000. Smith then had the unhappy task of confronting Stewart, and had to take difficult decisions about the future of his partner and of the firm.

Like Chapman faced with the problem of Powell, Smith was anxious to suppress scandal and did not prosecute. He even allowed Stewart to remain in the business, with the same salary as before, but without a partnership and without handling any of the firm's money. After two or three years of this unsatisfactory situation, when, as Smith said, "relations were friendly, though rather uneasy", Stewart's friends persuaded him to take a job in Calcutta. There he died, in 1852.

Smith was left with severe financial problems. His mother, his sisters and Alexander Elder all had their entire capital in the firm. Stewart's guardian, Aeneas Mackintosh, and his brother-in-law, Sir John Herschel, had both invested considerable amounts. To save the firm from bankruptcy, Smith negotiated for time to meet all the liabilities left by Stewart. To avoid further risks, he had to cut back on new publishing business – even, very regretfully, refusing to accept Browning's books. At the same time he found himself suddenly responsible for the Indian and Colonial business.

All this brought on nervous and physical strain. Smith used to get so agitated that he could not go to bed, frequently fainted and had difficulty getting a life insurance. His mother's help and encouragement, and his habit of horse-riding, were the things that kept him going through this exhausting time. "My mother's cheerful spirit never forsook her", he wrote.

In looking back I can see that she devoted herself to sustaining my courage; she even made fun of our perilous position. On one Sunday, when I was unusually depressed, she took me for a walk in Kensington Gardens; a more wretched creature than I felt, and I suppose looked, when we started for our walk could hardly be imagined, but my mother had evidently set her heart on cheering me. She had some gift of mimicry, and she drew such a humorous picture of the result of our utter ruin, when she expressed her intention, if the worst came, of having a Berlin wool shop in the Edgware Road, and so admirably mimicked one of my sisters – who was regarded in the family as having rather a taste for display – serving behind the counter, that I could not restrain my laughter, and returned home in a different and more hopeful condition of mind. . . . I worked with all the intensity and zeal of which I was capable. The correspondence was heavy, the letters were often both very long and very important. I used to dictate to two clerks, while two others were occupied in copying. It was a common thing for me with many of the clerks to work till 4 o'clock in the morning. I used to start work at 9 in the morning and did not leave my room, or cease dictating, until 7 the next evening, when the mail was despatched. During this twenty-two hours* of continuous work I was supported by mutton chops and green tea.

Looking back now I don't think I need have done so much work personally. Business methods have improved, and heads of firms have learnt to delegate to responsible clerks much of the work which in those days they did themselves. The perfection of business wisdom I have learned is never to do a thing with your own hand that other people can do as well, or nearly as well.

Smith kept up this great pressure of work until he was about thirty – through the time when he was publishing *Shirley* and *Villette*, having a lively correspondence with Charlotte Brontë, and widening his circle of literary friends. By 1851 he was beginning to emerge from his troubles, with the firm's turnover already £57,500 – nearly £10,000 more than it had been in 1846. Then the firm grew rapidly, until 200 clerks were employed. Turnover trebled in five years, more than doubled in the next five, and reached £627,129 by 1866.

It is not surprising that someone as perceptive as Charlotte Brontë should write in 1851: "I fancy there has been some crisis in which his energy and filial affection have sustained them all; this I judge from the fact that his mother and sisters are more peculiarly bound to him than ever and that his slightest wish is an unquestioned law."[1]

---

* *Sic* in typescript *Memoirs*; Leonard Huxley amends the arithmetic to thirty-four hours. Or did Smith mean seven the next morning, which seems formidable enough?

VI

Charlotte Brontë

Far the most distinguished writer introduced by Smith Elder & Co. was
Charlotte Brontë. Credit for appreciating her distinction must be shared
between George Smith and his reader William Smith Williams, both of
whom encouraged her and became her regular correspondents, in a series of
stimulating letters, until the last year of her brief life.

Smith Williams had only recently joined the firm. He seems to have been
a slightly sad character. Born in 1800, he had first been apprenticed to the
publishers Taylor & Hessey, where he came to know Leigh Hunt, Hazlitt,
and Keats; then he had tried to start his own bookshop. When George Smith
met him he was acting, not too successfully, as book-keeper to the firm of
lithographers who had illustrated the *Voyage of the Beagle*, and keeping in
touch with the literary world by writing reviews for the *Spectator*.

> I had a good many interviews with Mr Williams, [Smith wrote] and if he was
> not a good book-keeper he was a most agreeable and most intelligent man, a
> man with literary gifts wasted in uncongenial work. . . . I invited Mr Williams
> to my lodgings in Regent Street, and after tea I said to him, "Rightly or
> wrongly, I do not think you like your present occupation?" "I *hate* it," said Mr
> Williams with fervour. This reply made clear sailing for me, and before he left
> my room we had arranged that he should come to Cornhill as my literary
> assistant and general manager of the publishing department.

Smith Williams remained with Smith Elder & Co. until he retired. He was clearly still feeling sorry for himself in 1848, when Charlotte Brontë wrote sympathetically: "What you say respecting your own lot in life is very mournful . . . For thirty-five years to have filled a position where your tastes had no scope, and your faculties no exercise, is sad indeed."[1] This is from one of the more than a hundred surviving letters from Charlotte Brontë to Smith Williams, though, as with her letters to George Smith, we have only one side of the correspondence and must imagine the other.

The story of Charlotte Brontë's first communication to Smith Elder & Co., under the name of Currer Bell, has often been told, but it must be put here in George Smith's words.

In July 1847 a parcel containing a manuscript reached our office addressed to the firm, but bearing also, scored out, the addresses of two or three other publishing houses showing that the parcel had been previously submitted to other publishers. This did not tend to prepossess us in favour of the manuscript. It was clear that we were offered what had been already rejected elsewhere. But it was a rule that every manuscript sent to the firm should be faithfully considered.

The parcel contained the manuscript of *The Professor*, a book which was published after Charlotte Brontë's death. Mr Williams, the reader to the firm, read the manuscript and said that it evinced great literary power, but he had grave doubts as to its being successful as a publication. We together decided that he should write to Currer Bell a letter of appreciative criticism of the manuscript, declining the work but expressing an opinion that the writer could produce a book which would command success. Before, however, this letter was despatched there came a letter from Currer Bell, containing a postage stamp for our reply, it having been hinted to the writer by "some experienced friend" that publishers often refrain from answering communications unless a postage stamp was furnished for the purpose! Charlotte Brontë herself has described the effect the letter had on her: "As a forlorn hope he [Currer Bell] tried one publishing house more. Ere long, in a much shorter space than that on which experience had taught him to calculate, there came a letter which he opened in the dreary anticipation of finding two hard hopeless lines, intimating that 'Messrs Smith Elder and Co. were not disposed to publish the manuscript,' and instead he took out of the envelope a letter of two pages. He read it trembling. It declined, indeed, to publish that book for business reasons, but it discussed its merits and demerits; so courteously, so considerately, in a spirit so rational, with a discrimination so enlightened, that this very refusal cheered the author better than a vulgarly expressed acceptance would have done. It was added, that a work in three volumes would meet with careful attention."

Charlotte Brontë replied gratefully and said she was on the point of finishing another and longer book, which she would send. This was *Jane Eyre*, and it arrived on 24 August.

"The manuscript of *Jane Eyre* was read by Mr Williams in due course," George Smith continued:

> He brought it to me on a Saturday and said that he would like me to read it. There were no Saturday half-holidays in those days, and, as was usual, I did not reach home until late. I had made an appointment with a friend for Sunday morning: I was to meet him about 12.30 at a place some two or three miles from our house and ride with him into the country.
>
> After breakfast on Sunday morning I took the manuscript of *Jane Eyre* to the library and began to read it. The story quickly took me captive. At twelve o'clock my horse came to the door, but I could not put the book down. I scribbled two or three lines to my friend, saying I was very sorry circumstances had occurred to prevent my meeting him, sent the note off by my groom, and went on reading the manuscript. Presently the servant came to tell me that lunch was waiting; I asked him to bring me a sandwich and a glass of wine and still went on with *Jane Eyre*. Dinner came; for me the meal was a very hasty one, and before I went to bed that night I had finished the manuscript. My literary judgement was perfectly satisfied.

He backed his judgement energetically, and *Jane Eyre* was published in the astonishing time of six weeks. Charlotte Brontë was given an initial payment of £100, which was generous for an unknown author, and later a total of £400 more. For someone who had been earning £20 a year as a governess, £500 was wealth. £500, though, was also all Smith gave her later, when she was famous, for the copyrights of *Shirley* and of *Villette*; she never seems to have complained to him, although she did mention in a letter to Miss Wooler that she had hoped for £700 for *Villette*, "but when an author finds that his work is cordially approved, he can pardon the rest".[2]

Smith's enthusiasm for *Jane Eyre* was matched by that of the press, the public, and the literary world. The overwhelming success brought Charlotte Brontë not only happiness from seeing her book published and praised, but also a new life of intellectual friendship. Her correspondence with Smith Williams and George Smith let loose the side of her nature which had been held back from her dear, but not intellectual, schoolfriend Ellen Nussey. Visits to her publishers brought stimulating contacts with fellow-authors. The success transformed Smith Elder & Co. too, bringing them to the first rank of publishers, with distinguished new names, including Thackeray and Mrs Gaskell, soon on their lists. Charlotte Brontë's first visit to Cornhill, revealing her identity, did not take place until July 1848. There are many letters before that, mostly to Smith Williams. She was always glad to hear from Smith Williams – "he was my first favourable critic; he first gave me encouragement to persevere as an author, consequently I naturally respect him and feel grateful to him."[3] Altogether she was delighted with her publishers, particularly when she compared them to those dithering with *Wuthering Heights* and *Agnes Grey* – "Mr Newby does not do business like Messrs Smith and Elder; a different spirit seems to preside at 172, Mortimer Street to that which guides the helm at 65 Cornhill. Mr Newby shuffles, gives his word and breaks it; Messrs Smith and Elder's performance is always better than their promise."[4] By December she was writing to Smith Williams: "I cannot thank you sufficiently for your letters, and I can give you but a faint idea of the pleasure they afford me; they seem to introduce such light and life to the torpid retirement where we live like dormice."[5] Her letters to him became friendly and relaxed, ranging from politics, writers, and books to the education of his children.

Perhaps the letter that gave Charlotte Brontë the greatest pleasure was the one she had from Smith Williams enclosing Thackeray's praise of *Jane Eyre*. It seems a little odd, though, that when she decided to dedicate the second edition to Thackeray her publishers failed to warn her that, with his own sad problem of a mad wife, he might be hurt as well as flattered. Thackeray wrote to thank her for the great compliment, and also to tell her the true situation. Poor Charlotte Brontë was distressed.

She wrote to Smith Williams:

I suppose it is no indiscretion to tell you this circumstance, for you doubtless know it already, that his private position is in some points similar to that I have ascribed to Mr Rochester, that thence arose a report that *Jane Eyre* had been written by a governess in his family, and that the dedication coming now has confirmed everybody in the surmise. . . . I am *very sorry* that my inadvertent blunder should have made his name and affairs a subject for common gossip. The very fact of his not complaining at all and addressing me with such kindness . . . increases my chagrin. I could not half express my regret to him in my answer, for I was restrained by the consciousness that that regret was just worth nothing at all – quite valueless for healing the mischief I had done.[6]

All this time, though George Smith and Smith Williams suspected both from her style and from her handwriting that Currer Bell was a woman, they knew nothing about her. This changed when Newby offered *Wildfell Hall* to Harper Brothers of New York as by the author of *Jane Eyre*, claiming that all the Bell novels were written by the same person. Harpers, who already had an agreement with Smith Elder & Co. to publish Currer Bell's next book, were puzzled. George Smith wrote to Charlotte Brontë "to say that we should be glad to be in a position to contradict the statement, adding at the same time we were quite sure Mr Newby's statement was untrue".[7]

Mrs Gaskell has described how, the very day they received this letter, Charlotte and Anne set out walking to the station at Keighley to catch the night train to London at Leeds, then called in for breakfast at the Chapter Coffee House before hurrying to Cornhill. "That particular Saturday morning," wrote Smith,

> I was at work in my room, when a clerk reported that two ladies wished to see me. I was very busy and sent out to ask their names. The clerk returned to say that the ladies declined to give their names, but wished to see me on a private matter. After a moment's hesitation I told him to show them in. I was in the midst of my Indian correspondence, and my thoughts were far away from Currer Bell and *Jane Eyre*. Two rather quaintly dressed little ladies, pale-faced and anxious-looking, walked into my room; one of them came forward and presented me with a letter addressed, in my own handwriting, to "Currer Bell Esq". I noticed that the letter had been opened, and said with some sharpness, "Where did you get this from?" "From the post office," was the reply; "it was addressed to me. We have both come that you might have ocular proof that there are at least two of us." This, then, was Currer Bell in person. I need hardly say that I was at once keenly interested. Mr Williams was called down and introduced. . . .
>
> I must confess that my first impression of Charlotte Brontë's personal

appearance was that it was interesting, rather than attractive. She was very small, and had a quaint old-fashioned look. Her head seemed too large for her body. She had fine eyes, but her face was marred by the mouth and complexion. There was little feminine charm about her; and of this fact she herself was uneasily and perpetually conscious. It may seem strange that the possession of genius did not lift her above the weakness of an excessive anxiety about her personal appearance; but I believe that she would have given all her genius and her fame to have been beautiful.

Charlotte Brontë's first impression of Smith is written in her letter of 4 September to her friend Mary Taylor in New Zealand.[8] He was "a tall young man" and Smith Williams a "pale mild stooping man of 50"; there was "talk – talk – talk; Mr Williams being silent, Mr Smith loquacious". Charlotte and Anne refused George Smith's hospitable offer that they should stay at Westbourne Place, but in the three days that they were in London they dined there twice, the Smiths took them to the Opera, Smith Williams took them to church, they visited the Royal Academy and the National Gallery, bought presents to take home, and left "laden with books which Mr Smith had given us". "Mr Smith's residence is at Bayswater," the letter to Mary Taylor continued:

> the rooms, the drawing-room especially, looked splendid to us. There was no company – only his mother, his two grown-up sisters, and his brother, a lad of 12 or 13, and a little sister, the youngest of the family, very like himself. They are all dark-eyed, dark-haired, and have clear, pale faces. The mother is a portly, handsome woman of her age, and all the children more or less well-looking – one of the daughters decidedly pretty. . . . Mr Smith made himself very pleasant. He is a firm, intelligent man of business, though so young; bent on getting on, and I think desirous to make his way by fair honourable means. He is enterprising, but likewise cool and cautious. Mr Smith is a *practical* man. I wish Mr Williams were more so, but he is altogether of the contemplative, theorizing order. Mr Williams has too many abstractions.

Between that first visit to her publishers and her next, in the November of the following year, Charlotte Brontë's life was shattered by the deaths of Branwell, Emily, and Anne. In her loneliness she struggled to complete *Shirley*. Her letters to Smith Williams show increasing need for advice and criticism, now that she had none at home. She confided in him about Branwell's disastrous state; about all her fears for her sisters, the tragedy of their deaths. He must have written frequently; he urged homeopathy, which Emily rejected as "only another form of quackery".[9] She sent him the first volume of *Shirley* for comment "on two conditions; the first, that you give me a faithful opinion . . . the second, that you show it and speak of it to *none* but Mr Smith".[10] Later she added that the manuscript could also be shown to James Taylor, the manager in charge of the staff of clerks at Cornhill. There were letters to George Smith himself and to James Taylor, too, but these were on business matters – asking advice about her railway shares – or discussions of *Shirley*, or thanks for further parcels of books to read; at this stage the only intimate correspondence was with Smith Williams.

Charlotte Brontë defended herself against her publishers' criticisms of *Shirley*:

> My critics truly deserve and have my genuine thanks for the friendly candour with which they have declared their opinions on my book. Both Mr Williams and Mr Taylor express and support their opinions in a manner calculated to command careful consideration. In my turn I have a word to say. You both of you dwell too much on what you regard as the *artistic* treatment of a subject. Say what you will, gentlemen, say it as ably as you will – truth is better than art.[11]

She refused their suggestions, too, the she should write, in a preface to *Shirley*, about the deaths of Ellis and Acton Bell – "I can shed no tears before the public, nor utter any groan in the public ear. The *deep*, real tragedy of our domestic experience is yet terribly fresh in my mind and memory. It is not a time to be talked about to the indifferent."[12] But she did agree, on both George Smith's and Smith Williams' advice, to drop the idea of publishing, in the preface, an answer to the brutal criticism of *Jane Eyre* that had appeared in the *Quarterly*; they saved her from what would surely have been an undignified and upsetting quarrel.

Shirley was published on 26 October, and a month later Charlotte Brontë accepted her publishers' invitation to go for two weeks to London. This time, after some hesitation, she agreed to stay at Westbourne Place. As she wrote to Ellen Nussey:

> I found when I mentioned to Mr Smith my plan of going to Dr Wheelwright's it would not do at all, he would have been seriously hurt; he made his mother

write to me, and thus I was persuaded to make my principal stay at his house. I have found no reason to regret this decision. Mrs Smith received me at first like one who had received the strictest orders to be scrupulously attentive. I had fires in my bedroom evening and morning, wax candles, etc. etc. Mrs Smith and her daughters seemed to look upon me with a mixture of respect and alarm. But all this is now changed, that is to say, the attention and politeness continue as great as ever, but the alarm and estrangement are quite gone. She treats me as if she liked me, and I begin to like her much; kindness is a potent heartwinner. I had not judged too favourably of her son on a first impression; he pleases me much. I like him better even as a son and brother than as a man of business. Mr Williams, too, is really most gentlemanly and well-informed. His weak points he certainly has, but these are not seen in society. Mr Taylor – the little man – has again shown his parts; of him I have not yet come to a clear decision; abilities he has, for he rules the firm (which Dr Wheelwright told me the other day is considerably the largest publishing concern in London), he keeps 40 young men under strict control of his iron will. His young superior likes him, which, to speak truth is more than I do at present; in fact, I suspect he is of the Helstone order of men – rigid, despotic, and self-willed. He tries to be very kind and even to express sympathy sometimes, but he does not manage it. He has a determined, dreadful nose in the middle of his face which when poked into my countenance cuts into my soul like iron. Still he is horribly intelligent, quick, searching, sagacious, and with a memory of relentless tenacity. To turn to Williams after him, or to Smith himself, is to turn from granite to easy down or warm fur.[13]

There is a slight foretaste of Paul Emanuel in this description of James Taylor. He, too, is "the little man",[14] "so energetic, so intent, and above all so absolute",[15] with his mixture of kindness, intelligence and irritability. In fact James Taylor, who had first met Charlotte Brontë at Haworth when he had called in for the completed manuscript of *Shirley*, was strongly attracted to her. She did not respond. The next letter to Ellen Nussey, still from London, says, "You seem to suppose I must be very happy, dear Nell, and I see you have twenty romantic notions in your head about me. These last you may dismiss at once. . . . An attack of rheumatic fever has kept poor Mr Taylor out of the way since I wrote last. I am sorry for his sake."[16]

George Smith tells how his mother and sisters found Charlotte Brontë a somewhat difficult guest. "I am afraid she was not perfectly at her ease with them. Strangers used to say that they were afraid of her. She was very quiet and self-absorbed, and gave the impression that she was always engaged in observing and analysing the people she met." This was true, of course, and to some extent must always be true of novelists. Fanny Burney used to rouse the same fears – "Nothing is so formidable," she caused Lady Hesketh to remark, "as to be in company with silent observers".[17]

George Smith did all he could to be a good host. He took her to *Macbeth* and *Othello*, to the National Gallery and to the Turner Exhibition; Smith Williams took her to the new Houses of Parliament. For the first time, in spite of her horror of being "lionized", she met critics and fellow-authors. Because she longed, above all, to see Thackeray, Smith, who had not previously met him, invited him to dinner. The evening was not easy. Although Smith had begged Thackeray not to embarrass Charlotte Brontë by mentioning "Currer Bell" or his works, "to my dismay", Smith remembered,

> when we rejoined the ladies in the drawing-room, he approached Miss Brontë and quoted a passage from *Jane Eyre*. . . . The quotation in one sense was happy enough, and it did credit to Thackeray's memory of *Jane Eyre*, but not to his memory of his agreement with me. Miss Brontë's face showed her discomposure, and in a chilly fashion she turned off the allusion. But I was almost as much discomposed as Miss Brontë by this sudden assault on what she was so anxious to guard – her identity as the author of *Jane Eyre*. She cast an accusing look at me.

Charlotte herself seemed happy, though, describing the evening in a letter to her father:

> Yesterday I saw Mr Thackeray. . . . He was not told who I was, he was not introduced to me, but I soon saw him looking at me through his spectacles; and when we all rose to go down to dinner he just stepped quietly up and said, "Shake hands"; so I shook hands. . . . I get on quietly. Most people know me, I think, but they are far too well bred to show that they know me, so that there is none of that bustle or that sense of publicity I dislike.[18]

The other distinguished author Charlotte Brontë met on this visit was Harriet Martineau, but this was on her own initiative. Harriet Martineau had written an appreciative letter about *Shirley*, and when Charlotte found that they both happened to be staying near each other in London, she wrote to ask if she might call. From this call developed an important friendship for them both.

On the final evening of this London visit the Smiths gave her a farewell dinner party with seven literary men, including five critics, as the guests. She found it stimulating at the time, but totally exhausting. When she entered the dining-room she had not the courage to sit in her expected place, next to her host, but moved to the seat next to Mrs Smith. Mrs Smith helped her to manage such a formidable occasion. "She watched me very narrowly when surrounded by gentlemen," Charlotte wrote to Ellen Nussey,

> she never took her eye from me, I liked the surveillance, both when it kept guard over me amongst many, or only with her cherished one. She soon, I am convinced, saw in what light I received all, Thackeray included. Her "George" is a very fine specimen of a young English man-of-business; so I regard him, and I am proud to be one of his props.[19]

Charlotte Brontë's letters of thanks when she returned home show her relationship with the Smiths getting closer and more relaxed. There was one to Mrs Smith:

> It made me rather sad to leave you; regretful partings are the inevitable penalty of pleasant visits. I believe I made no special acknowledgement of your kindness when I took leave, but I thought you very kind. I am glad to have had the opportunity of knowing you, and, whether I ever see you again or not, I must always recall with grateful pleasure the fortnight I spent under your roof. Write a line to me when you have time, to tell me how you and your daughters are; remember me to them all.[20]

She enclosed a letter to George:

> I should not feel content if I omitted writing to you as well as to your mother, for I must tell you as well as her how much the pleasure of my late visit was enhanced by her most considerate attention and goodness. As to yourself, what can I say? Nothing. And it is as well; words are not at all needed. Very easy is it to discover that with you to gratify others is to gratify yourself; to serve others is to afford yourself a pleasure. I suppose you will experience your share of ingratitude and encroachment, but do not let them alter you. Happily, they are the less likely to do this because you are half a Scotchman, and therefore must

have inherited a fair share of prudence to qualify your generosity, and of caution to protect your benevolence. Currer Bell bids you farewell for the present.[21]

These letters were followed by a tentative correspondence with Mrs Smith – "Since you are kind enough to answer my letter, you shall occasionally hear from me, but not too often; you shall not be 'bored' (as Mr Thackeray would say) with too frequent a call for replies".[22] The next letter to George thanks him for criticism and books, and gently mocks his image as a businessman:

I have likewise got Mr Doyle's book in its beautiful lapis-lazuli cover. All comment on the circumstances of your sending a second copy after the first had been lost would, I feel, be quite unavailing. I leave the correction of such proceeding to the "man of business" within you: on the "close-fisted" Head of the Establishment in Cornhill devolves the duty of reprimanding Mr G-e S-th; they may settle accounts between themselves, while Currer Bell looks on and wonders, but keeps out of the mêlée.

. . . I regret exceedingly that it is not in my power to give any assurance of the substantial existence of Miss Helston. You must be satisfied if that young person has furnished your mind with a pleasant idea; she is a native of Dreamland, and as such can have neither voice nor presence except for the fancy, neither living nor dwelling except in thought.

N.B. – That last sentence is not to be read by the "man of business"; it sounds much too bookish.[23]

This correspondence, bringing friendship and memories of London to Haworth, became increasingly important in Charlotte Brontë's life. When there was a short break she wrote to Ellen Nussey,

I have had no letters from London for a long time, and am very much ashamed of myself to find, now when that stimulus is withdrawn, how dependent on it I had become. I cannot help feeling something of the excitement of expectation till the post hour comes, and when, day after day, it brings nothing, I get low. This is a stupid, disgraceful, unmeaning state of things.[24]

She knew she must avoid sinking to the state she had been in in 1845, frantic for letters from M. Heger. Six days later she was answering a letter from Smith Williams, and saying,

I always like your way of mentioning Mr Smith, because my own opinion of him concurs with yours, and it is as pleasant to have a favourable impression of character confirmed, as it is painful to see it dispelled: I am sure he possesses a fine nature, and I trust the selfishness of the world, and the hard habits of business, though they may and must modify his disposition, will never quite spoil it.[25]

In another letter to Smith Williams she asked him to pass on thanks to George Smith for helping John Greenwood, her Haworth stationer and friend, to add a bookselling agency to his shop – now he would no longer have to do wool-combing to make a living.[26]

By April 1850 the next visit to London was being discussed, the original plan being that Charlotte should stay with the Kay-Shuttleworths. "On no account should you have dreamed that I was coming to town", she wrote to Smith. "That there are certain organizations liable to anticipating impressions in the form of a dream or presentiment I half believe, but that you, a man of business, have any right to be one of these I wholly deny. 'No prophet can come out of Nazareth' (i.e. Cornhill)."[27] When, rather to Charlotte's relief, the Kay-Shuttleworth plan fell through, Mrs Smith invited her to stay once more with them, and she was anxious to accept.

After a few days with my "fashionable friends" as you call them, I believe I should be excessively disposed, very probably profoundly thankful, to subside into any corner of your drawing-room where I might find a chair of suitable height. I am sorry you have changed your residence, as I shall now again lose my way in going up and down stairs, and stand in great tribulation, contemplating several doors and not knowing which to open.[28]

Mr Brontë was willing for her to go, and in fact she spent the whole visit at the Smiths', in their new house in Gloucester Terrace. "Here I feel very comfortable", she wrote to Ellen Nussey. "Mrs Smith treats me with a serene equable kindness which just suits me. Her son is as before genial and kindly. I have seen very few persons, and am not likely to see many, as the agreement was I was to be very quiet."[29]

This turned out to be Charlotte's happiest visit – "I never remember to have enjoyed myself more in the same length of time,"[30] she wrote to Mrs Smith afterwards – and her friendship with George deepened. How deep this friendship went, on either side, has been much discussed and of course can never be known. George "found her conversation most interesting, her quick and clear intelligence delightful."[31] He clearly enjoyed being the confidant and patron of his dramatically shy and successful author. But "I do not think the relations between my father and Miss Brontë were ever sentimental," his daughter Mrs Reginald Smith said. "He regarded her from his youthful twenties as quite old, and besides he was a great admirer of beauty."[32] She was in fact eight years older than him, "past 30 and plain, with expressive grey eyes",[33] as Matthew Arnold said, and no one called her beautiful. When, in 1898, Mrs Humphry Ward was writing the preface for the Haworth Edition of *Villette* for Smith & Elder, the letters George Smith showed her led her to ask him outright whether he had ever been in love with Charlotte Brontë. "I was amused at your questions," he answered.

No, I never was in the least bit in love with Charlotte Brontë. I am afraid that the confession will not raise me in your opinion, but the truth is, I never could have loved any woman who had not some charm or grace of person, and Charlotte Brontë had none. I liked her and was interested by her, and I admired her – especially when she was in Yorkshire and I was in London. I never was coxcomb enough to suppose that she was in love with me. But I believe that my mother was at one time rather alarmed.[34]

Sir Tresham Lever, in an article in the *Brontë Society Transactions* in 1977, argued that correspondence in September 1851 showed George Smith on the point of proposing. This is on the strength of an otherwise unpublished letter of Charlotte's. Sir Tresham prints part of it but it must be quoted fully, because extracts from a discursive letter do not give a true impression of the whole. He leaves out the matter-of-fact reasons for not replying promptly, and interprets this letter as an attempt by Charlotte to "comfort but not quite encourage" George Smith. But it is lively letter, not at all what she might have written in a state of acute emotional stress. It reads:

My dear Sir,
People say it is wrong to write speak or act on the spur of the moment or

from first impulses – but I must do so for once. Your note of this morning is *so* like yourself – and – I must add – the best part of yourself – the *best* because the most individual – the least like ordinary-minded, ordinary feeling people who hardly ever doubt themselves – or think that what *they* have done can be in fault: but how far astray you are! How widely mistaken! <u>No</u> *indeed* your letter did not displease me – how could it? And you shall not find fault with what I like – for I *did* like the letter – nor shall you imagine me such a paltry-minded, porcupine-souled person as to fancy offence in what is genial, lifelike and full of pleasant spirit.

My reason for not immediately replying to it was partly because I had nothing gratifying to say about the Currer-Bell-Serial point – and partly because I felt sure you must have had quite enough of the Martineau–Brontë Correspondence – and decidedly needed some little repose – but I was not angry – *that* I was not.

I am tempted to say a little bit more on this subject – an explanatory metaphysical little bit drawing a sort of distinction. You mention the words "flippancy and impertinent licence". Allow me to say that you never need to mention these words because (it seems to me) that your nature has nothing to do with the qualities they represent – nothing in this world. I do not believe that except perhaps to people who had themselves a good deal of effrontery and hardness – you could be otherwise than kindly and considerate – you are always so to Currer Bell – and always have been, which is one chief reason why he has a friendship for you: you must leave a contrary line of conduct to people of another species – of the Mr Lewes order of instance. You are not like Mr Lewes – are you? If you are one atom like Mr Lewes – I will never trust my own instinct again – for I felt what he was through the very first letter he sent me – and had no wish ever to hear from – or write to him again – You appear to me something very different – *not* hard – *not* insolent – *not* coarse – *not* to be distrusted – all the contrary.

I have got "John Drayton" and when I write again will tell you what I think of him – So far I am struck by the excellence of many points and especially a magnitude of feeling and a graphic vividness of description – Then – there is no tendency to arraign class against class; you are made to sympathize with the poor without hating the rich – this proves a large heart in the author.

By the by – I always count the postage stamps on the back of every book you send. There were sixteen-pence worth on "J.D." alone – Circumstances of this kind cause one to think of Dr Brown* and to see him again in imagination with Mr Fraser's head between his hands – Mr Fr. looking down – conscious of a

* For the visit to the phrenologist Dr Brown, see p. 62.

large organ of extravagance amongst other erring developments. Mr Fraser shouldn't keep his own money – he isn't fit. These are all the thanks you get.

Never mind my spirits &c. I rub on – and only keep grudging myself the manna of an occasional letter from Cornhill and wishing I had strength of mind to cut off this indulgence and scorning myself pretty heartily because I have not this strength.

I am truly glad to hear that there are good news of Mr Taylor – that he is so well and that his business energies have so far stood the test of the Indian Sun.

I hope your "small troubles" will soon melt away – that paragraph in which you mention them brings to one's mind's eye the movements of a curbed-in eager steed. You must be patient – you must not champ your bit and rear in that way. Good-bye. I wish there was no more reality in any evil that can possibly come near you than there is in the idea of my feeling anything but gratitude for that unjustly accused letter.
Believe me always
Sincerely yours

C. Brontë[35]

It seems rather far-fetched to argue from this, as Sir Tresham Lever does, that the earlier unanswered letter must have shown George Smith anxious to propose and that the lack of an immediate answer made him back-pedal in panic and apologize for his "flippancy and impertinent licence". It is an odd interpretation of the letter, without any foundation, and totally out of character for Smith. He was a man of clear decisions and firm action; when he met his future wife his courtship was determined and unambiguous. Nor would Charlotte Brontë's letter, with its digressions on books and postage stamps, be a likely response – for all its friendship and warmth – to a letter which was almost a proposal.

If George Smith viewed Charlotte Brontë as a genius whose company he enjoyed, and whose confidence in him flattered him, her feelings towards him were more complicated. The first hint of something more than friendship came in a letter to Ellen Nussey towards the end of this London visit, in June 1850, when George had suggested that Charlotte should join him and his sister in a visit to Edinburgh.

I concluded he was joking, laughed and declined: however, it seems he was in earnest. The thing appearing to me perfectly out of the question, I still refused. Mrs Smith did not favour it; you may easily fancy how she helped me to sustain my opposition, but her worthy son only waxed more determined. His mother is master of the house, but he is master of his mother. This morning she came and entreated me to go. "George wished it so much"; he had begged her to use her influence, etc., etc. Now I believe that George and I understand each other very well, and respect each other very sincerely. We both know the wide breach time has made between us; we do not embarrass each other, or very rarely, my 6 or 8 years of seniority, to say nothing of lack of all pretension to beauty, etc., are a perfect safeguard. I should not in the least fear to go with him to China. I like to see him pleased, I greatly *dis*like to ruffle and disappoint him, so he shall have his mind, and, if all be well, I mean to join him in Edinburgh after I shall have spent a few days with you. With his buoyant animal spirits and youthful vigour he will make severe demands on my muscles and nerves, but I dare say I shall get through somehow.[36]

Perhaps Charlotte regretted the "perfect safeguard". During the course of the next year, when letters from Cornhill were again the drug she needed to keep her from sinking into depression in Haworth, she wrote revealingly to Ellen Nussey. In January 1851 she sent Ellen one of his letters for comment,[37] and then chides her for jumping to too many conclusions:

I think those "fixed intentions" you fancy – are imaginary – I think the "undercurrent" amounts simply to this – a kind of natural liking and sense of something congenial. Were there no vast barrier of age, fortune etc. there is perhaps enough personal regard to make things possible which are now impossible. If men and women married because they like each others' temper, look, conversation, nature and so on – and if besides, years were more closely equal – the chance you allude to might be admitted as a chance – but other reasons regulate matrimony – reasons of convenience, of connection, of money. Meantime I am content to have him as a friend – and pray to God to continue to me the commonsense to look on one so young, so rising and so hopeful in no other light. . . .

Good-bye, dear Nell, Heaven grant us both some quiet wisdom – and strength not merely to bear the trial of pain – but to resist the lure of pleasure when it comes in such a shape as our better judgement disapproves.[38]

The other clues to Charlotte's feelings for George Smith, as for M. Heger, are in *Villette*. "For those who knew Mr Smith," Sidney Lee said in an address to the Brontë Society in 1909, "Dr John is a speaking portrait." The personal appearance was absolutely right: "The well-proportioned figure, the handsome and manly face and brow, the imposing height, the blue eyes, the hair worn rather long", and so was the character, "strong and cheerful, firm and courteous, not rash yet valiant", with a "gay and sanguine" temperament, but human and "not perfect". The half-smile, the tremendous capacity for work, the thoughtfully arranged sightseeing, the charm and understanding of the relationship between mother and son – all these are taken from the Smiths for the Brettons. Here is Lucy Snowe's description of the Brettons' home:

> There are human tempers, bland, glowing, and genial, within whose influence it is as good for the poor in spirit to live, as it is for the feeble in frame to bask in the glow of noon. Of the number of these choice natures were certainly both Dr Bretton's and his mother's. They liked to communicate happiness, as some like to occasion misery: they did it instinctively; without fuss, and apparently with little consciousness; the means to give pleasure rose spontaneously in their minds. Every day, while I stayed with them, some little plan was proposed which resulted in beneficial enjoyment.[39]

Charlotte Brontë's books being, of course, all based on characters and events familiar to her, it is not surprising to find people and incidents of her London visits, as well as her Brussels experiences, in *Villette*. They are not described there simply by an observer, but by someone very much emotionally involved. The powerful account of Vashti at the Villette theatre, for example, is a memory of seeing Rachel at Covent Garden with George Smith, and the provision by Mrs Bretton of a new pink dress for the royal concert is, according to Sidney Lee, "true of an identical experience of Charlotte Brontë at Mrs Smith's Bayswater home".[40] Above all, for Lucy Snowe as for Charlotte Brontë, hiding a passionate nature under a self-effacing exterior, there was a yearning for the stimulating happy atmosphere of the lively ménage of mother and son, and an aching for the friendly letters which meant so much more to her than to the sender. There were five letters from Dr John, letters with "often very pithy thoughts, generally sound, and sometimes original opinions, set, without pretension, in an easily-flowing, spirited style . . . that genial, half-humorous vein, which to me gave such delight."[41] Lucy Snowe gave these letters a symbolic burial, and from that time Paul Emanuel, compounded from four parts M. Heger and one part James Taylor, replaces Dr John as the hero. "Lucy must not marry Dr John," Charlotte wrote to George Smith himself in

November 1852, "he is far too youthful, handsome, bright-spirited, and sweet-tempered; he is a 'curled darling' of Nature and of Fortune, and must draw a prize in life's lottery. His wife must be young, rich, pretty; he must be made very happy indeed."[42]

As Charlotte had shown in her letters to Ellen Nussey, anything more than friendship was unthinkable; romantic ideas had to be buried.

So friendship flourished, through the summer visits of 1850 and 1851 and through long letters between those visits – warmest in 1851, dwindling when *Villette* was, with many delays from poor health and low spirits, being painfully written, and ending soon after *Villette* was published. These letters, with their strength and liveliness, were unlike those she wrote to anyone else.

When Charlotte came to stay, George Smith continued to be the most thoughtful of hosts. In 1850, besides the conventional round of Opera, Royal Academy, Zoo and Parliament, he took her to the Chapel Royal in order to see her old hero the Duke of Wellington; they followed him out of the Chapel, carefully arranging their walk so that she met him twice on his way to Apsley House. George had Charlotte's portrait* drawn by Richmond for her father, he had G.H. Lewes to lunch, and Thackeray for a morning call when Charlotte "was moved to speak to him of some of his shortcomings (literary of course) . . . he did defend himself, like a great Turk and heathen . . . the matter ended in decent amity".[43] This led to the disastrous party, so marvellously remembered by Anny Thackeray, who was thirteen at the time, when Thackeray asked George Smith to bring Charlotte Brontë to dinner, and assembled a formidable collection of literary lions to meet her.

> We saw the carriage stop, and out of it sprang the active, well-knit figure of Mr George Smith, who was bringing Miss Brontë to see our father. My father, who had been walking up and down the room goes out into the hall to meet his guests, and then, after a moment's delay, the door opens wide, and the two gentlemen come in, leading a tiny, delicate, serious, little lady, pale, with fair straight hair, and steady eyes. She may be a little over 30; she is dressed in a

* A copy of this portrait and of Richmond's portrait of Mrs Gaskell were presented by Mrs George Smith in 1911 to Newnham College Cambridge, and now hang there in Clough Hall.

little barège dress, with a pattern of faint green moss. She enters in mittens, in silence, in seriousness; our hearts are beating in wild excitement. . . . The moment is so breathless that dinner comes as a relief to the solemnity of the occasion, and we all smile as my father stoops to offer his arm; for, though genius she may be, Miss Brontë can barely reach his elbow. My own personal impressions are that she is somewhat grave and stern, especially to forward little girls who wished to chatter. Mr George Smith has since told me how she afterwards remarked on my father's wonderful forbearance and gentleness with our uncalled-for incursions into the conversation. . . . Mrs Crowe, the reciter of ghost-stories, was there. Mrs Brookfield, Mrs Carlyle, Mr Carlyle himself was present, so I am told, railing at the appearance of cockneys upon Scotch mountain sides; there were also too many Americans for his taste, "but the Americans were as gods compared to the cockneys", says the philosopher. Besides the Carlyles, there were Mrs Elliott and Miss Perry, Mrs Procter and her daughter, most of my father's habitual friends and companions. In the recent life of Lord Houghton I was amused to see a note quoted in which Lord Houghton also was convened. Would that he had been present – perhaps the party would have gone off better. It was a gloomy and a silent evening. Every one waited for the brilliant conversation which never began at all. Miss Brontë retired to the sofa in the study, and murmured a low word now and then to our kind governess, Miss Trulock. The room looked very dark, the lamp began to smoke a little, the conversation grew dimmer and more dim, the ladies sat round still expectant, my father was too much perturbed by the gloom and the silence to be able to cope with it at all. Mrs Brookfield, who was in the doorway by the study, near the corner in which Miss Brontë was sitting, leant forward with a little commonplace, since brilliance was not to be the order of the evening. "Do you like London, Miss Brontë?" she said; another silence, a pause, then Miss Brontë answers, "Yes and No", very gravely. Mrs Brookfield has herself reported the conversation. My sister and I were much too young to be bored in those days; alarmed, impressed we might be, but not yet bored. A party was a party, a lioness was a lioness; and – shall I confess it? – at that time an extra dish of biscuits was enough to mark the evening. We felt all the importance of the occasion; tea spread in the dining-room, ladies in the drawing-room. We roamed about inconveniently, no doubt, and excitedly, and in one of my incursions crossing the hall, after Miss Brontë had left, I was surprised to see my father opening the front door with his hat on. He put his fingers to his lips, walked out into the darkness, and shut the door quietly behind him.[44]

Driving back from that party Charlotte, who had watched George

Smith talking with Adelaide Procter, startled him by leaning forward, putting her hands on his knees, and saying, "She would make you a very nice wife".[45]

The Scottish visit, looked forward to with trepidation in the letter to Ellen Nussey, did materialize, a brief three days but an entire success. "It furnished me with some hours as happy almost as any I ever spent,"[46] she wrote to Smith Williams; and later, after staying in the Lake District in less sympathetic company, she wrote to him again that in spite of even better scenery, that journey "did not give me half so much pleasure, because I saw it under less congenial auspices. Mr Smith and Sir J.K. Shuttleworth are 2 different people with whom to travel."[47] George Smith must have written to her with happy memories of Scotland too, for she replied:

> May I tell you how your mourning reveries respecting Glencoe and Loch Katrine will probably end? The thought has just come into my head and must be written down. Some day – you will be *even later than usual* in making your appearance at breakfast – your anxious mother, on going up to make enquiries, will find you deep in undeniable inspiration, on the point of completing the twelfth canto of "The Highlands; a Grand Descriptive Romantic and Sentimental POEM, by GS Esq."[48]

She tried to remember, in another letter that summer, that she must not intrude too much into his busy London life – "Were you still in Glencoe, or even in Edinburgh, I might write you a longer and more discursive letter, but, mindful of the 'fitness of things' and of the effect of locality, reverent too of the claims of business, I will detain your attention no longer."[49]

There were light-hearted letters that autumn about books, about Thackeray, Cardinal Wiseman, Mr Newby – "Poor Mr Newby! One is very sorry for him after all. I hope your conscience fined you in the sum of 5 shillings for that pun on the Nubian Desert."[50] "Forgive all the nonsense of this letter," she wrote another time, "there is such a pleasure and relief either in writing or talking a little nonsense sometimes to anybody who is sensible enough to understand and good-natured enough to pardon it."[51]

In the new year another possible journey with Smith was discussed – an idea of joining him and his family on a trip up the Rhine in the summer. "That hint about the Rhine disturbs me," she wrote to Ellen Nussey: "I am not made of stone – and what is mere excitement to him – is fever to me. . . . I cannot conceive either his mother or his sisters relishing it, and all London would gabble like a countless host of geese."[52] Fortunately for Charlotte's peace of mind the idea faded because of pressure of George Smith's work, removing the disturbing problem. At the end of March Charlotte wrote to him,

> What you say about relinquishing your proposed Continental trip stirs in me a feeble spirit of emulation. By way of imitation on a small scale I would fain give up all thoughts of going to London or elsewhere this spring or summer. Were I but as sure as you are of being able to work to some purpose, gladly, gladly would I make the sacrifice.[53]

Less than three weeks later she wrote again, having just accepted an invitation from Mrs Smith for a visit – "My scheme of emulation appears to have terminated in a somewhat egregious failure."[54] On 28 May 1851 she arrived in London, to spend a whole month at Gloucester Place.

One other letter from Charlotte to George Smith before her London visit must be quoted. It is an answer to one from him which presumably suggested using her knowledge of publishers in some future novel.

> Do you know [she wrote] that the first part of your note is most dangerously suggestive? What a rich field of subject you point out in your allusion to Cornhill, &c, a field at which I myself should only have ventured to glance like the serpent at Paradise; but when Adam himself opens the gates and shows the way in, what can the honest snake do but bend its crest in token of gratitude and glide rejoicingly through the aperture? But no! Don't be alarmed. You are all safe from Currer Bell – safe from his satire – safer from his eulogium. We cannot (or at least I cannot) write of our acquaintance with the consciousness that others will recognize their portraits, or that they themselves will know the hand which has sketched them. Under such circumstances the pencil would falter in the fingers and shrink alike from the indication of bold shades and brilliant lights (especially the last, because it would look like flattery); plain speaking would seem audacious, praise obtrusive. Were it possible that I could take you all fearlessly, like so many abstractions, or historical characters that had been dust a hundred years, could handle, analyse, delineate you, without danger of the picture being recognized either by yourselves or others, I should think my material abundant and rich. This, however, is no more possible than that the Nurse should give the child the moon out of the sky. So I repeat it – you are *very* safe.[55]

It is impossible to say how seriously George Smith's suggestion was made, and Charlotte of course never wrote a novel with a Cornhill background, but it was in the following year that the Smiths, and to some extent James Taylor, were written into *Villette*.

The 1851 visit was marred by headaches, and had not quite the happiness of the previous year. Charlotte found George Smith changed – "a little older, darker, and more careworn"[56] – and overloaded with work, sometimes staying in the City till three in the morning. Part of his trouble was that James Taylor had recently gone to India, to stay for five years on the firm's business. This sudden departure had startled Charlotte, and although she had decided, when Taylor had called at Haworth to say goodbye, that he was "second-rate"[57] and could never be acceptable as a husband, she yet was moved later when he wrote from India, and she became briefly in danger of once more centring too much of her life and emotions on waiting for the post. Smith, it seems, had found Taylor a difficult colleague, and complained of his temper. The result of banishing him was that Smith was now again carrying too much of the firm himself.

George Smith still found time to look after Charlotte. He escorted her to Thackeray's lectures – where Thackeray horrified Charlotte by introducing her to his mother as "Jane Eyre" – to see Rachel at Covent Garden, and to hear a variety of preachers, from F.D. Maurice to Cardinal Wiseman. He managed to take one whole day off for a family expedition with her to Richmond and even, under the pretence of being Mr and Miss Fraser, took her to a phrenologist.

The phrenologist's reports gave much amusement in later letters, and since Charlotte thought George Smith's was "*like – like – like* as the very life itself*",[58] it is worth quoting some of it:

He is an admirer of the fair sex. He is very kind to children. Is strongly attached to his home. Is of a very affectionate and friendly disposition. Has no care for riches for the sake of accumulation. Is of an open undesigning disposition, and requires to be careful of his own interest when sympathy for the distress of those he values demands a sacrifice. He is endowed with much benevolent feeling and would be liberal to those suffering in poverty. He is deferential and respectful and there is not a tincture of arrogance in his nature. He possesses a high sense of justice and much firmness; a strong love of distinction, but scarcely an adequate opinion of his own capabilities. . . . Is fond of the ideal and romantic and possesses a strongly developed organ of language. He has a just sense of the value of time, and is not prone to procrastinate. Is active and practical though not hustling or contentious. Whatever profession or business requires a quick perception of objects and circumstances and a readiness in citing examples would be well adapted to this intellectual development. . . . His feelings are easily moved but he has a very forgiving temper.[59]

Charlotte Brontë made a half-hearted resolution to ration her letter-writing after this visit, but was not very successful. There are many letters through the summer and autumn; warm, lively letters, trying to be cheerful – "Tell your mother I shall try to cultivate good spirits as assiduously as she cultivates her geraniums."[60] She wrote often about Thackeray and about Harriet Martineau, who was now, on Charlotte's introduction, writing a book for Smith & Elder. She rejected the idea of serial publication herself – she would like to, "but though Currer Bell cannot do this you are still to think him your friend, and you are still to be *his* friend. You are to keep a fraction of yourself – if it be only the end of your little finger – for *him*."[61] She sent Smith an amiable analysis of his character:

I will tell you a thing to be noted often in your letters and almost always in your conversation, a psychological thing, and not a matter pertaining to style or intellect – I mean an undercurrent of quiet raillery, an inaudible laugh to yourself, a not unkindly somewhat subtle playing on your correspondent or companion for the time being – in short, a sly touch of a Mephistopheles, with the fiend extracted.[62]

There were repeated invitations, both from George Smith and from his mother, for a further visit, but Charlotte would not go until she had "earned" it by finishing *Villette*. She could get on with it only when the right mood came – "Quakerlike waiting on the spirit"[63] as she wrote to George Smith – and in that autumn and the winter of illness and depression that followed, the mood failed her. In January George Smith even suggested coming himself to Haworth, perhaps to encourage her back to writing, but this happened to be during the one fortnight when she was away with Ellen Nussey; he was not willing to visit there instead, and the opportunity of their meeting at Haworth passed.

Books and letters still came from Cornhill, but in the spring these got fewer. "Cornhill is silent", Charlotte wrote sadly to Ellen Nussey on 1 July. "There has been bitter disappointment there at my having no work ready for this season."[64] In August there must have been a good letter, because she answers about her father's health, George's young brother going to India, and George himself overworking.

By 30 October she was able to send the first two volumes of *Villette*, waiting anxiously for the reaction. "I can hardly tell you how I hunger to hear some opinion beside my own, and how I have sometimes desponded, and almost despaired, because there was no one to whom to read a line, or of whom to ask a counsel . . . not that I am likely to alter anything."[65] She did not alter anything, but agreed with the criticism that there is a discrepancy between Graham's boyhood and manhood, agreed to give up the idea of publishing anonymously, and submitted "to the advertisements in large letters, but under protest, and with a kind of ostrich longing for concealment".[66] The last volume went on 20 November, and she was ready to consider London once more – "It is something to look forward to and to anticipate", she wrote to Mrs Smith. "I keep it, on the principle of the school-boy who hoards his choicest piece of cake."[67] But although letters from Mrs Smith were very kind, something unexplained was bothering Charlotte. "I almost wish I could still look on that kindness just as I used to do," she wrote to Ellen Nussey. "It was very pleasant to me once."[68] Then there was the worry of how the Smiths would react to their very recognizable portrayal. It is not surprising to find Charlotte reporting to Ellen that "something in the third volume sticks confoundedly in his throat, and as to the 'female character' about which I asked, [presumably Paulina, who became Dr John's wife] he responds crabbedly that, 'She is an odd, fascinating little puss', but affirms that he is 'not in love with her'."[69]

After Christmas, Charlotte wrote to Mrs Smith suggesting a January visit, and she arrived on 11 January. Before that – in December – her father's curate, Arthur Nicholls, proposed, though it was more than a year before she accepted him. It was Charlotte's last visit to the Smiths, and it followed a rather different pattern. George was absorbed by his heavy load of work, so much so that, as she wrote to Ellen,

The very lines of his features are altered; it is rather the remembrance of what he was than the fact of what he is which can warrant the picture I have been accustomed to give of him. One feels pained to see a physical alteration of this kind, yet I feel glad and thankful that it is merely physical; as far as I can judge, mind and manners have undergone no deterioration.[70]

Charlotte corrected proofs and chose her own unconventional sight-seeing, to the amazement of Mrs Smith and her daughters – Newgate, Pentonville, Bedlam, the Foundling Hospital, the Bank, the Exchange. George escorted her to some of these and has written of taking her to Newgate, where "she rapidly fixed her attention on an individual prisoner. This was a poor girl with an interesting face, and an expression of the deepest misery. She had, I believe, killed her illegitimate child. Miss Brontë walked up to her, took her hand, and began to talk to her."[71]

It is not possible to say how much George Smith knew then of the Brussels background to *Villette*, and of Charlotte's personal involvement with the Hegers as the inspiration of Lucy Snowe's love for Paul Emanuel. Charlotte asked George to prevent *Villette* from being translated into French, but he was not able to do so for long. The Hegers had a translation when Mrs Gaskell went there in 1856.

After this London visit letters are scarcer, though occasionally the old liveliness revived, for instance when Charlotte remembered their visit as Mr and Miss Fraser to the phrenologist, in this of 16 February:

> On the whole the critique I like best yet is one I got at an early stage of the work, before it had undergone the "Old Bailey", being the observations of a respected amateur critic, one A. Fraser Esq. I am bound to admit, however, that this gentleman confined his approving remarks to the 2 first volumes, tacitly condemning the third by the severity of a prolonged silence.[72]

Ten days later she was thanking George for the present of an engraving of Samuel Laurence's portrait of Thackeray, a portrait which Mrs Smith had taken Charlotte to see at the artist's studio. It was hung, "superb in his beautiful, tasteful, gilded gibbet",[73] with the earlier presents – the Wellington engraving and the Richmond drawing. In March she was able to write to him light-heartedly about the problem of Paul Emanuel's fate:

> every reader should settle the catastrophe for himself, according to the quality of his disposition, the tender or remorseless impulses of his nature: Drowning and Matrimony are the fearful alternatives. The merciful – like Miss Mulock,

Mr Williams, Lady Harriet St Clair and Mr Alexander Fraser – will of course choose the former and milder doom – drown him to put him out of pain. The cruel-hearted will, on the contrary, pitilessly impale him on the second horn of the dilemma, marrying him without ruth or compunction to that – person – that – that – individual – "Lucy Snowe".[74]

There is very little more. In July she thanked him for kind enquiries about her father, and for offers of help if they should want a London doctor. Another letter thanked him for Ruskin's *Architecture and Painting*, just published by Smith & Elder. But in November, when she was planning to go to London once more, Mrs Gaskell and Emily Shaen gave her advice about lodgings. This visit was cancelled and she did not go again. There was a brief letter to Smith Williams in December: "I forwarded last week a box of return books to Cornhill, which I trust arrived safely. To-day I received the 'Edinburgh Guardian', for which I thank you. Do not trouble yourself to select or send any more books. These courtesies must cease some day, and I would rather give them up than wear them out."[75]

A letter from Mrs Smith the following spring hinted at George's coming engagement:

> I was very glad indeed to receive a letter from you this morning . . . it is an age since I have heard of you. . . . I shall answer your kind enquiries about my son with a great deal of pleasure – he is quite well and very happy – he is thinking of taking a very important step in life, the most important and with every prospect of happiness. I am very thankful and pleased about it.[76]

The last long letter to George is a strange one, on 25 April 1854, congratulating him and thanking him for congratulations to her.

> It gave me sincere pleasure to be assured of your happiness though of that I never doubted. I have faith also in its permanent character – provided Mrs George Smith is – what it pleases me to fancy her to be – You never told me any particulars about her, though I should have liked them much, but did not like to ask questions. . . . What *I* have to say is soon told. The step in contemplation is no hasty one; on the gentleman's side, at least, it has been meditated for years, and I hope that, in at last acceding to it, I am acting right. My expectations however are very subdued – very different, I dare say, to what *yours* were before you married. . . . In the course of the year that is gone,

Cornhill and London have receded a long way from me; the links of communication have waxed very frail and few. It must be so in this world. All things considered, I don't wish it otherwise.[77]

Mr and Mrs George Smith, and Mrs Smith and her daughters, were on Charlotte's wedding invitation list; none of them went. Charlotte died, after less than a year of marriage, without seeing them again.

VII

Marriage

George Smith has left us his own account of his courtship and marriage. It gives a characteristic picture of his impulsiveness and determination – and of his business instincts.

I first met the lady who afterwards became my wife at a ball at Clapham Common on April 5th, 1853, at the house of her sister Mrs I. Anson. I remember it was on an Indian mail day and that I had been very hard at work until 4 o'clock that morning and up to 7 o'clock in the evening. I was consequently rather tired. It was, with me, a clear case of "love at first sight"! My mother, who got up early, had the habit of coming into my room almost every morning for a little talk, and I had no secrets whatever from her. Few sons and mothers, indeed, have ever been on terms of closer confidence. The morning after that memorable ball I said to her, "I have seen the woman I am going to marry." "That is all very well, you know," my mother replied, "but we have yet to know what the lady will say."

My habits of quick decision, joined with the warmth of the feeling kindled in me, made delay intolerable. I rode over to Clapham on the following Sunday and called at the house where the ball had been given, but Miss Blakeway, who had taken my heart captive, had gone home. I tried all sorts of plans to obtain a closer acquaintance with the object of my regard. I secured the assistance of my sisters and in this way I had one or two brief opportunities of seeing her. She lived at Clapton, and one day – in the following November – I got into a cab and drove off to the house. I found Mrs Blakeway was out, but the daughter was in. This suited my plans exactly. I asked to see Miss Blakeway. I think, by this time, she must have guessed my feelings, but I did not long leave them to be guessed. I frankly proposed, but did not succeed in winning, at first, a definite answer. I next went to see her father. Her father, a wine merchant in Bedford Street, heard me patiently out, but said little. By way of reply, at last, he said, "Well! Come and dine with us next Sunday." I went, and got permission to call every day. This probationary period lasted for ten days – and ten long days they were to me! – and then my suit was accepted. Three months after that we were married, and that marriage has given me life-long happiness. The bride's friends wished to make it a longer engagement, and my mother at first was of the same mind. But she was a keen observer and knew me well. She saw that as long as the object of my desires was unattained I was unsettled. "The fact is," she said, "if you don't let my boy marry he will fret himself into a fever!"

I was as energetic about my marriage as I was about every serious incident in my life. I used to ride over to my fiancée nearly every morning before breakfast. This was a distance of about eight miles, and from Clapton I rode to the City where the groom was waiting to take my horse back, and I had to purchase a horse specially for the performance. I bought one for £15 which had just come off a steeplechase, from the son of Sir Joseph Paxton, who built the Crystal Palace, and used to gallop on it to Clapton in the morning and then on to the City. This lasted during our engagement. I then sold the horse for £10.

So great was the strain of business at this time, and so great a burden had I to carry on my shoulders, that not even my honeymoon brought with it a holiday. We went after the ceremony to Tunbridge Wells, and the very next morning after our marriage down came a clerk with a bag full of letters by the Indian mail to be opened and looked through. My newly wedded wife had never been in personal contact with business affairs, and had no idea of what the conduct of a large business meant. At first she could not in the least understand the manner in which business cares pursued us.

We went on to Paris; but still in our tracks was an ever-flowing stream of correspondence. To copy the letters I had despatched in reply I had a press, but no screw arrangement. I had to secure copies by the primitive method of *sitting* on the press; and it was said by way of a joke in our family that when additional weight was required I used to secure my bride's assistance.

The charm and exhilaration of the honeymoon did not lull my business faculties into slumber. Just at that time the gold discoveries in Australia were reported. I told my wife we might as well extract the expenses of our honeymoon from Australian gold, and I sent to London instructions to buy a large number of revolvers and consign them to Melbourne. I felt sure that where there was so much gold revolvers would be needed. The consignment was sold at a large profit.

So right from the start Elizabeth Smith became involved in George's business life. She seems to have entered fully into the spirit of it, supporting and encouraging him as his mother had done when things went badly, and becoming a splendid hostess to help him entertain his authors and keep the friendly atmosphere to publishing that George so much enjoyed. She came from a Quaker family and was a strong character with, George said, "keen and sympathetic literary taste".

The Smiths lived for four years in George's old home, 112 Gloucester Terrace, and then, after a short time at Wimbledon, moved to 11 Gloucester Square, where they held the famous monthly Cornhill dinners. That house, Smith tells us, "had been previously occupied by Mr Sadleir, notorious for his frauds, who was found dead on Hampstead Heath with a silver cream-jug by his side which had contained prussic acid. By some defect in the construction of the house, when the front door was opened the drawing-room door also slowly opened, and the wind lifted the carpet in slight waves". This story appealed to Thackeray, who used it in his *Roundabout Paper* "On a Pear Tree" and, according to Smith, "was never tired of suggesting that it was Sadleir's ghost come in search of some deeds which had been hidden under the floor."

When, in 1863, the Smiths moved to Oak Hill Lodge, Hampstead, they were anxious that distance should not prevent friends calling on them; Thackeray proposed a regular "at home" evening, so they decided to keep open house on Friday evenings throughout the summer. There would be a cold dinner and guests would arrive unannounced and at various times – perhaps as few as five or six on one evening, or as many as thirty or forty. Smith's coach would take anyone who needed back as far as Swiss Cottage station. These were distinguished gatherings, with Thackeray, Millais, Leech, Trollope, Wilkie Collins and du Maurier among the regular guests. "Few authors or artists who gained reputation in the seventh decade of the nineteenth century", Sidney Lee wrote, "failed to enjoy Smith's genial hospitality at Hampstead on one or other Friday during that period."[1]

Du Maurier, who drew a menu card for the Friday dinners showing Mrs Smith driving a reindeer with a sleigh laden with food, had particular reason to be grateful to the Smiths. He was having trouble with his one functioning eye, and George Smith suggested that, instead of making minute drawings on wood blocks, he might try the new technique of making large drawings on cartridge paper to be photographed down. Du Maurier needed a lot of persuasion, feeling this would be a "sin against his art", but he was happy in the end to find that the result was acceptable and that at the same time he had produced a saleable drawing. Smith bought this first drawing himself for ten guineas; later, as stocks grew, George and Elizabeth Smith formed a committee with George and Emma du Maurier to fix prices for these drawings, ranging from ten to twenty-five guineas, and a great many were sold. Du Maurier was pleased with the extra income and even more pleased to find that, without the strain of wood-block drawing, his eye recovered.

Smith has described one Friday evening when, following two wet and empty weeks, he expected a particularly large party. He asked his butler to find extra tables, managed to organize seating for forty-two, and put his young daughter to count the coming guests. She counted forty,

and then one coach more was visible driving up the road! The child ran to her mother in great concern to report the coming tragedy! Here were guests for whom there would be no room! As it happened the approaching vehicle contained only two guests, there were no more arrivals, and the tables were exactly filled. But the interval was very narrow, and I fancy it was rather a lesson to my wife not to trust too much to what she called "the doctrine of averages". I said to my butler the next morning, "Where did you get all the small tables from?" "There *were* no small tables, sir!" he replied, "they were coffin tops. I borrowed them from the undertaker!"

It was understood by all our intimate friends they might bring with them anyone who was interesting. Turgeniev, the Russian novelist, was brought in this way and made himself very agreeable. Dr Blanc,* who was one of the Abyssinian captives, came, and brought with him his manacles. He put them on and walked about the garden in them, to the amusement of the company and the joy of the children. He brought with him a little copper-skinned Abyssinian, who showed amazing cleverness in picking up and playing games he had never seen till that evening. Thackeray's daughters stayed a great deal with us, and I suspect the earlier stages of the courtship of Leslie Stephen and Minny Thackeray were transacted in the garden at Hampstead. I had a high

* Freed, after three years' captivity, by Sir Robert Napier's expedition in 1867.

regard for Leslie Stephen, and when I noted that Friday after Friday he used to call and propose to walk out with me to Hampstead I was delighted. In my simplicity I quoted to my wife, as a proof of Leslie Stephen's growing friendship for me, the constancy with which, Friday after Friday, he gave me his company out to Hampstead. "Oh you goose!" said my wife; and then I began to notice that she always took care to put Leslie Stephen next to Minny Thackeray at table!

This gives something of the atmosphere of those Friday evenings, and it is pleasant to read that children in that very Victorian home were allowed to meet the guests and enjoy the party. It was, though, a carefully censored collection of guests. Charles Reade, author of *The Cloister and the Hearth*, who had contributed often to both the *Cornhill* and the *Pall Mall Gazette*, was kept strictly away from the family: "I got on well with Charles Reade", Smith wrote, "and he first gave me the name which has since been quoted – for and against me often – of 'the Prince of Publishers' . . . [but his] life was somewhat too Bohemian to permit him having a very wide social circle, and he never came as a guest to my house." George Eliot of course was never invited either, and although Smith went regularly to her Sunday salon and talked to her about his family, he only went so far as to take his eldest son with him once, but never his wife or his daughters. "Unpleasant social results might have followed", he wrote, "if young girls had been known as her visitors." "My wife", Smith continued, "sometimes said playfully she would not allow me to spend the best part of every Sunday afternoon with a lady at St John's Wood with whom she was not acquainted", but after Smith had pointed out George Eliot one day at the opera she changed her mind – " 'You may go every day in the week if you like,' said my wife with cheerful confidence, as she contemplated George Eliot's broad, heavy and melancholy face." The Smiths went frequently to the opera – it had been George's first idea for entertaining Charlotte and Anne Brontë, and they had at that time a regular box.

The Smiths' most famous theatre party was given at Christmas 1870, to celebrate George's recovery from a long period of illness and exhaustion. Believing, like Thackeray, that "a boy at a pantomime is always amused and amusing, and to see his pleasure is good for most hypochondriacs",[1] Smith booked the whole of the front of the dress circle at Covent Garden for a pantomime party for ninety children. Everything was done on a grand scale, even to the printing of a special playbill. Finding that, by an oversight, two strangers had seats at the end of his row, spoiling his vision of a complete block of young friends, Smith got the manager to try to persuade them to move; when that failed he high-handedly insisted that the house carpenters should turn these two seats into a private box so "the two obstinately discourteous visitors were literally built around with planks and cut off from contact with my child guests". There was a drawing of the party in the *Illustrated London News*, with Millais' children clearly in the centre.

Tributes and letters from many different people give some idea of Elizabeth Smith's involvement with George's authors. Browning, who became a close friend of the Smiths for the last twenty years of his life, wrote lines in her album and gave her the manuscript of *The Ring and The Book*. We find Henry James and Lowell both thanking her for welcoming baskets of fruit and flowers. Henry James indeed was an enthusiastic friend, as can be seen in a lively letter to Elizabeth from Anne Procter: "I met Mr Henry James at dinner on Wednesday and we sat next each other. I should have liked my dinner more if he had not admired you so much – I found Edmund Yates and Mr Escott wiser, they did not speak of you."[2]

Mrs Gaskell's letters to George Smith contain many messages to his wife and children; there is only one surviving letter to Elizabeth Smith, but it shows an easy relationship: "Florence brings us word of a most kind invitation from you and Mr Smith to a Greenwich Dinner for either the 20th or 21st, and if this good news is true, may we choose the former day? and how many of the Miss Gaskells will you accept in my train? Florence is brimming over with pleasant recollections of her doings at Hampstead."[3]

But Elizabeth Smith's closest literary friends were Thackeray's daughters. Naturally the two families saw much of each other in the early days of the *Cornhill*. There is a letter from Minny inviting the Smiths to the theatricals in Thackeray's new house in 1862: "We hope that you and Mr Smith will come and see Papa's play on Tuesday 25th at eight o'clock – Palace Green Kensington. Will you ask Mr Smith to be sure to applaud even if everything should go wrong."[4] Then in the sad time after their father's death, which cruelly soon followed the house-warmings and the celebrations, the Smiths were among the friends who helped the two sisters to re-establish their lives. Later Anny was writing many letters to "my dearest Lizzie" as well as to "my dear Mr Smith"; she was a constant visitor, and George eventually became godfather to her daughter. Her *Chapters from Some Memoirs*, published in 1894, were dedicated to George and Elizabeth.

When they had their Hampstead house the Smiths used to winter at Brighton, with George travelling daily to London, one of the earliest of commuters. This was not because they wanted to retreat from constant entertaining, but because Elizabeth was considered to be in delicate health and doctors advised her to live in the country. We read of plenty of guests staying there with them – Thackeray's daughters, John Leech, Theodore Martin, Frederick Burton. There is a story that Leech witnessed Elizabeth Smith being unwilling to ride a rather lively horse, and her bolder eight-year-old daughter offering to do it for her; Leech used the incident, but not the Smith family, for a drawing in *Punch*.

Poor Elizabeth was always having trouble with horses. When she and George stayed with Trollope, "he proposed, out of mere kindness of heart, that they should put a bar up and my wife might then relieve the dullness of her country visit by jumping over it on his favourite hunter for an hour or two each morning! This was, for my wife, a very alarming proposition indeed."

In 1872 the Smiths left both Hampstead and Brighton and moved to South Kensington, where they rented various houses until they bought the Duke of Somerset's mansion in Park Lane in 1891. They also had a house at Weybridge for a while, from 1884 to 1897.

Elizabeth Smith was by all accounts very beautiful, and, Mrs Humphry Ward wrote, "beautiful even as I remember her last, in the year of the outbreak of war, 1914, when she was over eighty."[5] Julia Cameron had heard about her, Anny Thackeray reported to George from Freshwater in 1865: "She says, 'Why does not Mrs Smith come to be *Photographed*. I hear she is *Beautiful* – Bid her come here and she shall be made *Immortal*.' "[6]

Mrs Cameron did not photograph Elizabeth Smith, but there are portraits. Frederick Walker intended to do a painting of her with three children but was unhappy about his preliminary sketch, slashed at it with a carving knife, and never got any further; George liked the sketch, though, and kept it. A grander portrait was done by Frederick Burton, and hung in the Royal Academy. The Smiths had met "the proud and fastidious Burton"[7] in 1864, had come to enjoy his friendship, and admired and bought his paintings. Elizabeth Smith's portrait – the last he ever painted – was, according to George, a wonderful likeness and took three years and something like a hundred sittings. Paying for it was a problem; no price had been agreed, so Smith sent Burton a blank cheque, with a very complimentary letter. Burton filled it up for five hundred guineas, which Smith considered "wholly inadequate", but he only offended Burton when he offered a further five hundred. Here Smith failed to learn from experience, for he had similarly offered a blank cheque to the sculptor Alexander Munro, whom he had commissioned to do a marble figure of his four-year-old daughter. Munro had asked if he might also do a head of his wife, and a profile portrait in *alto-relievo*. This portrait gave trouble, as the first two attempts were spoiled by marks in the marble, though Smith was delighted with the final one and thought Munro had filled in his cheque for an "unreasonably modest sum". Munro then asked whether he might alter the earlier efforts, and sell them as idealized faces. Evidently they were not altered enough, because terra-cotta reproductions were recognized by a friend of Smith's, who was surprised to see Mrs Smith's portrait for sale in a shop window. Smith was not upset, but happily bought several as presents for his daughters and his friends.

There are various signs that Elizabeth Smith had considerable influence in George's publishing life. Irritating gossip-writers wrote in the *Literary Budget* that Thackeray had withdrawn from the editorship of the *Cornhill* because "Mrs Smith edits the Cornhill Magazine". This was wildly untrue, but it does at least imply that she had some reputation as a power behind the scenes. Certainly Mrs Smith encouraged Thackeray to write his *Roundabout Paper* "On Screens in Dining Rooms", as a counter-attack to Edmund Yates's rude references to George, when George himself would have left the matter alone.[8] She outlived George by thirteen years but she kept a strong interest in the firm to the end, especially in the *Dictionary of National Biography* which, as it was his personal property, George had bequeathed to her.

On George's death, a moving tribute was written to Elizabeth by Leslie Stephen:

> I cannot think of your dear husband without the warmest sense of personal gratitude – in which you too have your full share. I think of the old days when I saw you at Hampstead, and met Anny and Minny and saw how you loved them

and felt how you sympathized with my love. I think of all your unvarying kindness since . . . you can hardly know how much you have done for me and others by showing unconsciously the beauty of a perfectly harmonious union.[9]

In her will, Elizabeth Smith left great treasures to the British Museum Library in memory of George, including autograph manuscripts of Charlotte Brontë's novels, Emily's *Gondal Poems* (bought by Mrs Smith in 1907), Thackeray's *The Wolves and the Lamb* (the play that celebrated Thackeray's new house in 1862), some poems by Elizabeth Barrett Browning, and Robert Browning's present of *The Ring and The Book*.

The year of George Smith's engagement was also the year when he took a partner into his rapidly growing firm. He chose Henry Samuel King, a bookseller from Brighton whose wife Ellen was Elizabeth Blakeway's sister. King remained a partner with a quarter-share of the profits, active in the Indian agency and banking as well as publishing, for fifteen years. His chief literary distinction was the arrangement and editing of Robertson's *Sermons*, which have been called the most widespread literature of that kind which has ever issued from the press.[10]

In spite of the family connection – or perhaps when it altered, for by 1865 King was married to a well-connected Miss Hamilton – it was not a happy partnership. Friendship dwindled until, although they met weekly in committee for business, Smith and King never exchanged a word more than they had to. Neither Smith in his *Recollections* nor Leonard Huxley in *The House of Smith Elder* mentions that Smith and King were brothers-in-law.

VIII

Mrs Gaskell

It was the death of Charlotte Brontë that first brought Mrs Gaskell in touch with George Smith. It says much for both of them that from the writing of the biography, in spite of the hornets' nest it stirred, grew not just a good business relationship but a lasting friendship between the Gaskell and Smith families.

The first of more than a hundred surviving letters from Mrs Gaskell to George Smith is a request, written in May 1855 just after Charlotte Brontë had died, for a copy of the Richmond portrait. The letter goes on to say: "sometime, it may be years hence – but if I live long enough, and no one is living whom such a publication would hurt, I will publish what I know of her, and make the world (if I am but strong enough in expression) honour the woman as much as they have admired the writer."[1] Mrs Gaskell had not yet met Smith but, shattered by Charlotte's death, she seems to have felt an impulse of friendship towards him as Charlotte's publisher and friend, and a need to write to him about her. A few days later she wrote again, enclosing a letter from John Greenwood and pouring out her own memories. "My children, who all loved her would like to have what I could write about her," she said, "and the time may come when her wild sad life, and the beautiful character that grew out of it may be made public."[2]

[87]

The time came unexpectedly soon. Urged on by Ellen Nussey, Mr Brontë himself wrote to Mrs Gaskell, in his matter-of-fact restrained way, asking her to undertake a biography.

> Finding that a great many scribblers, as well as some clever and truthful writers, have published articles in newspapers and tracts respecting my dear daughter Charlotte since her death, and seeing that many things that have been stated are true, but more false; and having reason to think that some may venture to write her life who will be ill-qualified for the undertaking, I can see no better plan under the circumstances than to apply to some established author to write a brief account of her life and to make some remarks on her works. You seem to be the best qualified for doing what I wish should be done.[3]

This initiative from Mr Brontë, the man Mrs Gaskell had thought would shrink from any idea of a published memoir, changed the whole scope of her plan. It was now, as she wrote to Smith, "a more serious task", which she was determined to do "well and fully".[4] She decided to start writing during her six weeks' summer holiday in Silverdale, and went first for "a most painful visit"[5] to Mr Brontë and Mr Nicholls in Haworth. As she left, Mr Brontë warned her rather ominously, "No quailing Mrs Gaskell! No drawing back!"[6]

Mrs Gaskell did not want to draw back. She passionately wanted to tell the world the truth about Charlotte Brontë – the harsh drama of her life, her goodness, her suffering and her genius. Impulsive by nature and impatient to get all possible information, Mrs Gaskell pestered Smith for material and was irritated with him at first for not producing as much as she thought he could – though the irritation did not last long. In November she wrote to Ellen Nussey,

> "At last – and by dint of a very cross letter, I have heard from Mr Smith apologizing etc., and enclosing about twenty letters, some of them only fragments of dear Miss Brontë's. The remainder, he says contain matter of too purely personal a nature to be generally interesting, but with these he says I may do as I like if I will only take care to return them to him. He is very civil, more civil than satisfactory . . . I am sure I have not got half of what Mr Williams and he together *might* give: and what they *shall* give, or I'll know the reason why . . . . I still retain the arguments you suggest as weapons against the refractory Dr John.[7]

[88]

It seems likely that, in spite of his growing friendship with Mrs Gaskell, "Dr John" never did show her all his letters from Charlotte. Certainly, whether from delicacy or from lack of opportunity, she never used more than twenty or mentioned any others in any of her surviving correspondence; sixty-five more letters to Smith and to his mother, the liveliest and most personal, appeared for the first time in Clement Shorter's notes to the Haworth Edition of the *Life* in 1900. It is frustrating too to find that Smith must have asked Mrs Gaskell to avoid personal references to himself or his mother. Mrs Gaskell wrote to him promising they would be mentioned only in order to illustrate Charlotte Brontë's character, "and not in any ways referring to your private employments habits or circumstances – far less to your appearance."[8]

Searching for information from everyone who had known Charlotte, always with determination and thoroughness, Mrs Gaskell was generally more successful and found much material that was difficult to handle. The stories of criminal negligence at school and of cruel treatment to the sisters as struggling governesses she knew already from Charlotte herself; now she heard tales of their childhood and home, and vicious gossip about Branwell. All this she faced firmly, with a strong indignant sense of justice. The one thing she suppressed – and George Smith knew she was suppressing it – was the upsetting discovery of Charlotte's letters to M. Heger that M. Heger had kept, and which he showed her in Brussels. These were not published until 1913.

It seems to have been assumed, without any discussion of contract, that Smith & Elder would publish the *Life*. It was not until December 1856, when the work was nearly done, that Mrs Gaskell got round to asking Smith "what would be a proper remuneration?"[9] Then, surprisingly, Smith made the rather ungenerous suggestion of £600 – less than she had expected, and in her reckoning inadequate for the time, worry and expenses of the work. He immediately raised the offer to £800, which satisfied her.

From the start Mrs Gaskell wrote full accounts to Smith of her ideas and her progress, with a relaxed friendliness that had never appeared in her correspondence with her former publisher, Edward Chapman. By May 1856 he was sending her presents of books. Shortly after that they met for the first time and, she reported to Ellen Nussey, she "found Mr Smith an agreeable, genial-mannered man, with a keen eye to business; he is rather too stout to be handsome, but has a pretty, Paulina-like little wife, and a little girl of eighteen months old".[10] George certainly had put on weight since his schooldays; his mother, disguised as Mrs Bretton but speaking in phrases that surely ring true, commented to Lucy Snowe, "Has he not rather the air of an incipient John Bull? He used to be slender as an eel, and now I fancy in him a sort of heavy dragoon bent – a beef-eater tendency. Graham, take notice! If you grow fat I disown you."[11]

After that meeting her letters generally include family greetings and become thoroughly conversational and charming. Sadly, once again, no letters of his survive, though they seem to have given her pleasure – "The laughing I had over that letter of yours was as good as a bottle of medicine",[12] she wrote in September, when she had been ill from overwork. What had amused her was Smith's account of his meeting, at the Chapter Coffee House, with the waiter who had looked after Charlotte and Anne Brontë on that first famous visit.

Another letter ends with a sentence warning of trouble to come: "Do you mind the law of libel. – I have three people I want to libel – Lady Scott (that bad woman who corrupted Branwell Brontë), Mr Newby, & Lady Eastlake, the first & last not to be named by name, the mean publisher to be gibbeted."[13] Smith did mind, and did warn her, but she would not accept all his warnings. She did not feel too strongly about gibbeting Mr Newby – "*Do* let me abuse Mr Newby as much as I dare, *within the law*. Your legal adviser will I trust keep me from a libel"[14] – but her indignation got the better of her common sense when writing about Lady Scott, who was clearly identifiable even if she was not named. Smith has been blamed for allowing the *Life* to appear in its original libellous state, but his job was not easy and he had done his best. "Tell me if there is anything you would like taken out," Mrs Gaskell had written to him, "but I don't *promise* to alter what you do not like. I only promise to consider of it."[15] Very little was altered, the *Life* was finished, and Mrs Gaskell left England on 13 February 1857, with an advance payment of £250 from Smith, to recover from the strain by an idyllic holiday in Italy with her two elder daughters. She left instructions that no reviews or business letters should be sent on, and did not return until the end of May. In Venice she saw a copy of the Tauchnitz edition of the *Life*, and she must have been happy when she was sent Mr Brontë's letter telling her: "You have not only given a picture of my Dear daughter Charlotte, but of my Dear wife, and all my

Dear children, and such a picture too as is full of truth and life. The pictures of my brilliant and unhappy son, and his diabolical seducer, are masterpieces.''[16] Altogether it was the happiest of holidays. Writing later to her hosts, the Storys, she said, "I don't think I was ever so happy before. My eyes fill with tears when I think of those days, and it is the same with all of us. They were the tip-top point of our lives.''[17] It was not until she reached Paris on her way home that Mrs Gaskell learnt about the storm that had burst, and the emergency action Smith had taken without her.

At first all had gone wonderfully well. The *Life* was published on 25 March and widely praised by the critics; Smith & Elder quickly issued a reprint of Currer Bell's novels at six shillings and of the poems of the three Bells at four shillings, and announced a second edition of the *Life*. The first sign of trouble came when George Smith was shown a letter from Sir James Stephen discussing the possible libel on Lady Scott. George himself must tell the rest of the story:

> I had more or less been anxious about passages in Mrs Gaskell's book concerning this lady, and, while the book was being printed, I had written to her at some length with reference to them. I expressed my doubts as to her being able to justify the statements made, and argued that, after so many years, it was scarcely fair to revive the scandal. The wrongdoer might well have repented of the wrong. In any case it was not for Mrs Gaskell, acting as Charlotte Brontë's biographer, to assume the judicial office in regard to this case, re-try it in public, and sentence the woman to perpetual ignominy. But Mrs Gaskell was obstinate. She argued that it was her "duty" in dealing with Branwell Brontë's character and condition of mind to expose the woman who had ruined him. The trouble I had foreseen had now arrived, and I was much perplexed. Sir James Stephen's letter was followed by one from a gentleman more directly representing the person concerned, threatening legal proceedings; next came formal letters from his solicitors, etc. Mrs Gaskell had gone away to the Continent, as was her custom after she had completed any work; and, as was also her custom, she had left no address. As there were no means of communicating with her, I wrote to her husband, the Rev. W. Gaskell, and he came up to London. But he could not help me and would take no responsibility. In effect he said, "you must act on your own judgement; I can do nothing.''

Her husband did know her address, of course, and had forwarded Mr Brontë's approving letter, but he kept her holiday, as she had asked, free from business worries. Smith continued:

Mrs Gaskell's solicitor and my own had a conference, and it was determined to employ detectives in order to ascertain what evidence was available to justify the alleged libel. Much gossip, it was found, existed, but it was gossip of the kind which is apt to dissolve into mere vapour when tested in a court of law . . . . In the end, and after infinite trouble, we decided to withdraw the edition, destroy all existing copies of the book and publish a new edition without the libel.

Before Mrs Gaskell returned to England the whole business was settled in the manner I have described. On her arrival she expressed content with what had been done, but one matter, it seemed, grieved her. She wrote me a letter of reproach, mildly and graciously expressed. "With all my experience" – which, by the way, was only about half her own – she wrote, "I must have realized from the first the dangerous character of the passages which had brought on us all this trouble. Why," she asked, "had I not cautioned her that in writing them she was straying into the realms of libel?" I had of course done this very thing. I had taken so much pains, indeed, with my letter on the subject, that, having made some alterations in the first draft, I had rewritten it, and still had the original draft by me . . . . Human nature urged me to send her my draft, and prove that her reproach was undeserved. It is always pleasant to be able to say to some one else, "I told you so!" But I resisted the temptation. I liked Mrs Gaskell very much indeed, and I knew that the receipt of the original draft of my letter, while it would prove me to be right, would give her keen discomfort. I simply made the best excuse I could, expressed my regret and took my scolding, in short, "lying down".

Smith thought Mrs Gaskell must have remembered afterwards what had really happened. When, some years later, she was staying in Paris, she went to enormous trouble to borrow a pamphlet he needed for the *Pall Mall Gazette* and sat up all night copying it for him. "Well," she said in answer to his thanks, "you know I owed you something, for you once showed extraordinary consideration for me." "That was all that passed," wrote Smith, "and I can only guess that Mrs Gaskell was thinking of that letter which she reproached me with *not* having sent, and the meekness with which I had endured the accusation!" Meekness did not come easily to him.

For Mrs Gaskell there was much distress and much hard work before the *Life* was sent out again, in its third and revised edition, on 22 August. Lady Scott had been appeased by a letter from William Shaen, the Gaskells' solicitor, in *The Times*, retracting "every statement contained in that work which imputes to a widowed lady, referred to, but not named therein, any breach of her conjugal, her maternal, or of her social duties."[18] But other complaints poured in – from Carus Wilson about Cowan Bridge School, from Harriet Martineau about the portrayal of her relationship with Charlotte Brontë, from the servants at Haworth who had been described as "wasteful", from someone in Toronto who said his mother "Miss Scatcherd" had been insulted. Mr Nicholls sent a list of omissions wanted by Mr Brontë. "Everyone who has been harmed in this unlucky book complains",[19] Mrs Gaskell wrote; "and *I did so try to tell the truth*."[20]

It was, as Mrs Gaskell later called it, a "terrible summer". Ecstatic memories of the Italian spring were buried under a pile of worries – as well as the "unlucky book" there was her daughter Meta's very sudden engagement to Captain Hill, an officer who was shortly to return to India, and an endless invasion of visitors, in Manchester for the great Exhibition of World Masters. Through it all she was "taking all possible pains" to make the revised edition a success.

In the long run, of course, this new edition became an enormous success. It did restore peace on the whole, though echoes of the earlier storms were heard from time to time. In March 1858, to Mrs Gaskell's surprise, Smith sent a further cheque for £200 – "I had always felt that you had behaved to me most liberally in the first instance," she wrote, "& that in some respects, the book must have been a great source of annoyance & vexation to you . . . . As *money* it is very acceptable just now, but I am even more touched by the kindness & liberality, which will always make me feel beholden to you."[21]

There had been no recriminations or bad feeling between George Smith and Mrs Gaskell. She had even invited him and his wife to Manchester for the Exhibition, had confided in him about Meta, and was delighted to find him knowledgeable about India and helpful to Captain Hill. He had sent her books about India, as well as copies of the *Homeward Mail*, the journal of news from India published by Smith Elder.

With her charm, her wide sympathies, and her intellectual and domestic life, Mrs Gaskell must have been the most likeable of the Victorian women novelists; it is not surprising that George Smith and his family enjoyed her company or that she brought out the best in him, finding him "full of frolic and bright light wit".[22] The Smiths frequently invited her to their London home and she loved the outings they gave her – to operas, to supper parties, or best of all, after they had moved to Hampstead, driving fast through country lanes in an open carriage. Anny Thackeray, who first met Mrs Gaskell in that Hampstead home, has described a happy morning there, with the Smiths and their guests listening while Mrs Gaskell told endless wonderful ghost stories – "mystery was there, romantic feeling, some holy terror & emotion, all combined to keep us gratefully silent & delighted."[23] When the Smiths visited Mrs Gaskell in Manchester she showed them another side of her life by taking them to lunch at a coffee house which provided cheap food for the poor, and Smith told how they ate at the same table as a postman and a sweep.

Perhaps some extracts from Mrs Gaskell's letters give the best picture of George Smith's friendship with her – it was a correspondence which, while never reaching the full intimacy of her letters to her close friend the American art historian Charles Norton, increasingly showed a relaxed relationship, as well as a respect for his business advice and help:

4 February 1859: We were so very glad to receive the news of the birth of your little son. Don't you feel proud? How many times have you spoken of "my son". I hope a great many already, because, if so I should conjecture from that that Mrs Smith was going on being well . . . . Is there no chance of your ever coming to see us here? It would give us all such great pleasure; & I think there are things in Manchester you would care to see, and that in fact you ought to know about in order to teach your boy to know more than a young friend who has been staying with us this week, & who proposed to me this question "Mrs Gaskell, is there any difference between cotton and linen?" Only think if young Master Smith should ask such a question and his Papa not be able to answer him!

14 February 1859: I hope Mrs Smith is going on bravely and well . . . will you let me have a copy of Charlotte Brontë's Memoirs, – the prohibited 1st edition will do, as it is to be sent immediately into Hungary, to a young friend (of Sir James Stephen's as well as mine,) who is just marrying an Austrian in command of some utterly unpronounceable place, – where neither The Times nor my name nor Lady Anybody's has ever penetrated.

21 June 1859: [after Smith had met her four daughters]. You have won four young hearts. What will Mrs Smith say, if you go on at the rate of so many a day?

29 June 1859: [Auchencairn] You never no, *never* – sent a more acceptable present than *Cousin Stella* and *The Fool of Quality*, – and that irrespective of their several merits. But books are books here, – where potatoes have to be sent for from Castle Douglas, nine miles off – where we are uncertain what King or Queen reigns in England, – where we are far away from newspapers or railways or shops, or any sign of the world: where we go to bed by daylight, and get up because the cocks crow, & cows low to be milked, & we can't sleep any longer. Thanks many for your kind thought of us. I am sorry to say Meta lies at this present moment fast asleep with *Cousin Stella* in her hand; but that is the effect of bathing and an eight mile walk; not of the book itself . . . . I mean to be so busy here; but I am, at present, continually tempted out of doors. I can hardly believe that we were in London two days ago. Oh! I will so try & write you a good novel; as good as a great nosegay of honeysuckle just under my nose at present, which smells not only of honeysuckle, but of very good cake into the bargain. My girls send you all manner of pretty messages. Please write to us, – an old man whistles at the end of the field, if he has any letters for us, – and some one races down for them, holding them in triumph, if there are many. But suppose the day should arrive when there is no whistle! Heaven & Mr Smith avert that evil time.

1 October 1859: *The* box came; I was so thankful there was only one daughter (Julia) at home; for the squeal, & scream of delight she set up, multiplied by four, would have been perfectly deafening . . . we worked on through the box, screaming & laughing & talking, and half checking ourselves to wish for the others. And now Julia is sitting in silent admiration before rolling up her sisters' presents in paper – I suggest that she should write her own thanks, – to which at first she acceded with grateful alacrity – but suddenly she said "But is he not an author, or something of that sort" – and I think she fancies writing to you may be like rushing into print, and rather shrinks back. So once for all in the name of the four daughters

THANK YOU.

5 April 1860: Oh Mr Smith! your grandfather was a brick, and your grandmother an angel; your – (how can I go higher? it is inexpressible in the next generation) – how *very* charming you are! If I lived near Cornhill I would go and pay you a call of two hours & a half long, and offer to read to you in the evening, – only think of having the *Mill on the Floss* the second day of publication, & of my very own. I think it is so kind of you, & am so greedy to read it I can scarcely be grateful enough to write this letter; which now shall begin all properly – My dear Sir, Mrs Smith is very very charming & kind and sweet & pretty, – and you are a bright warm genial witty man – but – I (privately) don't believe that Sir J.P.K. Shuttleworth seeks your acquaintance

[95]

& society for any of these reasons, simple & pure – (he has generally a double set of motives for all his actions –) but he has a novel, – partly read to Mrs Nicholls the last time she was at Gawthrop, – partly to me, – *wholly* to many of his friends – a novel of Lancashire society, which is at present in MS & which he wants you to publish I have no doubt.

25 July 1864: In my hurry I am afraid I have taken up a very bad pen wherewith to write a letter to one who writes so exquisitely neatly himself. There! we will try this, which is a shade better! because I want to propitiate you before I make a request, which I may as well plunge into at once. Will you advance me £100 of the payment of *Wives & Daughters*. I want it to take Meta (& the others too) into Switzerland; but it is on *Meta*'s especial account that we go.

30 July 1864: You may have 20 good marks added to the number already gained for this lovely paper. It is a regular embarras de richesse all the colours. The blue and the red & chocolate divide my affections equally so whichever you like best I like best. I don't think the G. one bit too big and I do think the monogram quite as perfect as Mr George Smith & Mr Harrington Balfour; what higher praise can it have? As I am to command and have owing to your kindness, I like the monogram both on paper & envelopes, but if I may, I should like a very small quantity with 46 P. Grove, but not much please as the principal amount of my correspondence is carried on from home. Don't insult my powers of cooking. You always believe I can do nothing useful. If you will come won't I make you lobster sauce with Brodignagian [*sic*] pieces in it, and melted butter for you to wash your hands in like the little boy in the story book, to say nothing of a Mayonnaise like one I made the other day, and which met with universal kudos. I am obliged to praise myself because you give me credit for not being able to do a thing. For our sakes I hope you will both be too ill to cross the channel and so will have to end your travels by coming to us. But for your sakes I hope you will get to Switzerland. When am I to have a G.S. monogram for a cigar-case?

Towards the end of Mrs Gaskell's life, George Smith was taken into her confidence about her secret plan to buy a house in the country to move to when her husband retired. He helped her in every possible way. He lent her the money to make the whole scheme possible – £1,000 towards the total cost of £2,600 – which she was to repay gradually, not telling her husband until it was complete; he advised her about tenants and details of leasing land – "Mr White says incoming tenant ought to pay something for standing crops," she appealed to him, "apples, potatoes, onions?";[24] and, with his many trade connections, he got 22½ per cent discount for her off all furniture and equipment she bought through him.

Very occasionally, Smith seems to have irritated Mrs Gaskell. This does not appear at all in her letters to him, but in one or two comments to others; and it was always only a passing annoyance. Writing to Smith Williams in February 1862 about *Sylvia's Lovers*, she said, "Mr Smith who has had it [the MS of the first two vols] for a month has never said a word about it; which has made me fear he does not like it . . . . I do not imagine him to be any great judge of it from an artistic point of view."[25] This was a surprising remark, and not her usual opinion – on the whole she agreed with Charlotte Brontë, who had written to Smith, "I see plainly nature made you a critic."[26]

Impatience with Smith also flared up when he had, evidently on his own initiative, sent a rejected manuscript on to Froude. In a letter to her daughter Marianne in June 1863 she wrote,

> I am sorry that MS has gone to Mr Froude, as I don't like his having to take Mr Smith's refuse for old friendship's sake. But I have done my best to remedy this by writing to Mr Froude to bid him send the MS back to Mr Smith, & to desire the latter to seal it up *at once*, & send it to me, care of W. Shaen. At any rate dear you did your best, but I am *very* angry with Mr Smith.[27]

These are only minor incidents in a correspondence lasting ten years which was, as A.W. Ward said in the introduction to the Knutsford Edition of Mrs Gaskell's works, "one of the gayest ever carried on between author & publisher".

As well as the friendship and the literary gossip these letters also, of course, contain business matters. After the *Life of Charlotte Brontë*, Smith published all Mrs Gaskell's major works and the best of her minor ones. She wanted to give him only the best. She told him in June 1859 that Sampson Lowe had astonished her by offering £1,000 for a three-volume novel, which "does a little bit tempt me, it is such a great sum . . . but I would much rather have £800 from you than £1,000 from them . . . I mean literally what I say".[28] Smith replied by offering £1,000, and she launched happily into *Sylvia's Lovers* – "I will so try and write you a good novel".[29]

The attitude that nothing but the best was fit for Smith & Elder, or the *Cornhill*, was shown in Mrs Gaskell's letter of 23 December that same year; it seems that Smith had offered her more for one of her stories than

Dickens would give for putting it in *All the Year Round* but, she wrote firmly,

> I *would not take* a penny more advantageous terms than Mr C.D. offers. So there! and there's an end of that part of the subject. Now please clear your mind for the next branch. I have three things begun. (Very bad management I know: but there are excuses for all things if you know them.) 1st in order of time was begun a story, 120 pages of which are written & have been this year & a half; *not very good*, & that would not be above 1 vol: in length. *It is not good enough for the C.M.* – I am the best judge of that, please, – but might be good enough for H.W. [*Household Words*] . . . . 2nd a story of perhaps 40 (of my pages) long. Begun & I *think* good; intended *for* C.M.; but delayed because of extreme dislike to writing for Mr T. [Thackeray] & also because I do want to make it as good as I can, & so only to write at it in my best moments . . . . 3rdly The Specksioneer in 3 vols. Published by Smith & Elder (it is to be hoped –).[30]

Smith evidently objected to the awkward title – "Mr Gaskell says if you will come & pay him a visit of a week he will undertake to teach you how to pronounce 'Specksioneer' before the end of that time," she wrote. "What do you think of 'Philip's Idol'; – then again you may say people will call it 'Philip's idle', . . . 'Monkshaven' might do, might it not? very stupid though – 'Sylvia's Lovers', – but then there is a 'Nanette & her lovers', is there not? & published by you, too."[31]

Smith published Mrs Gaskell's short story "Curious if True" in the second number of the *Cornhill*. Another short story, "Six Weeks at Heppenheim", appeared in the *Cornhill* two years later, and then the longer "Cousin Phillis". There is a Valentine, sent by Smith to Mrs Gaskell in 1864, showing the publisher on his knees begging for his manuscript from a Mrs Gaskell dressed as a dairywoman. This, together with the offer of £2,000, helped her to agree to undertake her last great novel, *Wives & Daughters*, which started as a serial in the *Cornhill* that summer.

So Mrs Gaskell came to respect Smith's standards and his critical judgement. It was Smith who persuaded her to abandon her projected story *Two Mothers* "because I thought you did not seem to like it fully"[32] and to start *Wives & Daughters* instead. The fee of £2,000 seemed splendid payment until she heard that Smith was giving Wilkie Collins £5,000 for *Armadale*; it made her, as she wrote to Marianne, "less scrupulous"[33] about accepting the 22½ per cent discount on household equipment. Her strong sense of justice made her feel she should be treated no worse than other authors but she was, as Smith knew, in no way grasping. There is a story of Smith sending her a blank cheque for one of her stories and getting a reply, written by her daughter, that she "would much rather not fill up a cheque for herself: for never having had such an opportunity she knows that she should put in £100,000, or something of that sort, and that you would be too gentlemanly to demur, and when you moved to a smaller house and began to retrench she should not feel quite comfortable".[34]

Shortly after the *Life of Charlotte Brontë* was published, Smith asked if he could take over the copyrights of Mrs Gaskell's earlier works, which had been published by Chapman. He gradually acquired these and after her death brought out collected editions of her works – in 1872–3 an eight-volume edition illustrated by du Maurier, and in 1897 an eight-volume pocket edition; the 'Knutsford Edition', with introductions by A.W. Ward but without the *Life of Charlotte Brontë*, was brought out by Smith & Elder after Smith's death, in 1906.

Some new authors came to Smith through Mrs Gaskell, not on the spectacular scale of the great who were introduced by Charlotte Brontë but several who joined his list, either as novelists or as contributors to the *Cornhill* – Hamilton Aidé, Henrietta Jenkin, John Addington Symonds.

Mrs Gaskell died in November 1865, in the house at Alton that Smith had helped her to buy and furnish as a present for her husband. The last surviving letter from her to Smith, in characteristic form, was written from Dieppe in October –

This place gets more and more charming as the weather becomes rougher & wilder, & the people (smart ones, I mean) disappear. We are becoming highly authorial (if there is such a word), in this hotel. Mrs Crowe; and a M. Alfred de Brehat who has sent me his romans, as a compliment to the author of Ruth (pronounced Roit,). I never heard of him before in my life, – but he says you are a great editeur & a "brave homme" so I suppose you know him, & I shall consider you responsible for the morality of his works, which now lie on the table close by Meta & Julia . . . . Hearn sends word one of the tops to a sauce tureen & one of the chairs is broken in carriage; all else right.[35]

IX

Ruskin

Ruskin links the early days of Smith Elder & Co. with the flourishing times of the *Cornhill* and the *Pall Mall Gazette*. He had published his first poems in *Friendship's Offering* when George Smith was only eleven; George himself came to know him when the Ruskins and the Smiths were neighbours on Denmark Hill, and the friendship lasted for thirty years. But in the seventies, Ruskin's eccentric views on bookselling provoked even such a patient man as Smith into a quarrel, and their business and personal relations never recovered.

The first volume of *Modern Painters* appeared in 1843, just before George Smith took over the publishing side of the firm. George inherited an exciting author, and through him gained an introduction to the artistic world. At Ruskin's house he met Millais, Burne Jones, John Leech, George Richmond and Alexander Munro, the sculptor who was to do the fine bust of Elizabeth Smith. Under Ruskin's influence he bought watercolours, and must have built up an enviable collection; we find Ruskin advising him not to pay more than £150 each for two drawings – "a large drawing is always better worth its price"[1] – and Mr Ruskin senior asking him to accept a drawing by Lewis, "The Mantilla", which George had admired.[2] For George, as for many others, Ruskin became the dictator of taste:

whenever he asked me my opinion on any work of art, or architecture, I used to say: "No, no, tell me your opinion first, and then I will agree with it." Ruskin destroyed all my pleasure in my room at Waterloo Place which I had furnished with what I fondly hoped was sound taste. His admiration of two marble busts supporting the mantelpiece was so enthusiastic that I said: "I am so glad you like them, what do you think of my carpet? Are not the flowers beautiful?" "Flowers!" he said with a look of the deepest scorn, "Flowers! Pickled cabbage, you mean!" I never liked that carpet afterwards.[3]

Ruskin was happy with his publisher. The second volume of *Modern Painters* was published in 1846, followed by the *Seven Lamps of Architecture* three years later. There were twenty-five volumes and pamphlets in the fifties, eight in the sixties, and five in 1871 and 1872 before the quarrel, besides many letters for the *Pall Mall Gazette*. Ruskin's letters to Smith are lively and amiable, with good-tempered criticism of the *Gazette* and a mixture of business and social matters. He was pleased with Smith & Elder's clear print and handsome bindings – and he was not easily pleased. He was irritated, understandably, when in his absence abroad in 1861 Smith & Elder published *Selections from the Writings of John Ruskin*, chosen by Smith Williams and W.L. Harrison: "My crest [a boar's head] is all very well as long as it means Pork," wrote Ruskin, "but I don't love being made into sausages."[4] But the irritation did not last, and the book was successful and often reissued.

Smith described Ruskin as

essentially a man of surprises. You never knew what paradox he would produce next, nor how ably he would sustain it. That he was a brilliant talker goes without saying, especially on his own subject, art. Later on, when absorbed in social economy, his talk lost something of its charm. Of all the surprises – literary and other – that came to me at his table, the greatest occurred one evening when he volunteered to sing a nigger song, and sang it with great energy![5]

The absorption in social economy brought problems. Ruskin had contributed to the third number of the *Cornhill* a very acceptable article on "Sir Joshua and Holbein", but his next offerings were the stormy economic sermons "Unto This Last". Of course these essays, preaching the need for responsible care of the workers on the part of the employers and for fair pay, do not now seem in any way outrageous; but trouble was expected then and it came, from all quarters – the *Saturday Review*, the *Scotsman*, the *Manchester Examiner*, *The Times*. After three essays, Thackeray and Smith yielded to the criticism and decided to publish only one more, though they allowed it to be twice as long as the others, to conclude the arguments. The *Cornhill* was already having enough trouble with Jacob Omnium's attacks on Eton, so Thackeray had suggested Ruskin's essays should be signed with initials instead of keeping to the convention of anonymity because, as John Ruskin senior said, "the Editor would not be answerable for opinions so opposed to Malthus and *The Times* and the City of Manchester."[6] Altogether this side of Ruskin's life was an embarrassment to his father, who wrote to George Smith in 1860 that his son was "very hot on Political Economy" and that this might harm the success of the *Stones of Venice* and of *Modern Painters*:

> He is scarcely aware of the utter unfitness of these Papers for a magazine. They are solemn sermons and will be for the beautiful writing much admired in a few quarters but they will be "caviare to the general" – denounced by Thousands as Cant and Humbug. They will besides give offence to Mill and his friends from their sarcastic Tone but Being for the present brought to a close I trust they will not hurt Sale of Cornhill Magazine.[7]

The *Cornhill* retreated but was not hurt, Ruskin's personal friendship with Thackeray and Smith survived the crisis, and Smith published *Unto This Last* as a book in 1862.

Smith tells a story of Ruskin's belief in himself as a social economist:

> On his birthday, two interesting events always occurred; his father always gave us a glass of the "Nelson" sherry, and one of us had to propose John Ruskin's health; and we listened with keen pleasure to the son's always eloquent response. On one occasion I was asked to propose Ruskin's health; and, having had a glass of the famous "Nelson" sherry, I thought I had made – in spite of my usual diffidence – a rather neat little speech. But to my amazement, John Ruskin was indignant. I had said, he declared in his reply, the kindest things – much more than he deserved – in respect to his writings on art and the influence of those writings on the world generally; but I had left out the only thing he had done worth mentioning – his contributions to the science of social economy!

> The famous "Nelson" sherry deserves, perhaps, a word of explanation. Shortly before the Battle of Trafalgar, Nelson sent an order to Mr Ruskin's

firm for some sherry. They sent him the finest they had; then, on sentimental grounds, the partners decided that not another glass from that particular butt should be sold. Each member of the firm, however, was allowed his portion, paying for it at the price at which it stood in the firm's ledger. The first time I was present when the famous sherry was produced, and its history narrated, I said to Mr Ruskin: "I am bold enough to ask you a question which every one at the table would like to ask, but lacks the necessary courage to do so. At what price does the 'Nelson' sherry stand in the ledger?" "Ah," said Mr Ruskin, "I was thinking of that as I drove into the City this morning, and I made a rough calculation which shows that at present it stands at about a guinea a glass." "And very cheap at the money too," said a Mr Pritchard, at that time Member for Broseley. "I'll have another glass!"

It was Ruskin's attempt to apply his theories of social economy to bookselling that brought a rift between Ruskin and Smith. In his monthly letter, *Fors Clavigera* (1871), Ruskin attacked current business methods, including the commissions, advertising and discounts which were standard practice in the book trade at that time. Logically this meant that *Fors* itself and all Ruskin's future books should have a fixed price to all booksellers or direct buyers, and a standard profit to retailers. Ruskin therefore set up his friend George Allen as his agent, to manage his publishing in his own way. Following this, to be clear of past business worries he offered to sell Smith the copyright of all his earlier works. He put a higher value on his copyrights than Smith could accept, and this led to a correspondence[8] which has survived intact and is worth quoting fairly fully as a unique example of Smith in action.

From J.R., 21 January 1873:
I have had a difficult year, and many things to arrange, or wade through the unarrangeable disorder of. And my own old books encumber my thoughts and ways – and I see no chance of getting them into the shape I want in any nameable time, – and what people say to me about the use of cheap editions weighs somewhat with me. I had been long thinking off and on about it, but must now come to some decision. What would you give me for the copyright of the whole lot of my books, published before 1870, in their original text – to do what you liked with, and publish cheap and nasty and any sort of edition that the public seems to want – leaving to me always the power of republishing as I am able, any of them I choose in my own series? I would give you all the plates of everything, and wash my hands and brains quit of it all: saying so much in

clear terms in Fors. I do not want to retract anything I have written, but to say it better. If I can't say it better, it is better said somehow – anyhow.

Only you must be bound to introduce none of my new notes or additions, which give what value it may have to my own series.

From G.S., 29 January 1873:
I was very glad to receive your letter of the 21st instant, being anxious to see your larger works again in circulation. And I am desirous of meeting your offer of the Copyright of all your published works up to 1870 in a liberal spirit. I have therefore gone into a careful [word missing] of the cost and probable results of their republication.

It will be obvious to you that your reservation of a right to reprint any portions of *Modern Painters, The Stones of Venice, The Seven Lamps of Architecture* etc. in your new series of works, very materially lessens the commercial value of your former books. Nevertheless I shall be happy to purchase the copyright of your works published before 1870 and your interest in the plates for £2,500. I hope you will consider this an equitable arrangement, for it is based upon a liberal estimate of the probable profit from the sales. I should not, of course, be entitled to make any use of your new notes or additions but simply to reprint the old editions of the work.

From J.R., 30 January 1873:
I am not able, of course to judge of the matter, but the offer being somewhat less than I expected, I am going to try what other booksellers will offer. – Meantime – as soon as may be – will you let me have our accounts up to the end of '72.

I'm having a lark with Mr Greg in the Pall Mall.

From G.S., 31 January 1873:
I must confess to feeling some surprise and mortification at the contents of your note of yesterday. The idea of your offering your copyright to other booksellers is really painful to me.

I am sorry that the sum I offered you is not so large as you expected, but if you will name the amount that you think you should receive, I will endeavour to meet your views.

You will, I think, on reflection, perceive that there are other considerations involved than relate to mere bargain and sale in the course you contemplate. Our relations as between Author and Publisher have subsisted on the most friendly footing for more than a quarter of a century, and I have had reason to hope from your continued kindness to me, that they have been satisfactory to you. I cannot think, therefore, that you are at all aware of the detriment to the reputation of my Firm as well as the injury to my personal feelings which would result from the removal of your books from us. Indeed I may say it would be a cruel injury.

It is not impossible that you might find a publisher willing to give more than I have offered you and more than the value of the copyrights for reasons apart from considerations of legitimate profit, indeed rather than that they should be taken out of my hands, I would, so far as my means afforded incur a considerable loss in their purchase: or should you prefer to have the stock and copyrights valued, I would purchase them at the amount of the valuation.

I feel sure that this matter has not before appeared to you in the light in which I naturally regard it, and I hope therefore you will excuse any undue stress that I may have laid on it.

From J.R., 1 February 1873:
I am very glad of your letter, and pleased that you care to have me still in connection with your house, – Nor am *I* at all without feeling on the subject. I have always had the most true pleasure in all my *personal* relations with you (and with Mr Williams) – nor do I see the least reason why these should be interfered with by any change in our business relations. With the latter, I never *have* been quite satisfied; people were always abusing me for selling my books dear, and congratulating me on the enormous income I must be making out of them. I could not plead guilty to the accusations – nor smilingly receive the felicitations – my experiences being mostly, of late – of a quarto volume of accounts giving a balance in my favour of two pounds ten. However; this may be the best that can be expected of books such as mine – and I really never have hitherto thought them worth more than I got. But now – I begin to feel as if the public would want them a little; and it seems to me there are many houses who would be able to make more of such a copyright as I offer, than you could. I don't in the least know its worth in the market, and I doubt if, without trying, anybody can know – some people might have a fancy for experiments – or a knowledge of workable means – very different from those which either you or I have been in the habit of trying. I think much the fairest and simplest way is to put the thing up to auction. – If the old connection is worth an extra bid to you, well and good – but for my own part, I would almost rather that the new modes of proposed publication should be carried out by some other firm – with which I had no personal associations, than that I should see you either losing by your last bargain with me, or deriving a flourishing trade in spoiled plates and flame-coloured bindings.

From G.S., 6 February 1873:
Before replying to your letter of the 1st instant, I wished to look through the

accounts of your works, and I trust you will excuse my expressing my own opinion that you have not only derived a fair share of the profits of their publication, but that considering the expensive manner in which they have been produced they have yielded quite as much profit as any one acquainted with publication business would have expected.

I learn with surprise and regret, and now for the first time, that you have not been satisfied with the pecuniary results of the publication of your books; but this dissatisfaction on your part must be of a recent date for it gratified me to find on referring to our correspondence, expressions of your and your Father's entire satisfaction at the liberality of my business arrangements respecting your books, and it will be admitted by you that his perfect knowledge of business and affairs would enable him to form a sound judgement on such a matter.

Referring to your remark on the small balance of late appearing at your credit in the accounts of your publications – I hardly know whether you wrote playfully or in earnest; but in either case I cannot leave such a remark unanswered. Permit me then to remind you that in the very last account rendered to you there was an amount at the credit of the account of more than a thousand pounds for the works published by us – It is true that this sum was to a great extent used for the payment of the accounts for printing, binding, etc. of Fors Clavigera and your new series – which works have been sold through Mr Allen, and from whom you will have received whatever returns there may have been from the Sales. If they have not yielded a profit on the cost of production I not only repudiate any responsibility on the subject but I say that I have frequently – until in fact I began to fear I gave you offence – advised you that such would be the result of your mode of publication. – In regard to these books I am only concerned in insisting that all the prices charged by me for the production of the Books are not only fair but so moderate that I can hardly be said to have received any adequate return for the time and trouble bestowed upon them. This statement I am prepared to substantiate. When we make up our accounts we may have a sum to claim from you for printing and binding these books but you surely will not therefore suppose that your publications in my hands are producing you less than nothing.

So far as regards the detriment to my Firm and the disappointment to myself personally arising from the breaking up of the business relations between us, I have nothing to add to what I said in my last letter. But before putting the copyrights into the hands of an Auctioneer, it will be necessary that an arrangement should be come to between us with respect to the stock of your Books in our hands, and some arrangements should be arrived at respecting the plates of the Illustrations.

From J.R., 9 February 1873:

I had your beautifully written and expressed letter. – I wish you didn't always write so neatly.

I wasn't in play. I very seldom am in play, nowadays, more's the pity. But all the world is such a stage – and such a play, that I don't think you need take what I said quite so seriously.

I never said you were illiberal. I said I thought I wasn't getting as much as I should like to get. Many people in this [word unclear] dramatic world are of the same mind – no offence to anybody. You say I've been getting a lot of money. – All I *know* is that for the last ten years I've never calculated on my books as furnishing me the least help in my expenses. It is true I'm an extravagant dog – and lately, a hundred pounds here or there didn't much matter. But a thousand – if it had ever come in my way – I should have licked my lips over – I'm very glad to hear there was that to my credit "in the very last account" – but if so – surely I should be a goose to give you the copyright for 2500? [word unclear] You know – that offer meant that the whole lot – to *me* were only worth £80 a year – and were indeed not worth that, now, but only *would* be worth that if I went in for the cheap and nasty . . . . Please – it won't bother you and it would me – to get at what I really *have* had for the last five years. It will be a guide to copyright value and everything – just send me word of that, with the other accounts . . . . Of course, with respect to the arrangement to be come to with regard to the stock in your hands, – you will ask nothing – other than is ordinarily the practice in such cases . . . .

From G.S., 11 February 1873:

The contents of your letter of the 9th instant are rather confusing to me.

You seem in some way to have arrived at the conclusion that the Profits of your works have been a thousand pounds a year; I never told you anything of the kind, and do not know where you get your figures from. Of course it is not pleasant for a Publisher to be told by an Author that he (the Author) would be a goose to accept an offer made to him by his Publisher, or to have his own words tossed back to him with the ironical question whether he calls it meeting the Author's proposal in a fair and liberal spirit to offer him £2500 for a thousand a year; but, as all this seems to have arisen from a mistake I feel the good nature to feel and the generosity to express regret for the pain it has caused me. Your remark that I must know the offer meant that all your Copyrights were only worth £80 a year to you, is altogether beyond me. I have puzzled my brains over it in vain. If it be a conundrum I give it up.

With respect to the amount of £1035.2.0 which appeared at your credit when the accounts were made up to December 31 1871 and over which you say you would have licked your lips "if it had ever come in your way", you surely

[108]

cannot mean to imply that that amount has not been paid to you as certainly as if it had been placed in your hands in bank notes; you have had it and spent it in printing the "Fors Clavigera" and the books of your new series. . . .

Now as to the spirit in which I met your offer – the value of a copyright is always estimated at so many years purchase of the profits of previous years; in a letter which I received some time since from Mr George Bell, the publisher, an experienced valuer of publication stock and copyrights, he says "according to the steadiness of the sale and the probability of its continuance I estimate the copyright at one, two, three or four years purchase. Few books are worth more than four years purchase, but there are special cases in which five or even six would not be too much". Mr Bell's remarks apply to copyrights sold in the usual manner and in which the purchaser therefore has the entire property, without any restrictions or conditions whatever; but you have annexed to your proposed sale peculiar conditions. You proposed to retain the right of reprinting any portions of your books, and indeed avowed your intention of reprinting in your new Series all that you deemed really valuable in them; the purchaser of the copyright had therefore to face not only the risk of finding the property rendered almost worthless in the course of a few years, but also of incurring a heavy loss from having on his hands a large quantity of unsaleable stock. I did not myself consider the fact that under such a reservation it would be possible for you, or your executors at any time to reprint the whole of the books with the fresh matter from your new series as affecting the value of the copyrights but even that circumstance might be taken into account by a purchaser.

Moreover as soon as you commenced reproducing in your new series any portions of your former works, the original editions of such books would be discredited with the public for they would be led to infer that you did not yourself regard the portions of those editions which you omitted from your new series, as valuable, and the commercial value of the copyrights would consequently be depreciated.

As regards cheap editions of your books they would doubtless have a large sale, notwithstanding the above circumstances if they were *very* cheap: but the cost of printing the illustrations, and the necessity of adhering to the present large size of many of the books in order to give the illustrations, would in my opinion preclude the hope of any considerable profit being derived from them; besides, a cheap edition would destroy the sale of the more expensive books; whatever profit might be derived from the former would therefore not be additional profit, as you seem to suppose. That would be assuming the proprietor of your copyright could "eat his pig and have his pig" with a vengeance which cannot be done with due regard to the proprieties even in the "dramatic world".

If I have made the matter clear to you, I hope you will be able to dismiss from your mind the erroneous, and I must be allowed to say, the injurious and unjust suspicion you entertained that I did not meet your proposal in what I conscientiously believe to be a fair and liberal spirit – As to the value of your copyrights, there may of course be various opinions; but that is another matter altogether . . . with respect to those plates which are the property of my firm, it would I think suit your interest to include them in the sale of the copyrights, and if you carry out your present intention of selling your copyrights by auction, I shall be happy to make an arrangement with you for that purpose when the proper time arrives.

. . . You must permit me to say in conclusion that though it may seem to you that I take your comments too anxiously, I cannot do otherwise. The matter is a serious one to me, in respect of my personal feelings and as well of my commercial interests; and I am not ashamed to confess that I am sensitive to remarks implying a want of confidence in my fair dealing; I am little accustomed to them from any one, and I did not expect to receive them from the hand of one who has known me so long as you have done.

From J.R., 13 February 1873:
I am busy this morning: – were it otherwise, I should not think it necessary to pursue the points of discussion which are opened in your letter. For its clearness of statement I thank you: one sentence in it however requires explanation. You speak of certain plates as "the property of your firm". I could not have been more surprised if you had spoken of my Turner pictures as the property of your firm.

You have certainly acted as if they belonged to you, and the tone in which you attempted to justify that action might have prepared me for a claim such as that implied by the sentence in question. But my ignorance of any conceivable ground on which such a claim could be advanced is so total that I still find myself capable of very serious astonishment.

You are too good a man of business to have used the words without purpose. I can only in conclusion express my most profound regret for whatever purpose you had in using them. Your answer will find me here till tomorrow. I would call upon you, but it is now evidently necessary that we should write what we mean.

Smith replied to Ruskin the same day, saying that the plates belonged to Smith & Elder because they had been paid for, either direct to the engravers or to Ruskin in repayment of what he had paid the engravers. When Ruskin claimed that anything Smith paid the engravers had been deducted from what Smith had owed him, Smith replied (15 Feb): "It is by no means true that on some or any occasions you allowed my firm to pay your engravers. – The costs of engraving the plates were paid for by my firm as the other expenses of producing the books were paid . . . . I quite agree with you in thinking that it is needless to prolong our correspondence."

So in the course of six weeks their friendship came sadly to an end, and on 19 February Ruskin wrote to say that further contact should be through representatives; he suggested that his cousin W.W.S. Richardson should act for him.

There were occasional letters later, but never again with the earlier relaxed friendliness. In January 1875 we find Smith giving some advice, and fishing to get his custom back; this was answered amiably but firmly, and it is not clear what prompted Smith's letter. He wrote:

Your new books would I am sure be as largely sold and as eagerly read as your older books if they could be obtained with the same ease. People don't know where to get them, and they don't like the trouble of getting them in the only manner in which they can be got. As evidence of the former assertion I may mention that a good deal of the time of one of my clerks is occupied in answering letters of inquiry about your Books. I do not want to bother you with suggestions or proposals but I would gladly pay for the right to print editions of twice the number of copies you have printed of your recent works and I have no doubt whatever I should come to you for permission to arrange for new editions within eighteen months or two years – but then I must be allowed to sell them in the usual manner. Of "Fors Clavigera" I could easily sell 3000 or 4000 copies monthly.[9]

Ruskin thanked him for his kind letter, adding:

I quite believe that you know incomparably better than I how far my present mode of sale checks the sale of books essentially dull. – but if I chose to write a sensation novel, and I *could* write a good one, do you think people wouldn't find out when it was to be got? . . . One thing I do wish that booksellers *could* see, that I am acting in their interest as much as my own, in the endeavour to establish a fixed price – and good quality.[10]

In 1878 Ruskin removed all his books from Smith's charge but, as Smith wrote in his *Recollections*:

Notwithstanding all this I have every reason to suppose that Mr Ruskin has always cherished kindly feelings towards me, as I certainly have towards him. I know that on one occasion when he was requested to furnish particulars for a newspaper or magazine article, he told the writer that "whatever he said he must not say a word against his old publisher". In one of his papers, written with all his usual discursive eloquence while talking in his exalted manner of joys and sorrows of life, he says, "for my part, what I should like best at the present moment, would be to be sitting at one side of the table, and my old publisher at the other, with a bottle of my father's sherry and a plate of walnuts between us, listening to some of his good stories."

X

Money

Before turning to the birth of the *Cornhill Magazine*, it is helpful to look briefly at the financial background that made such a gamble possible.

The astonishing figures given by George Smith in his *Recollections* show that in the decade 1851–1861, after the recovery from the chaos left by Patrick Stewart, the amount passing through the banking account of the firm rose from £57,506 to £405,163. With Charlotte Brontë joining the firm's list the publishing business was expanding, but the main reason for the enormous growth was very successful overseas trade.

> At this period, [Smith wrote] . . . our operations covered an ever widening area. We had a branch at Bombay, an agency at Java, another on the West Coast of Africa. Some of our transactions were large and a single letter from the East would sometimes cover remittances to the amount of £10,000 or £12,000.
>
> The business ran into the oddest forms. We had to buy everything our clients needed; and as they belonged to almost every profession and calling, the articles they required were of the utmost possible diversity. Someone said to me once, "You seem to be a Jack of all trades and deal in everything in the world; but I think I can name something you don't deal in." "What is that?" I asked. "Skeletons," he said with an air of triumph. I replied, "If you will come to Cornhill I will show you two skeletons hanging up in a room waiting to go out to Java."

I took a contract for supplies to the hospitals in the Crimea of medicines, medical comforts and other necessaries. The army doctors who were to go out, who were new to the service, used to come to Cornhill to examine samples of the supplies.... We supplied large quantities of scientific instruments to India. I believe we sent out to the Ganges Canal Works the first telegraphic equipment. We had a room at Cornhill, kept at a uniform temperature winter and summer, and stored with theodolites and surveying instruments of every kind, so as to ensure them being perfectly dry before shipment. When after the Mutiny Her Majesty's Government took the business of supplying these things into its own hands I am afraid I was rather pleased to learn that the first two or three shipments of these articles were found to be useless, because they had not been properly treated before shipment.

The Indian Mutiny cost me a fortune. It not merely wrecked one great branch of our business. Our customers were mostly men in the army. We supplied them with pistols, saddles, provisions, books, equipment of every kind; indeed anything they wanted. We bought for them on commission, always securing for them the best goods at the lowest rates, and charging them a commission on the actual cost of the articles. This plan suited them and the business was profitable to us. But in the Mutiny so many of our debtors were killed that a large amount was lost to us. The Mutiny brought in its train another change which greatly affected my business. The whole system of England in the East was altered. The old East India Company vanished, and with the new Government came new arrangements. Under the new administration stores were supplied by the Government itself, and this practically wiped out, at a stroke, a great branch of business for me.

But there is no need to be too sorry for Smith. Although he could no longer supply Jacob's Horse and Hodson's Horse, the Mutiny was for him only a temporary setback. The turnover figures quoted by Smith, given at five-yearly intervals, certainly show no signs of disaster:

1846	£ 48,088
1851	£ 57,506
1856	£175,989
1861 (four years after the Mutiny)	£405,163
1866	£627,129

New markets were found, there was continuous increasing prosperity, and it was the profits from this trade that made Smith able to offer such generous payment to his authors and to afford such a formidable collection of talent for the *Cornhill* and the *Pall Mall Gazette*.

XI

Thackeray and the Cornhill Magazine

"I have a vivid recollection of the first time I ever heard of Thackeray or his writings some fifty years ago", Smith wrote in his *Recollections*.

It was the custom of publishers and of large dealers in "remainders" to have what were called "coffee-house sales". A publisher would invite the booksellers to dinner at an early hour – three or four o'clock in the afternoon – and after dinner he, or an auctioneer acting on his behalf, offered his books one after another from a printed list at a lower price than that at which they were usually sold to the trade. Orders were taken in the room, and each bookseller – even if he were not a buyer – entered the price of the work on his catalogue with the names of the larger purchasers, as a guide to the sources whence he might afterwards supply his demands.

Shortly after my appearance at Cornhill, and while I was still very young, I was sent to represent the firm at Messrs Tegg and Son's coffee-house sale, with instructions to mark my catalogue. This I did conscientiously, until Mr Thackeray's "Paris Sketch Book" was handed round. When the copy reached me I opened it, and my eyes fell on the sketch of Mr Deuceace. I commenced to read and I was fascinated! I forgot the scene around me. I read on till the end of the sale, and then awoke to the fact that my catalogue was unmarked. I asked Mr Tegg if I might have a copy of the book for the price at which it had been offered to the trade. Its original retail price had been a guinea: the price at which it was offered was 1s 9d. My joy at the possession of this treasure was chastened by the thought of how I should face my father with my unmarked catalogue; but I persuaded a good-natured confrère to lend me his list, and I copied his prices on to mine before I went to bed that night. I still preserve the book which first introduced me to the writings of Thackeray, whose name I had never heard till it fell from the lips of the auctioneer in that coffee-house sale. I fondly – though perhaps not quite accurately – believe I then resolved if ever I became a publisher I would publish the works of that writer.

So when Thackeray was still relatively unknown, before the days of *Vanity Fair*, Smith sent Smith Williams to see him and "say simply that, if ever he was in need of a publisher, I was his man on his own terms." Smith was then too shy to go himself; Smith Williams was not sufficiently persuasive, and this offer came to nothing.

It was not till Charlotte Brontë's second visit to London, in 1849, that Smith met Thackeray for the first time. The difficult dinner party when Smith introduced Charlotte Brontë to her hero, the morning call from Thackeray the following year, and the terrible evening when he took her to dinner with Thackeray led Smith to one of the most important literary friendships in his life. Although Smith, according to Gordon Ray,[1] was never in the inner circle of Thackeray's intimates, he became an esteemed friend; his reliable businesslike nature was a reassuring help to Thackeray's chaotic genius. Thackeray, for his part, introduced Smith to a far broader literary and artistic life, and was warmly admired by him.

Smith wrote of the first book he published for Thackeray, *The Kickleburys on the Rhine*, a Christmas Book for 1850:

> I came down rather late one morning to breakfast, and my mother told me that, while she was standing at the open window of the dining-room, Mr Thackeray rode up on his cob. He called out "Good morning" across the pavement, and asked: "Is your son in?" "I told him," said my mother, "that you were not in bed till four o'clock this morning and so had not come down yet. Thackeray said 'O-h-h' in a quizzical tone, and made such a funny face that I could not help laughing. I hastened to explain that you had been very hard at work in the City till late in the morning, on the *Indian Mail*. He seemed to accept my explanation, but I rather doubt if he believed it. He went on to say, 'I want to ask him if he would publish a book for me?' I told him I was sure you would, and that, if he was going home, I had no doubt you would come round to his house in an hour."

I was eager to publish for Thackeray; and, after I had hastily breakfasted, went to his house in Young Street, Kensington. Thackeray explained that his last Christmas Book, *Rebecca and Rowena*, had not been successful, and, as a result, Chapman and Hall could not see their way to paying him his price for the next book.

After this rather unpromising explanation, Smith accepted the book, wrote a cheque for £150, and agreed to publish an edition of 3,000. The book was severely attacked in *The Times*, but it sold out, and Smith had to persuade Thackeray to tone down the counterattack on *The Times* critic which Thackeray insisted on publishing as a preface to the second edition.

Smith published three more books for Thackeray before the start of the *Cornhill* – *Henry Esmond*, the *Lectures on the English Humourists*, and the most successful of all his minor books, *The Rose and The Ring*.

With the publication of *Esmond* (1852), Smith for the first time gave a four-figure sum for a novel. He called on Thackeray to make the offer at a time when, in spite of the success of the *English Humourist* lectures, Thackeray still had serious money worries. Anny Thackeray remembered the visit:

> One day my father came in, in great excitement. "There's a young fellow just come," said he; "he has brought a thousand pounds in his pocket. He has made me an offer for my book, it's the most spirited, handsome offer, I scarcely like to take him at his word; he's hardly more than a boy, his name is George Smith: he is waiting there now, and I must go back;" and then, after walking once up and down the room, my father went away, and for the first time, a life-time ago, I heard the name of this good friend-to-be.[2]

The agreement was for a three-volume novel, £400 to be paid straight away, £400 on receipt of the manuscript, and £400 on publication; if the full 2,750 copies of the first impression sold within eighteen months, Thackeray was to get an extra £100; further impressions were to be paid on half profits, after 5 per cent had been taken by Smith; Thackeray was not to publish a serial or other work within six months of *Esmond*'s publication; American profits, if any, were to go to Smith. This was in fact only half what Bradbury and Evans had given Thackeray for *Pendennis* – £100 each for twenty-four instalments – but it was very generous for three-volume publication, and it enabled Thackeray to write a great book without the strain of serial writing.

The publication of *Esmond* brought Thackeray and Smith closer. Smith's tribute to his great author, as to Charlotte Brontë earlier, was to commission a portrait, this time from Samuel Laurence – a drawing which so pleased Thackeray that he recommended Laurence to new patrons on both sides of the Atlantic. The portrait was given to Anny and Minny Thackeray to console them when their father set off for his first lecture tour in America, and reproductions were sold by Smith Elder for two guineas as part of the advertisement campaign for *Esmond*. Just before the boat sailed Smith was able to send Thackeray a copy of the first edition of *Esmond* together with a fine leather writing-case – a more appropriate present than the silver punch bowl sent to the ship by Bradbury and Evans, and certainly a more welcome one than the lifebelt sent by Thackeray's mother, which he loyally kept in his cabin in spite of its powerful smell.

It was not any dissatisfaction with Smith that made Thackeray turn back to Bradbury and Evans for his next major work, *The Newcomes*. The trouble was simply that before the days of the *Cornhill Magazine* Smith did not go in for serial publication, and Thackeray wanted the money that only serials could bring. Bradbury and Evans offered £3,600 for twenty-four numbers, with £500 more to come from Harper and Tauchnitz. As Thackeray happily wrote to his mother, "It's coining money, isn't it?"[3]

Smith was left with the minor job of publishing the *Lectures on English Humourists*. He gave Thackeray £200 for the right to print any number of the *Lectures* in one or more editions in any one size or form, with Thackeray keeping the right to publish them in any other size or form; but, Smith wrote, "I assume you will not allow an edition to be interfered with by another reprint of the Lectures for a few years."[4]

About this time, in April 1854, there is an amiable letter from Thackeray to Smith on his marriage:

> On my return home yesterday I found the twin glazed cards which announced your happiness. As I expect that you will add to mine (by numberless cheerful commercial transactions between us) you know I can't be indifferent to yours. May G. Smith and partner be happy in Gloucester Terrace, and G.S. and Co. continue to prosper in Cornhill! I am very glad indeed to hear of your settlement in life; and hope at a very early day you will be so kind as to

introduce me to Mrs Smith, and that she will like your old friends and reckon among them, Yours very sincerely and much obliged.[5]

The Rose and The Ring, written to amuse Thackeray's children and their friends through winter holidays and illnesses in Naples and Rome, became the much-loved Christmas Book for 1854. This time reviews were good everywhere, though a letter from Thackeray to Smith shows that sales were at first disappointing:

> I am very sorry to hear that the Xmas Book will produce such small results: and of course take whatever share my publisher can afford me. Will you kindly put £150 as a set off against my debt to you; and if we sell the American edition or another here I shall be able to wipe off all but the kindness of that obligation.

This letter ends, however, with a hopeful prophecy – "In spite of the war and the badness of literary times I feel as if we could make a success with a new periodical."[6]

The sources of the new periodical can be seen separately in both Smith's and Thackeray's ambitions, and as their friendship grew in the fifties it became natural that the two streams should join to produce the *Cornhill Magazine*. Thackeray, with his varied experience of journalism, had recurring ambitions to run his own magazine. In 1854 he had suggested to Smith that they should produce a daily sheet of general criticism, and this had been enthusiastically considered for a while until Thackeray got cold feet at the thought of an editor's life. Now it was Smith's turn to have an idea, and to suggest a magazine that would be a combination of serial fiction and a monthly review.

We have Smith's own account of the birth of the *Cornhill*, adapted from his *Recollections* and published in the *Cornhill Magazine* of January 1901, and also Anny Thackeray's account, published both in her Introduction to *Philip* and in the *Cornhill* of January 1910. "Early in 1859 I conceived the idea of founding a new magazine", Smith wrote.

> The plan flashed upon me suddenly, as did most of the ideas which have in the course of my life led to successful operations. The existing magazines were few, and when not high-priced were narrow in literary range, and it seemed to me

that a shilling magazine which contained, in addition to other first-class literary matter, a serial novel by Thackeray must command a large sale. Thackeray's name was one to conjure with, and according to the plan, as it shaped itself in my mind, the public would have a serial novel by Thackeray, and a good deal else worth reading, for the price they had been accustomed to pay for the monthly numbers of his novels alone.

I had, at first, no idea of securing Thackeray as editor. In spite of all his literary gifts I did not attribute to him the business qualities which go to make a good editor. But a novel by Thackeray was essential to my scheme. I wrote on a slip of paper the terms I was prepared to offer for his co-operation, and I went to him with it. I said I wanted him to read a little memorandum, and added, "I wonder whether you will consider it, or will at once consign it to your wastepaper-basket!"

Here are the *ipsissima verba* of my proposal:

"Smith, Elder & Co. have it in contemplation to commence the publication of a Monthly Magazine on January 1st, 1860. They are desirous of inducing Mr Thackeray to contribute to their periodical, and they make the following proposal to Mr Thackeray:

1. That he shall write either one or two novels of the ordinary size for publication in the Magazine – one-twelfth portion of each novel (estimated to be about equal to one number of a serial) to appear in each number of the Magazine.

2. That Mr Thackeray shall assign to Smith, Elder & Co. the right to publish the novels in their Magazine and in a separate form afterwards, and to all sums to be received for the work from American and Continental Publishers.

3. That Smith, Elder & Co. shall pay Mr Thackeray £350 each month.

4. That the profits of all editions of the novels published at a lower price than the first edition shall be equally divided between Mr Thackeray and Smith, Elder & Co.

65 CORNHILL: February 19th 1859"

Thackeray read the slip carefully, and, with characteristic absence of guile, allowed me to see that he regarded the terms as phenomenal. When he had finished reading the paper, he said with a droll smile: "I am not going to put such a document as *this* into my wastepaper-basket."

We had a little talk of an explanatory kind, and he agreed to consider my proposal. He subsequently accepted it, and the success of this part of my plans was assured.

My next step was to secure an editor. I applied in the first instance to Mr Tom Hughes, who received me with the genial manner for which he was remarkable, but he would not say "Yes". He had thrown in his lot, he explained, with Macmillan's, and with characteristic loyalty did not feel free to take other literary work. Several other names came under consideration, but none seemed to be exactly suitable, and I was at my wits' end. All my plans, indeed, were hung up pending the engagement of an editor. We were then living at Wimbledon, and I used to ride on the Common before breakfast. One morning, just as I had pulled up my horse after a smart gallop, that good genius which has so often helped me whispered into my ear, "Why should not Mr Thackeray edit the magazine, you yourself doing what is necessary to supplement any want of business qualifications on his part? You know that he has a fine literary judgement, a great reputation with men of letters as well as with the public, and any writer would be proud to contribute to a periodical under his editorship."

After breakfast I drove straight to Thackeray's house in Onslow Square, talked to him of my difficulty, and induced him to accept the editorship, for which he was to receive a salary of £1,000 a year.

"I am told that my Father demurred at first to the suggestion of editing the Cornhill," Anny Thackeray wrote.

Such work did not lie within his scope, but then Mr George Smith arranged that he himself was to undertake all business transactions, and my Father was only to go on writing and criticizing and suggesting; and so the first start of the Cornhill was all gaily settled and planned. The early records of the start are of a cheerful character – no time is lost – business questions are adjourned to Greenwich, to dinners, to gardens – meetings abound. . . .

I have an impression also, besides the play, of very hard and continuous work at that time; of a stream of notes and messengers from Messrs Smith and Elder; of consultations, calculations. I find an old record which states that "in sixteen days" the Cornhill was planned and equipped for its long journey.

My Father would go to Wimbledon, where the young couple Mr and Mrs George Smith were then living. Later on it was Mr Smith who used to come to see my Father, driving in early, morning after morning, on his way to business, carrying a certain black bag full of papers and correspondence, and generally arriving about breakfast-time.[7]

So Thackeray became the editor, determined, he said, that "the Magazine must bear my *cachet* you see and be a man-of-the-world Magazine",[8] but agreeing not to have sole right of decision on contributions; either Smith or Thackeray could use a veto – a very necessary arrangement, since Smith's tougher nature made them able to reject articles that Thackeray might have accepted from sentiment or pity. Thackeray's frequent illnesses and his chaotic manner of work – with notes on backs of envelopes and odd scraps of paper, and constant mislaying of manuscripts and last-minute crises – made it entirely right that Smith should keep the business management, a situation which he clearly enjoyed. The arrangement worked because, Smith said, "Thackeray's nature was so generous, and my regard for him was so sincere, that no misunderstanding between us ever occurred." Thackeray, for his part, found Smith "a splendid fellow and a clever tradesman".[9] Together they assembled a wonderful collection of talent.

While Smith was offering terms "lavish almost to the point of recklessness", Thackeray was writing endlessly to colleagues and friends to collect contributions for an outstanding magazine. "There can never have been a more brilliant partnership of cause and effect, of philosophy, fancy, and enterprise," Anny Thackeray wrote, "than during that too short time while the editor and the originator of The Cornhill Magazine worked together."[10]

They had agreed on the general scope and outlook of the magazine, and Thackeray set out their ideas in an advertisement letter in November 1859:

> . . . fiction of course must form a part, but only a part of our entertainment. We want, on the other hand, as much reality as possible – discussion and narrative of events interesting to the public, personal adventures and observation, familiar reports of scientific discovery, descriptions of Social Institutions – *quicquid agunt homines* – a Great Eastern, a battle in China, a Race-Course, a popular Preacher – there is hardly any subject we *don't* want to hear about, from lettered and instructed men who are competent to speak on it. . . . At our social table, we shall suppose the ladies and children always present; we shall not set rival politicians by the ears; we shall listen to every guest who has an apt word to say; and, I hope, induce clergymen of various denominations to say grace in their turn.

There is the same appeal, put more informally, in a private letter from Thackeray to Trollope who, although he did not yet know either Smith or Thackeray personally, had written to offer short stories for the *Cornhill*:

> Whatever a man knows about life and its doings, that let us hear about. You

must have tossed a good deal about the world, and have countless sketches in your memory and your portfolio. Please to think if you can furbish up any of these besides a novel. When events occur, and you have a good lively tale, bear us in mind. One of our chief objects in this magazine is the getting out of novel spinning, and back into the world. Don't understand me to disparage our craft, especially *your* wares. I often say I am like the pastry-cook, and don't care for tarts, but prefer bread and cheese; but the public love the tarts (luckily for us), and we must bake and sell them.[11]

At the same time Smith responded to Trollope with the offer of £1,000 for *Framley Parsonage*, twice as much as Trollope had ever had for a novel before. So in fact there were two large tarts in the *Cornhill*, and since Thackeray's serial, *Lovel the Widower*, was not a major novel, *Framley Parsonage* was to be the "stately herald" opening the first number.

Contributions showered in, and Thackeray had to urge Smith to keep some back and not put too much in the first issue – "Pray, Pray don't give more than you intend in other numbers."[12] It was certainly a well-packed magazine for a shilling, and there was plenty more in store. The accounts of the literary expenditure for the *Cornhill* are preserved in the National Library of Scotland, and it is interesting to look at the contents of this first number and at the sums paid to the authors:

Anthony Trollope	Framley Parsonage	25pp	£ 62 10
Sir John Bowring	The Chinese and the Outer Barbarians	18pp	18 18
W.M. Thackeray	Lovel the Widower	17pp	150
G.H. Lewes	Studies in Animal Life	14pp	17 10
F.S. Mahoney ("Father Prout")	Ode	2pp	5 5
Gen. Sir John Burgoyne	Our Volunteers	8pp	5 5
Thornton Hunt	A Man of Letters (about his father, Leigh Hunt)	11pp	10
Allen Young	The Search for Sir John Franklin	26pp	32 11
Mrs Archer Clive	Poem	2pp	4 4
W.M. Thackeray	Roundabout Paper (a monthly essay)	5pp	41 13 8
			£342 11 8
Editor (W.M.T.)			83 6 8
			£425 18 4

So out of a total literary expenditure of £425 for the first month Thackeray himself received £275, and the knowledgeable amateurs – Sir John Bowring, General Sir John Burgoyne, or Allen Young – were not treated so very generously.

The "lavish expenditure" may have been largely for Thackeray to begin with, but no one seems to have complained; the magazine was a startling success and Smith was delighted. A record 110,000 copies of the first number were sold – compared with 10,000–15,000 for *Macmillan's Magazine*, which had started just before, in November 1859. The only problem was that the *Cornhill* was so successful that Smith actually lost money on the advertisements, which had been accepted at a rate calculated for a far smaller sale. He had been away with his wife on a three-week holiday in the Lakes recovering from the strain of preparing the *Cornhill* when his office had agreed an advertisement rate of six or seven guineas a page; with such a large sale this did not even cover printing costs. Later he raised the charge to twenty guineas, but lost considerably on those early contracts which had been committed for a year. "I can remember messengers arriving during the day when that first number was published", Anny Thackeray wrote, "to tell the Editor of fresh thousands being wanted by the public; then more messengers came, and we were told how the printers were kept working till all hours. I have also heard of the binders fixing on the yellow wrappers all through the night."[13]

From the fourth number Thackeray's salary as editor was doubled. J.T. Fields, the American publisher, described him holidaying in Paris in a wildly excited state:

> "London," he exclaimed, "is not big enough to contain me now." . . . We dined at all possible and impossible places together. We walked round and round the glittering court of the Palais Royal, gazing in at the windows of the jewellers' shops, and all my efforts were necessary to restrain him from rushing in and ordering a pocketful of diamonds and "other trifles", as he called them; "for," said he, "how can I spend the princely income Smith allows me for editing the Cornhill, unless I begin instantly somewhere?"[14]

But Thackeray, as Smith pointed out, "was not a good business manager of his own affairs", and the problem of having too much money to spend was not his usual one: "He would walk into my room in Pall Mall with both his trouser pockets turned inside out, a silent and expressive proof of their emptiness. I used to take out my cheque-book and look at him enquiringly. He mentioned the sum required and the transaction was completed."

Thackeray remained editor of the *Cornhill* until April 1862. The circulation could not keep at the great heights of the first number but it stayed healthy, settling down to 87,500 at the end of 1860 and 72,500 at the end of 1861. During this time the proprietor as well as the editor was responsible for introducing an impressive list of contributors. It was Smith who first tried approaching Tennyson, with a grand offer of five thousand guineas for a poem as long as *Idylls of the King*; nothing came of this, though Thackeray persuaded Tennyson to give him *Tithonus* (for fifty guineas) for the second number. It was Smith, too, who rightly insisted that Trollope's novel must be, not Irish as Trollope would have liked, but "an English tale, on English life, with a clerical flavour",[15] to follow up the success of *Barchester Towers*. In fact in his *Autobiography* Trollope states: "What I wrote for the Cornhill Magazine I always wrote at the instigation of Mr Smith." Since Thackeray, with his sympathy with the Southern States, was suspicious of Harriet Beecher Stowe, it is probable that *Agnes of Sorrento* came to the *Cornhill* through Smith's initiative. G.H. Lewes, who had been Smith's friend since the days of Powell's Museum Club, was asked by him to do the series *Studies in Animal Life*, to appear first in the *Cornhill* and later as a book. Many writers contributed out of friendship for Thackeray, but Mrs Gaskell, who had "extreme dislike to writing for Mr T.",[16] sent her stories entirely out of friendship for Smith.

These first two years of the *Cornhill* produced a splendid mixture of articles. Always there were two serials, one by Thackeray and one other – *Lovel the Widower* was followed by *The Four Georges* and then by *The Adventures of Philip*, while *Framley Parsonage* was followed by *Agnes of Sorrento*. There was an assortment of instructive essays – "it's curious", Thackeray wrote to Smith, "to see how the useful-knowledge mongers begin alike with a lively anecdote"[17] – and there was generally a *Roundabout Paper* from Thackeray, short stories, poems, travellers' tales and natural history. All the mid-nineteenth-century literary figures except Dickens were there – Matthew Higgins ('Jacob Omnium'), Richard Monckton Milnes, Elizabeth Barrett Browning, Lord Lytton, Charles Lever, Richard Doyle. Charlotte Brontë had died five years earlier, but her father was comforted by the touching tribute to her in Thackeray's "The Last Sketch"; this was his introduction to *Emma*, the fragment which Mr Nicholls authorized Smith to publish in the *Cornhill*. A new author, diffidently offered to Smith but happily accepted, was Anny Thackeray, whose first essay, "Little Scholars", appeared in the fifth number. Thackeray was proud of Anny's writing, but not too proud to be critical, and he did not think his younger daughter Minny's efforts were good enough to submit – "the author is very doubtful about it; so is her Papa."[18]

There is one curious gap, in a magazine that set out to discuss scientific discoveries and all matters of general importance to mankind. *The Origin of Species* had been published in 1859, and the first year of the *Cornhill* saw the heated arguments that followed and the great Huxley–Wilberforce debate at the Oxford meeting of the British Association in June; but in the magazine produced by the publisher of *The Zoology of the Beagle* the only mention of Darwin was a careful discussion in G.H. Lewes's fourth and fifth *Studies in Animal Life* (April and May 1860). Perhaps Thackeray was simply trying to avoid religious controversy, in the same way that he shied away from stormy political articles.

Thackeray was also over-anxious to avoid upsetting the most touchy moral sensibilities. For this reason he refused both Trollope's *Mrs General Tallboys* and Elizabeth Browning's *Lord Walter's Wife*; Smith in his *Recollections* clearly and reasonably implies that this last decision was an unnecessary fuss. Smith seems to have been bolder than Thackeray, too, about the criticisms of Eton in the article "Paterfamilias to the Editor of the Cornhill Magazine", written by Matthew Higgins; this article, Thackeray wrote to Smith, "had best be left alone, and I am sure if we publish it we have the worst of the controversy. Could it be stopped?"[19] It was not stopped; it made, as Thackeray said, "an awful row at Eton",[20] and led to a literary battle with the *Quarterly*, but the *Cornhill* emerged as a triumphant champion of public school reforms.

Both Thackeray and Smith cared very much about the standard of illustration in the *Cornhill*. The drawings in the early *Cornhills* were in fact so distinguished that in 1863 a selection, by Millais, Leighton, and Walker, was republished as *The Cornhill Gallery*. It was Smith's happy idea to invite Millais to illustrate *Framley Parsonage*, to Trollope's great delight. "Should I live to see my story illustrated by Millais," Trollope wrote to Smith, "nobody would be able to hold me";[21] and although there is a despairing letter from Trollope about the June number – "the picture is simply ludicrous. . . . I presume the fact to be that Mr Millais has not time to devote to these illustrations"[22] – yet in his *Autobiography* Trollope remembered the illustrations with pleasure, and told what trouble Millais had taken to get the spirit of the work right and how he himself had been helped by the drawings when carrying the characters on from book to book.

Smith had met Millais first at Ruskin's house, and a close friendship had grown between the two families. "He sent for me a few days before he died", Smith remembered:

> He could not speak owing to a recent dreadful operation on his throat. But the extraordinary courage he had shown all through his illness still shone in his eyes. He took a slate, and with his feeble fingers, scrawled a few sentences on it, asking if I could remember the fun we had together on such and such an occasion, and with so and so.

Frederick Leighton was known to the Smiths because he was distantly connected to Elizabeth Smith. Thackeray suggested inviting him to do drawings for the *Cornhill*, but at that time he was away from London and did not contribute until, after Thackeray had resigned from being editor, Smith asked him to illustrate *Romola*.

Frederick Walker, who was to do so much for the *Cornhill* before his death at the age of thirty-five, first appeared on the scene as a shy young artist asking for work. Smith remembered introducing him to Thackeray:

> My first acquaintance with Frederick Walker was in 1860. I was at that time under a great and constant strain of work, and my room at Cornhill was rather jealously guarded against interruptions. On leaving my room on one occasion I caught a glimpse of a youthful-looking figure, portfolio under arm, passing through the outer office. The artistic profile – keen, clear, refined – somehow prepossessed me, and I left instructions that when he called again he was to be shown to my room.
>
> He came and showed me his drawings, and I realized their artistic thoroughness and promise. It happened just then that Thackeray was beginning to find it troublesome to draw on wood. His last two or three drawings for *The Adventures of Philip* were made on paper, and these had to be re-drawn on wood by an artist, and the result, so far, had not been very satisfactory. It occurred to me that my youthful visitor was precisely the man to re-draw on

wood Thackeray's sketches, and I proposed the task to him, and understood that the task was acceptable. But Walker's nervous agitation while I was speaking to him was almost painful, and though I did my best to set him at his ease, he left my room without my being sure that he understood the arrangement I wished to make with him. The plan was to be subject to Thackeray's approval, and I explained to him how painfully nervous his new assistant was. "Can't you bring him here," said Thackeray, "and we can prove whether he can draw." I wrote to Walker and said I would call and drive him to Thackeray's house. The drive was almost a silent one, Walker's agitation being very obvious. When we reached our destination Thackeray set himself in a most genial fashion, but with very partial success, to put Walker at his ease. At last he said, "Can you draw? Mr Smith says you can. I am going to shave, would you mind drawing my back?" Thackeray went to his toilet glass and commenced shaving, while poor Walker took a sheet of paper and began sketching his subject's broad back. The sketch is a proof at once of his artistic skill and of his nervous state of mind.

I looked out of the window while Walker worked, in order that he might not feel he was being watched. Thackeray's idea of giving his back to Walker as a subject was as ingenious as it was kind; for I believe, if Walker had been asked to draw Thackeray's face, instead of his back, he would hardly have been able to hold his pencil.

Walker passed this exam with flying colours, later doing another drawing of Thackeray's back which Anny said was more like her father than any other ever made. After two or three drawings on wood from Thackeray's designs Walker asked for more creative work, and was happier when he was promoted to take over the illustrations for *Philip* altogether.

For both Smith and Thackeray, the best way of running any enterprise was to keep everyone happy with good dinners. So there were various occasions when Thackeray would suggest that "he always found his mind clearer for business at Greenwich than elsewhere, especially if his digestion were assisted by a certain brown hock, at 15s a bottle";[23] and there were the monthly dinners, for principal contributors, at Gloucester Square – great literary gatherings where Smith much enjoyed acting as host.

These dinners led to an incident which caused some upset at the time, and caught Smith up in Thackeray's past quarrels. Edmund Yates, an old enemy who had been expelled from the Garrick Club after a previous attack on Thackeray, wrote an article in the *New York Herald*, later

[130]

quoted in the *Saturday Review*, sneering at the "tremendously heavy dinner parties", saying that if the *Cornhill* had gone up like a rocket it was coming down like the stick, and referring to Smith as "a very good man of business, but totally unread; his business has been to sell books, not read them, and he knows little else". Smith would have ignored all this but his wife was deeply upset, and Thackeray, after "lying awake half the night in a sort of despair",[24] produced his *Roundabout* "On Screens in Dining Rooms" in reply, where he loyally defended Smith as "a gentleman to the full as well informed as those whom he invites to his table", and pointed out that the sales of the magazine were not 40,000 but more than 90,000. "Attack our books, Mr Correspondent, and welcome," wrote Thackeray. "They are fair subjects for just censure or praise. But woe be to you if you allow private rancours or animosities to influence you in the discharge of your public duty."

Thackeray was always loyal and, Smith said, "prepared to stand by me, not only when I was right but when I was wrong". On one occasion Thackeray rebuked Smith for writing too strong a letter to Lucas, editor of *All The Year Round*: "Now, from the little insight I have into the character of George Smith, he has as strong a desire to go his own way as any man I ever saw. You dwell on this and that, and things grow more ugly in your mind as you think of them . . . you have ridden too roughly at Lucas and hurt your case by so doing."[25] But this was private criticism; in public Thackeray supported Smith.

It was Thackeray who put Smith's name forward for election to the Reform Club, causing Smith to write: "I am told there is a report at the Reform Club that I am Smith of the Strand* and that if it is not contradicted I am pretty sure to be pilled – I don't know if you can do anything in the matter, but if the description could be made complete I might have a chance of failing on account of my own demerits, and not those of my namesake."[26]

Thackeray was a wonderful colleague in the early days of the *Cornhill*, when his great prestige and enthusiasm helped launch it so successfully. But this very success had brought such wealth that he could now afford to give up the editorial chair. The first excitement was over, and endless problems increasingly worried him: his recurring illness, his dislike of the

*W.H. Smith.

constant pressure of a monthly magazine, and his worry at the "thorns in the editorial cushion"[27] – the need to say "no" so often to deserving or struggling or charming would-be contributors. After much heart-searching he resigned in May 1862, though he and Smith remained on the best of terms for the remaining eighteen months of Thackeray's life. Perhaps there had been some disagreements – it would be surprising if there had been none – and there may be a hint of unspecified problems in Thackeray's resignation letters:

4 March 1862:
My Dear Smith, – I have been thinking over our conversation of yesterday, and it has not improved the gaiety of the work on which I am pretty busy. To-day I have taken my friend Sir Charles Taylor into my confidence, and his opinion coincides with mine that I should withdraw from the magazine. To go into bygones now is needless. Before ever the magazine appeared I was, as I have told you, on the point of writing such a letter as this. And whether connected with the Cornhill Magazine or not, I hope I shall always be sincerely your friend.

6 March 1862:
My Dear S, – I daresay your night, like mine, has been a little disturbed: but "Philip" presses, and until this matter is over, I can't make that story so amusing as I would wish.
   I had this pocket-pistol in my breast yesterday, but hesitated to pull the trigger at an old friend. My daughters are for a compromise. They say: "It is all very fine Sir Charles Taylor telling you to do so and so. Mr Smith has proved himself your friend always." *Bien.* It is because I wish him to remain so, that I and the Magazine had better part company. Good-bye and God bless you and all yours.[28]

Thackeray continued to write for the *Cornhill*:

Though editor no more I hope long to remain a contributor to my friend's magazine. I believe my own special readers will agree that my books will not suffer when their author is released from the daily task of reading, accepting, refusing, losing, and finding the works of other people. To say "no" has often cost me a morning's peace and a day's work. I tremble *recenti metu*. Oh, those hours of madness spent in searching for Louisa's lost lines to her dead piping bullfinch, for Nhoj Senej's mislaid essay! I tell them for the last time that the late editor will not be responsible for rejected communications and herewith send off the chair and the great Cornhill Magazine tin box, with its load of care.[29]

Roundabout Papers, for which he was now paid twelve guineas a page, appeared for another year; *Philip* lasted until August 1862; and one more serial, *Denis Duval*, started for the *Cornhill* but never finished, was published there after his death. There was much talk of a great history of the reign of Queen Anne, a sort of continuation of Macaulay's *History*, to be written for Smith Elder in Thackeray's new Queen Anne house at Palace Green "all built out of Cornhill money", but this never even started.

The Smith family were at the theatricals that celebrated the completion of Thackeray's house in March 1862. Smith must have helped in the search for furnishings or, ever a great present-giver, must have offered a very grand house-warming present indeed, for we find Thackeray writing, "Please don't buy those beautiful chandeliers. I think they are too big for my rooms"[30] – and they were very big rooms. Another letter from the new house, in July 1862, asks: "Will you let Laurence make another drawing of you? I should like to hang it here."[31] Thackeray's last letter to Smith, typically part about *Denis Duval* and part personal, was written on 17 December 1863, just a week before his death:

> I was just going to be taken prisoner by Paul Jones when I had to come to bed. If I could get a month's ease I could finish the eight numbers handsomely with the marriage of Denis and Agnes, after the capture of Toulon by the English. "The Course of True Love" I thought of as a pretty name. . . . Yesterday BURGLARS entered our house and robbed my poor mother and girls of watches, trinkets, diamonds – all my little presents, lockets, bracelets, to poor Anny since she was fifteen.[32]

Thackeray's death did not change the *Cornhill* because already he was no longer the editor, or the dominant contributor he had been in its early days; but it was a great personal loss to Smith, as to so many of his fellow writers. As Trollope, who had become Thackeray's friend through the *Cornhill*, wrote in his tribute in the February 1864 number, "He was the kindest of guides, the gentlest of rulers, and as a fellow-workman, liberal, unselfish, considerate, beyond compare." It was Smith who asked Dickens also to contribute a memorial essay – an essay for which he refused any payment.

Smith's connection with Thackeray's family and his works grew, if anything, even closer. He was one of a group of Thackeray's friends, with

Herman Merivale, James Fitzjames Stephen, and Henry Cole, who tried to help Anny and Minny by looking after their business affairs. Thackeray had always been painfully aware of the need to accumulate sufficient capital to leave for his mad wife and young daughters. Thanks largely to the *Cornhill* he had managed to do this, but the capital was in the form of his great house and its contents, and such copyrights as were still his, including his half-share in the books published by Chapman and Hall and by Bradbury Evans & Co. The house was sold, his possessions auctioned.

> Anne Thackeray [wrote Smith] had a sentimental wish to keep a particular Queen Anne tea kettle, as her father had been very fond of it. I privately determined to purchase that particular kettle at the sale for her. It happened that another friend of the family, Mr Russell Sturgis, made up his mind to do the same thing. He commissioned a broker to buy the kettle without mentioning any limit of price. I went to the sale myself and we went on bidding against each other long after all other bidding had ceased. The kettle fell to me at last, and I do not think a kettle has ever been sold at such a price before or since.

Thackeray's seventeenth-century *Portrait of a Lady*, by Pourbas, must have been bought by Smith for himself, as we read later of it hanging in his dining-room in Park Lane.

Smith was anxious to buy all the copyrights, and here too negotiations were through the same group of friends. Thackeray himself had reckoned his copyrights worth £4,000, and on Anny and Minny's behalf Merivale, Cole and Stephen were happy to accept Smith's offer of £5,000, provided that Anny and Minny did not have to hand over any of their father's unpublished work that they wished to remain unpublished. Later Smith showed himself sensitive to their feelings by helping to see Thackeray's letters were kept private, until Mrs Brookfield forced his hand by publishing hers in America.[33]

Thackeray's mother, Mrs Carmichael-Smyth, was delighted that Smith was taking over:

> Give me leave to express to you as best I may my great satisfaction that the literary labours of my most dear son are placed in your hands . . . my hope is that you and yours will gather as you have sown, so abundantly, that you will realize the substantial as well as the moral reward of so much kindness. I wish I

could tell you how much I thank you and rejoice that such a friend is assured to my grandchildren.[34]

So far all was generous and amiable; but there was less goodwill in the negotiations with Chapman and Hall and with Bradbury and Evans for the remaining half-share in their copyrights, and we see a harder and less likeable side of Smith's nature. With his authors he was always deferential and anxious to please, but with other businessmen he could be peremptory and tough. Chapman and Hall only owned half-shares in relatively minor works such as the early *Christmas Books*, and the *Irish* and *Paris Sketch Books*, which, Chapman nobly or mistakenly wrote to Fitzjames Stephen, "are not of that lasting character as his other works, and we therefore think that a high value should not be put upon them."[35] To complete his copyright of these Smith gave £400, with £95.13.2 for the remaining stocks, including the plates and blocks. This seems an astonishingly good bargain, but even so the letters on Smith's side become increasingly bad-tempered, with complaints of delays and demands to see Chapman's legal title to the copyrights. When Chapman said there was never any assignment from Thackeray, only an informal agreement and "equitable copyright", Smith replied that clearly in that case Chapman had never had a legal title to any interest in the copyright of any of Thackeray's works, and was entitled neither to print them himself nor to prevent Smith & Elder from doing so for their exclusive advantage;[36] but he did not push this claim any further.

Arguments broke out again in 1888 when Chapman offered to sell Smith, at what he called the low price of £100, eight further essays by Thackeray which had previously appeared only in the *Foreign Quarterly* and had been forgotten at the time of the earlier transactions. Smith was irritated: "It seems to have escaped your memory that in the year 1865 your firm sold to Smith Elder & Co. all their interest in works written by the late W.M. Thackeray. Therefore the articles printed in the Foreign Quarterly Review or any profit to be made from them belong to us and not to you."[37] Smith's legal adviser gave his opinion that although Smith was probably in the right, it was hard to prove that Chapman had been aware of these articles in 1865, so for once – perhaps he was getting old – Smith gave way. "The question of our legal claim to have the article printed in the Foreign Quarterly Review . . . handed to us is a complicated one, and I am advised not to endeavour to enforce it."[38]

With Bradbury and Evans there was even more trouble. It is not clear what the terms of the final agreement were, but Bradbury and Evans turned down Smith's first offer of £2,500 and there was an increasingly heated series of letters – "This correspondence", Smith wrote, "has now extended over a period of more than six months and we think that we have strong reason to complain of the manner in which it has been protracted by you."[39] Eventually Bradbury and Evans put forward a counter-offer of £3,500 for Smith Elder's share in their copyrights – a larger offer, but Smith Elder held a rather larger share. This produced a very angry reply from Smith:

> It is now quite clear that no satisfactory arrangement will result from any further discussion and we will only consider with you the mode in which the whole of the Property in which we are jointly interested shall be offered for sale – and as we presume that you would wish, as we do, to have an opportunity of bidding for the property, we would propose that the sale should be conducted by some one chosen by both of us.[40]

There was no auction, and shortly after this ultimatum Bradbury and Evans sold their copyrights and stocks to Smith Elder. The total paid to Bradbury and Evans and Chapman and Hall was, Smith said, less than the £5,000 given to Anny and Minny.

Smith now had the copyrights of all Thackeray's works and he did indeed, as Mrs Carmichael-Smyth had hoped, eventually gather a substantial reward. Standard editions of Thackeray's works started to appear in 1867. Nearly thirty years later, after Thackeray's wife had died and Anny had looked out old diaries and letters for her *Chapters from Some Memoirs*, George Smith encouraged her to delve still further into her overwhelming mass of family manuscripts and notebooks to write the marvellous biographical introductions to the Biographical Edition of Thackeray's works that was published, in thirteen volumes, from 1894 to 1899. In 1911, to mark the centenary of Thackeray's birth, Anny revised these Introductions, and newly identified manuscript material was added to make the fine Centenary Edition, under the direction of George Smith's son-in-law and successor, Reginald Smith.

[136]

XII

The Cornhill after Thackeray

From Thackeray's resignation as editor in 1862 until Leslie Stephen's appointment in 1871, George Smith himself was the guiding spirit of the *Cornhill Magazine*. At the beginning of this period he had Frederick Greenwood's help as sub-editor and later, after Greenwood became fully busy with the *Pall Mall Gazette*, he had Dutton Cook. For the first two years, as well, George Smith persuaded G.H. Lewes to act as consulting editor. An undated letter from Lewes to Smith[1] shows that this arrangement with Lewes, which had to have George Eliot's blessing, was at first to be unofficial and was not easy to negotiate:

> I find that Mrs Lewes's objections were not directed so much against the idea of odium to be incurred, as against the idea of secrecy and equivocalness. She very truly says that any attempt at secrecy would look like a shrinking from real responsibility, and might imply that an office honourable in itself was thought by us either discreditable or too dangerous for avowal. Neither of which implication could be tolerated.
>
> Were my position clear and distinct, she thinks, I could with propriety see a contributor, now and then, whenever it was desirable to explain more fully our wants in a particular case, or the reasons of our rejection of a particular article. I should at no time object to incur the responsibility of a rejection which was based on an opinion of my own; nor to state personally the grounds of my

opinion to the contributor himself. . . . Remember always that you are to be Editor in reality, as in name, my position must be one absolved from all responsibility beyond my own judgement and acts; and to have none of the *representative* duties which would necessitate dining out, grand receptions, much correspondence, or any other serious alteration in my mode of life. . . . If I join you my first thought naturally will be the strength of the Magazine and therefore I should endeavour to persuade Mrs Lewes to publish her new work in it. . . . She is, as you know, reluctant and diffident; but she will I am pretty sure be guided by my wishes, even against her own preference for the other form of publication.

With this carrot dangling in front of him Smith was happy to agree to all Lewes asked. As Lewes's diary entry for 8 May 1862 put it, "I am to act as his chief Literary Adviser in the selection of articles, and suggestion of subjects, he bringing them to me and I only taking responsibility as is implied in my judgement. Salary £600 per annum. This is very handsome, as the whole work promises to be light, and not disagreeable."

£50 an issue for Lewes and only £25 for Greenwood meant a big drop in editorial expenses, but fees for star authors remained high, most conspicuously when Lewes did "persuade Mrs Lewes to publish her new work in it". The £7,000 given for *Romola* entailed a monthly payment of £583.6.8 – over £150 more than the total literary expenditure for the first number of the *Cornhill* – and sent the monthly figure rocketing to more than £1,000. The initiative had come from Smith. It was not an attempt to compensate for the loss of Thackeray, since George Eliot recorded in her Journal that Smith's first approach came on 23 January 1862, nearly three months before Thackeray resigned. Smith, she wrote, asked "if I were open to a 'magnificent offer'. This made me think about money – but it is better for me not to be rich." The following month, according to Lewes,

> he made a proposal to purchase Polly's new work for £10,000. This of course includes the entire copyright. It is the most magnificent offer ever yet made for a novel; and Polly, as usual was disinclined to accept it, on the ground that her work would not be worth the sum! Moreover she felt it impossible to begin publication in April or May – the period when Smith wishes it to begin to appear in the "Cornhill Mag.". Unless she sees her book nearly completed and such as she considers worthy of publication she objects to begin printing it. I went down to Smith to tell him of her difficulties. He was much put out, April or May being the months when the Magazine will stand in need of some

reinforcement, as Thackeray's story is quite insufficient to keep up the sale. Smith then proposed to print her story of *Brother Jacob*, written in 1860, if it can be split up into three numbers, and thus tide over the three months; and then to commence in August or September with the new work. She has consented to let him see the story to see if this arrangement will do. If not some other proposal will be made by him.[2]

The arrangement would not do, and Smith's next proposal, in March, was a tentative one to publish the novel in weekly numbers, at sixpence with one plate, as he felt he was not interested in an autumn serial for the *Cornhill*. The May visit, when Lewes was already consulting editor, was more productive; George Eliot read Smith several chapters of *Romola*

> in order that before finally making any proposals he should know the kind of work it was to be. He dissuaded us from the notion of a serial, believing that it would not tell in small portions. He wishes to publish it in the "Cornhill Magazine" but in considerable instalments – of 45 or 40 pages each number, with two illustrations . . . tonight we go to the opera to see Rigoletto, George Smith having given us his stalls.[3]

So *Romola* appeared in the *Cornhill* in twelve long monthly parts. The payment of £7,000 was to include the copyright and foreign rights for six years, and after that the right to sell the stock and to reprint the book in any one form only.

This agreement was £3,000 less than Smith's original offer, and the modification of the copyright arrangement does not seem sufficient reason for such a large reduction. Smith's own version of the story, admittedly written thirty years later, gives a different account. According to him, the £10,000, offered impulsively under the charm of hearing George Eliot read, was to have been for sixteen instalments, but George Eliot would not divide her book into more than twelve, even if this meant it would be worth less to Smith and would therefore bring her considerably less money. "She was cheerfully content", wrote Smith, "to accept the smaller sum for the sake of an artistic division of her novel. Lewes himself by no means shared George Eliot's artistic scruples. He seconded me heart and soul; for he was not so indifferent to money considerations as the woman of genius."

To illustrate *Romola* George Smith chose Frederick Leighton, who had lived in Florence as a boy, and paid him £20 for each drawing. George Eliot herself had visited Florence only briefly, but Smith claimed that she had remembered it so well and that the descriptions were so good that he and his wife were able to use *Romola* as a guidebook on their first visit.

George Eliot now had to confess to her friend and publisher John Blackwood how she had deserted him for "an offer which I suppose was handsomer than almost any terms ever offered to a writer of Fiction".[4] Blackwood replied sadly, "Hearing of the wild sums that were being offered to writers of much inferior mark to you, I thought it highly probable that offers would be made to you, and I can readily imagine that you are to receive such a price as I could not make remunerative by any machinery that I could resort to."[5] To salt the wound, Smith Elder & Co. sent an advertisement to be inserted in *Blackwood's Magazine*: "A New Novel by the Author of 'Adam Bede' Will Be Commenced in the Next Number of the Cornhill Magazine."[6] Blackwood's London manager, Joseph Langford, thought the whole thing "a disgusting transaction, which certainly does not surprise me on her part, but does rather on the part of Mr Smith."[7] Blackwood himself took the desertion well, refusing to quarrel and adding, in a letter to Langford, "Besides if the story is the one I suppose, I have no doubt it will be a fine thing but it was doubtful in my mind how far it would bear being given in fragments in the Magazine and certainly it would not suit the readers of the Cornhill."[8]

Blackwood was right. *Romola*, the most expensive serial published by the *Cornhill*, did nothing to revive sales, which had slumped badly when Thackeray resigned. "It has", Lewes admitted, "unfortunately not been so generally popular as I hoped and believed its intrinsic beauty would have made it."[9] George Eliot herself tried to make up for the failure by sending Smith *Brother Jacob* as a present for the *Cornhill* – the story for which Smith had earlier offered two hundred and fifty guineas.

As a book, *Romola* sold respectably but not with any of the startling success of *Adam Bede* or *The Mill on the Floss*. It took two years to sell the 2,288 copies of the three-volume edition that Smith & Elder printed in July 1863. Then came a six-shilling edition in one volume, with 1,519 copies printed in September 1865 and a further five hundred in January 1869. Smith & Elder's copyright ran out in June 1869, leaving them with the right to issue the book in one form only, and they chose a cheap edition at two shillings and sixpence. In 1880, by agreement with Blackwood,

Smith & Elder also produced a "grand edition" of *Romola* in two volumes, on special paper, limited to a thousand numbered copies. Acknowledging Smith's cheque for £100 for this, George Eliot wrote, "I did not expect to receive any honorarium at present, if at all, but it is so much in your well-remembered way to exceed the expectations even of those who know you, in acts of delicate consideration, that your letter hardly surprised me. I thank you for both word and deed."[10]

Apart from four articles in the *Pall Mall Gazette*, Smith did not publish anything more for George Eliot. He lost his opportunity in 1866 when Lewes offered him *Felix Holt*, with a warning that George Eliot wanted £5,000 for it. "I read the MS to my wife, and we came to the conclusion it would not be a profitable venture and I declined it."[11] Blackwood agreed to the £5,000 and regained his place as George Eliot's publisher.

Lewes resigned his consulting editorship of the *Cornhill* in August 1864, not after any disagreement but, it seems, more from general disappointment and from a feeling that it was a sinking ship, damaged by rivals arising from its own success and failing to recover from the loss of Thackeray's prestige. It would be best to economize, he advised Smith, by reducing the number of illustrations and by dispensing with his services.[12] In his Journal, Lewes wrote: "With this month ceases my consulting editorship of the Cornhill Magazine began May 1862 . . . the diminished and constantly diminishing circulation no longer permitting the Mag. to be at such an expense which could be spared. I regret the loss of the income very much, the more so because the duties were so light and agreeable but on the other hand it is a tie loosened."[13]

Lewes continued to write articles for the *Cornhill*, and it was not long before his services were given to Smith in a new capacity – in December of the same year Smith appointed him as adviser to the newly formed *Pall Mall Gazette*. He kept the salaried post for only a year, but he remained a very active contributor until an unsympathetic review[14] of George Eliot's *Spanish Gypsy* upset him, causing him to stop writing for the paper and making a temporary break in his friendship with Smith. The friendship revived, but never quite on the old terms, and there were no more *Cornhill* articles. George Smith continued to send bon-bons at New Year but not, as before, oyster dishes or initialled travelling bags.

It was not easy to keep up the standard of serial fiction set by the opening batsmen Trollope and Thackeray. For the first half of Smith's editorship there was still a distinguished and mostly familiar list. Trollope himself was the mainstay, with *The Small House at Allington* (1862) and *The Claverings* (1866), while Thackeray's *Denis Duval* ran in 1864; there was Mrs Gaskell's *Cousin Phillis* (1863) and *Wives and Daughters* (1864). The newcomers, apart from George Eliot, were Anny Thackeray with *The Story of Elizabeth* and *The Village on the Cliff*, Frederick Greenwood with *Margaret Denzil*, and Wilkie Collins with *Armadale*.

Anny Thackeray was an inevitable choice; she wrote with liveliness and Victorian charm in a distinctive style of her own and became a regular *Cornhill* contributor, loved for her father's sake and for her own.

With Wilkie Collins, then at the height of his fame, Smith was making another bid for a sensational success. Ruskin had introduced Collins to Smith in 1848, but Smith had at that time refused the historical novel *Antonina* on the grounds that he did not want a story with a classical subject. Later he lost the opportunity to publish *The Woman in White*, one of the most popular of all Victorian novels, through uncharacteristic incompetence. In 1855 Smith had published a collection of Collins's short stories, and had been promised the offer of his next novel; in 1860, when *The Woman in White* was appearing in *All the Year Round*, Collins made good his promise, but Smith failed to make a remotely adequate response. In his *Recollections* Smith confessed his failure:

On receiving Wilkie Collins's letter I asked three or four of my clerks if they had read the tale, but none of them knew anything about it. Wilkie Collins had asked for an early decision; I had to go out to dinner that night, and I dictated a hasty note, making him an offer of £500, and told my clerk to send the letter off.

The lady sitting beside me at dinner that night was a bright and lively talker, and she somewhat startled me by asking, "Have you read that wonderful book *The Woman in White*? Everybody is raving about it. We talk Woman in White from morning till night!" If I had heard that piece of gossip a couple of hours earlier, it would have multiplied my offer to Wilkie Collins fivefold.

I went to town earlier than usual next morning, and asked directly I reached my office, "Have you sent that letter to Mr Wilkie Collins?" "Yes," was the reply; "you said you wanted it sent quickly and it was delivered by hand." If my offer had been multiplied tenfold I should have made a large sum by the transaction; but my hasty original offer cost me the pleasure and profit of publishing *The Woman in White*.

So, hoping to secure the next best seller, the following year George Smith offered Collins £5,000 for the copyright of "a work of fiction a little longer than *The Woman in White*" for the *Cornhill*. "No living novelist (except Dickens) has had such an offer as this for one book", Collins wrote to his friend Charles Ward – this was before the offer for *Romola* – and an agreement was made for the first part of the book to be delivered on 1 December 1862. Collins's constant ill-health pushed this date on nearly two years, and *Armadale* did not in fact start in the *Cornhill* until November 1864, and one month later in *Harper's Monthly*. It is said that *Armadale*'s success probably saved *Harper's* from extinction, but for the *Cornhill* it seems at best only to have slowed down the decline. As with *Romola*, Smith had once again gone to a popular novelist but had unluckily not got a popular novel. Some sales figures for the last month in each year tell the sad story:

Cornhill	No. 24,	December 1862:	72,500 (copies)
,,	36,	December 1863:	50,000
,,	48,	December 1864:	41,250
,,	60,	December 1865:	40,000
,,	72,	December 1866:	38,000
,,	84,	December 1867:	36,500
,,	96,	December 1868:	32,250
,,	108,	December 1869:	27,000

After 1866, until Meredith, already a regular writer for the *Pall Mall Gazette*, started *Harry Richmond* in 1870, it seems almost as if Smith gave up trying to find first-class serials for the *Cornhill*. Possibly he was too absorbed with the *Pall Mall* for a time, and then the *Cornhill* must have had problems when Smith suffered a severe breakdown at the end of 1868; possibly also Dutton Cook may have proved less helpful than Frederick Greenwood. Whatever the cause, 1867, 1868 and 1869 show a very uninspired fiction list in the *Cornhill*, with three novels each from Charles Lever and Lady Verney and one each from Charles Reade and A.I. Shand. At least costs were down, total payment to authors being less than £300 an issue. Trollope's association with the *Cornhill* had ended with *The*

Claverings; *The Last Chronicle of Barset* at Trollope's suggestion was brought out by Smith & Elder in 1866 and 1867 in sixpenny numbers.[15]

There was not the same falling off in general literature. Indeed, George Eliot wrote to Smith in July 1867,

> I rejoice to see how many valuable articles you get for the Magazine. I don't read the fiction, but if that is at all in keeping with the good matter I often find in other contributions it will be a public benefit if "natural selection" turns out to be in favour of the Cornhill. But natural selection is not always good, and depends (see Darwin) on many caprices of very foolish animals.

The mixture of excellent essays and general articles was maintained to a remarkable degree, and interesting new names, as well as the old ones, constantly appeared. The most influential recruit was Leslie Stephen, who sent his first article in 1866 and soon became a regular contributor, appearing in seven of the issues for 1869.

Among the huge range of writing in the *Cornhill* at this period we find poems from Tennyson, Swinburne, Sir John Herschel, Lord Houghton and Frederick Greenwood; short stories from Anny Thackeray, Mrs Oliphant and Mrs Sartoris; articles from Matthew Arnold (an increasingly important *Cornhill* figure), Fitzjames Stephen, G.H. Lewes, Frederick Greenwood, James Hannay, Hamilton Aidé, W.S. Gilbert, Fanny Kemble, John Addington Symonds, Harriet Martineau, Samuel Laurence, G.O. Trevelyan, F.T. Palgrave, Arthur Helps, and G.A. Henty. Much of this is still good reading today. But the "many caprices of very foolish animals" had to be contended with, and high-quality essays, as Leslie Stephen was to find in an even greater degree, did not sell a magazine.

It must have been a relief to Smith to find Leslie Stephen willing to take over as editor. Stephen afterwards wrote that in 1871 he was offered the editorship of *Fraser* but "I consulted George Smith, who thereupon offered me the Cornhill, which I accepted the more willingly from its connection with Thackeray."[16] Stephen had never met Thackeray, but his marriage to Minny Thackeray had taken place in 1867 and both Minny and Anny (who lived with the Stephens) were delighted at being once more involved in the *Cornhill*. Though Stephen did not start his new job with great enthusiasm – "What can one make of a magazine which excludes the only subjects in which reasonable men take any interest; politics and religion?"[17] he complained – he became in time thoroughly absorbed in the work of literary essays and criticism and made his mark on the character of the magazine. He himself while editor contributed the "Hours in a Library", and according to Maitland at least twenty other papers, though this, Edward Cook wrote later, was "only a tithe" of the whole number, some even appearing over false initials lest there should seem to be "too much Stephen".[18] "From Thackeray's day to our own," A.W. Ward wrote in 1904, "no English magazine has been so liberally interfused with literary criticism of a high class, and at the same time remained such pleasant reading as the Cornhill under Stephen's management."[19]

There was a revival in the quality of serial fiction in this decade, with R.D. Blackmore (not, unfortunately, with *Lorna Doone*), Thomas Hardy, Henry James, and W.E. Henley. A prolific new writer was Robert Louis Stevenson, with the essays later collected as *Virginibus Puerisque*; "R.L.S. is not the Real Leslie Stephen, as some of my friends insist, but a young Scotchman whom Colvin has discovered,"[20] Stephen wrote to Gosse. Stephen did not claim to have made great discoveries himself, but he was happy to feel that he had helped authors at the start of their career.

It was Frederick Greenwood who showed Stephen *Under the Greenwood Tree*. Stephen read it, as he wrote to Hardy,

> with very great pleasure indeed . . . such writing would probably please the readers of the Cornhill Magazine as much as it has pleased me. *Under the Greenwood Tree* is, of course, not a magazine story. There is too little incident for such purpose; for, though I do not want a murder in every number, it is necessary to catch the attention of readers by some distinct and well-arranged plot.[21]

The result of this encouragement was that Hardy offered *Far From the Madding Crowd*. Stephen was delighted with it, though the puritanical traditions established by Thackeray and Smith gave him some problems. The doctrine was, in Stephen's words, "thou shalt not shock a young lady", and the threshold for shock was low: "I have ventured to leave out a line or two in the last batch of proofs, from an excessive prudery of which I am ashamed; but one is forced to be absurdly particular."[22] It was illustrated by Helen Paterson (later Helen Allingham). The *Hand of*

Ethelberta also appeared in the *Cornhill*, but after seeing the opening of *The Return of the Native* Stephen said, according to Hardy,

> he feared that the relations between Eustacia, Wildeve, and Thomasin might develop into something "dangerous" for a family magazine, and he refused to have anything to do with it unless he could see the whole. This I never sent him; and the matter fell through. . . . Our correspondence as editor and edited was thus broken off, but when I had published *The Trumpet Major*, he expressed, with some perversity I thought, his regret that I had not given him the opportunity of bringing it out. . . . "Though," he added in a saturnine tone, "the heroine married the wrong man." I replied that they mostly did. "Not in magazines," he answered.[23]

Henry James marked his arrival on the English literary scene with *Daisy Miller*, published in the *Cornhill* in 1878, two years after he had settled in London. It had been rejected by *Lippincott's* in Philadelphia, but was welcomed by Stephen. Then followed the short story "An International Episode", and finally *Washington Square*, in eight parts illustrated by du Maurier. Henry James's growing social round in London soon included George and Elizabeth Smith, and the interminable sentences began to be heard at their dinner parties.

Throughout his editorship Stephen was on the best of terms with the Smiths. Various letters show constant consultation about writing and accepting papers. "If I have shown confidence in you I have shown no more than I felt," Stephen wrote to Smith in 1880. "I have once or twice found that you might be allowing friendship to interfere with business: but I have never had any other doubts."[24] To Charles Norton he wrote, "One of the best pieces of luck that I have had is in finding an employer like G.S., who is also a warm friend and a thorough gentleman."[25] According to Maitland "the publisher was for near forty years one of Stephen's best friends, and in public and private Stephen spoke of Smith in terms of warm affection".[26]

If George Smith had hoped that Stephen would restore the fortunes of the *Cornhill* he certainly never reproached him with the sad truth that, though it might be intellectually distinguished, the magazine was becoming a business disaster. Fortunately, at the same time Smith was making huge amounts of money by other business enterprises and could afford to support a disaster. When Stephen resigned, to devote himself to the *Dictionary of National Biography*, the circulation had dropped to 12,000. In his resignation letter to Smith, Stephen wrote:

> After what you told me about the state of the Cornhill I feel that I must in any case retire. The difficulties in the way of making it a serious magazine, like the Fortnightly, seem to me enormous. To take the Fortnightly tone in regard to politics and theology would be to frighten away all our old readers, and I should necessarily take that tone or something like it. Nor do I fancy that at present there is much room for such an organ. On the other hand, I think that it may very well be made lighter; but I am equally clear that I am not the man who could do it. As our present road leads downhill, and I cannot take either of the ways which might possibly lead upwards, the conclusion is clear. . . . I am very ill qualified to be the editor of such a periodical.[27]

In the Jubilee Issue which celebrated the fiftieth year of the *Cornhill* in January 1910, W.E. Norris gave Stephen better marks than this as an editor. Stephen was, Norris wrote,

> not indulgent. He himself was at infinite trouble over the discharge of his duties, and he did not mind calling upon his contributors to be equally painstaking. More than once he made me re-write whole chapters, and often I was required – a little against the grain I must confess – to strike out passages or incidents which he thought likely to jar upon the susceptibilities of his readers. One's tidy manuscripts used to come back scrawled all over with alterations and emendations in his diminutive script, which was not always over-legible. . . . That his judgement in literary matters was a very fine and accurate one does not need to be said. Whether he was absolutely the right man in the right place as editor of a magazine may be open to question; he himself seemed to think that he was not. I have never heard him actually say that the task of editorship bored him; his complaint was rather that he was conscious of inability to discern the shifting currents of public taste. . . . What will not, in any case, be denied is that the Cornhill under Leslie Stephen's rule attained and kept an extremely high level of literary excellence.

And this, after all, was what he and Smith were both wanting.

James Payn, Stephen's friend since undergraduate days at Cambridge, was the man Smith chose to make the *Cornhill* less heavyweight, and to steer it back to popularity. As Payn's own *Lost Sir Massingberd* was said to have put up the circulation of *Chambers' Journal* by 20,000,[28] and as he himself had been successfully working with Smith as reader since the retirement of Smith Williams in 1874, he seemed to be a good choice. The new-style *Cornhill* planned by Payn, with larger print and costing only sixpence, gave the public fewer essays and more short stories, with plenty of illustrations. It was a brave gamble at a time when literary fashion was turning away from the old magazines – *Fraser's* had given up in 1882, and was soon to be followed by *Murray's*, *Longman's*, *Temple Bar*, and *Macmillan's*.[29]

To produce the *Cornhill* at such a price there had to be far greater sales, and this Payn did not achieve; he lost some of the highbrow market, while failing to make the magazine popular. The first number sold 47,000 – far fewer than had been hoped – and the figures went steadily down until they were even lower than when Stephen had resigned. This was sadly disappointing, but the *Cornhill* survived because Smith still thought it worth supporting – and he could afford to support it – perhaps partly from sentiment, but also because it still brought prestige and new authors to the firm. Through all this difficult time there was a high standard of serials – three from Payn himself, and others from a new generation of writers: Rider Haggard, Anstey, Conan Doyle (with *The White Company*), Stanley Weyman, Seton Merriman; Mrs Humphry Ward, already on Smith & Elder's list, contributed *The Story of Bessie Costrell*. For economy, illustrations had to be given up in 1886.

Payn retired in 1896, with crippling arthritis which kept him an invalid for the remaining two years of his life. Throughout his illness both George and Reginald Smith were among the many friends who regularly came to see him, to help him forget his pain with games of whist or with talk.

After Payn's retirement the down-market experiment was abandoned. The *Cornhill* again cost a shilling, and once more carried a good supply of essays and general articles. It was edited for two years by John St Loe Strachey, until he moved to take over the *Spectator*, and the *Cornhill* then settled for seventeen years with Reginald Smith, who thus became, as his father-in-law had become in 1862, both editor of the *Cornhill* and head of the firm of Smith Elder.

XIII

The Pall Mall Gazette

We have followed the story of the *Cornhill* through to the end of George Smith's life, but it was of course only one strand in the pattern of that life. Even by 1863, when Smith was struggling with the problems of running the *Cornhill* without Thackeray, he was prepared to tackle a new scheme. The huge success of his overseas trade, then spreading in India, Java and West Africa, gave a strong financial background which encouraged him to take risks. With plenty of money, plenty of magazine writers among his friends, and a still unsatisfied urge to organize and run something demanding, Smith was easily persuaded into the newspaper world.

The idea of running a newspaper had appealed to Smith for some years. In 1855, with John William Kaye as editor, he had successfully started the *Overland Mail*, to take news to India, followed the next year by the *Homeward Mail*, edited by E.B. Eastwick, to distribute Indian news in England. Smith seems to have been personally involved in the detailed running of these papers and has described his distress at the time of the Mutiny, when "as mail after mail came in charged with the dreadful tidings I had to go through the files & select items for the Homeward Mail".

He was ambitious to run something on a larger scale. He wrote in his *Recollections*:

I had some years before tried to induce Thackeray to edit a little daily sheet, something after the style of the *Spectator* and the *Tatler* of the days of Addison and of Steele. We got far enough to invent a title for the proposed paper: we decided to call it "Fair Play". . . . I think it is possible that our discussion as to the kind of articles which could be written for "Fair Play" may have been the germ of the famous "Roundabout Papers" which Thackeray contributed to the Cornhill. "Fair Play" was to have been non-political – or rather non-partisan: it was to try all parties and all policies by the test of honesty and good sense; and it was to carry that spirit into the realms of literature and of criticism. There was, at that time, much of jobbery in literary criticism as well as in politics, and we proposed to wage relentless warfare upon it. . . . All these circumstances made me willing to listen to the proposal for an honest and courageous daily still.

Now that Smith was at the centre of the literary circle of the *Cornhill*, a new proposal was made, this time for an evening paper. Frederick Greenwood, Smith's energetic colleague on the *Cornhill*'s editorial board, had already had plans for a paper, to be called the *Evening Review*, and had earlier suggested it to the publishers of *Fraser's Magazine*. These plans had not materialized, but Smith was very ready to respond when the idea was brought to him in 1863. His partner, Henry King, was less enthusiastic but agreed that the firm might take it on, with Smith having the control and management of the paper, if King could at any time ask for it to be stopped or to have his interest bought out. The recent abolition of the "taxes on knowledge" – the advertisement tax in 1853, the newspaper duties in 1855, and the paper duty in 1861 – made this the right moment for a good cheap newspaper.

Smith and Greenwood started to discuss policy and contributors. One early problem was the title. "Fair Play" was reconsidered, but rejected as "too bumptious; it would not do", said Smith, "to proclaim the virtue of the paper in every issue". With memories of Thackeray, Smith suggested the "Pall Mall Gazette", the journal "written by gentlemen for gentlemen" in *Pendennis*. Greenwood was not keen, but Anny Thackeray, according to Smith, "was enchanted with the idea. 'Oh! how pleased,' she cried, 'Papa will be!' Thackeray had been dead for two years, but his daughter cherished the idea most vividly that her father kept his interest in those he had loved, and knew everything that happened here."

Two years later, the following Prospectus appeared in *The Times*, the *Athenaeum*, and elsewhere:

It is difficult to describe the plan of an enterprise like the PALL MALL GAZETTE without seeming to boast, or to decry the efforts of others. But we are unwilling to lose the advantage of a few words of explanation, and we trust the candour of the Reader for a just interpretation of our meaning. The PALL MALL GAZETTE will contain all the news proper to an Evening Journal. But addressed as it will be to educated men and women, the space of the Paper will not be occupied by trifling chronicles, nor by that excess of words which adds nothing to the interest of newspaper records, while it destroys their significance. Literary considerations alone would determine us to have our News Reports written in plain English; but beyond these there is the fact that the lessons to be found in many an accident of human life or social polity are lost in the turgid language in which they are commonly narrated.

Events made known by the Morning Papers may be discussed in the PALL MALL GAZETTE of the same day, but they will not be reported anew. Trustworthy advices from the Money Market will be included in the News of the Day. The rest of the Paper (by far the greater part) will be made up of original articles, upon the many things which engage the thoughts, or employ the energies, or amuse the leisure of mankind. Public Affairs, Literature, the Arts, and all the influences which strengthen or dissipate Society, will be discussed by men whose independence and authority are equally unquestionable, and who are accustomed to regard the public expression of opinion as a serious thing. This is the chief aim of the PALL MALL GAZETTE: to bring into Daily Journalism that full measure of thought and culture which is now found only in a few Reviews. At the same time, we by no means intend to make the Paper pedantic or solemn. Humour is too powerful, as well as too pleasant, to be left out of the design; which will lose none of the advantages of occasional trifling. If a thing can be said better in verse than in prose, it will be said in verse. Epigram, but not spite – burlesque, but not vulgarity – will be readily admitted into its columns; and since a joke is often as illustrative as an argument, good jokes will be welcome too.

It will be understood that this advertisement is rather a proclamation of idea and of effort than of promise. But the proclamation is not made before a large number of able writers have accepted the idea, and pledged themselves to the effort.

This was not a bad description of the *Pall Mall Gazette*. It was unashamedly highbrow – to rank with *The Times*, but published in the evening, smaller in scale, and costing 2d not 3d. The approach was totally different from that of the popular evening papers of the end of the century, which aimed to write for "the meanest intelligence",[1] or from that of the

Daily Mail, which was mocked in 1896 by Lord Salisbury as "a newspaper for office boys written by office boys".

All the details of the *Pall Mall Gazette* were planned, slowly and carefully, by Smith and Greenwood; proprietor and editor worked together and it is not now possible to separate their ideas. The distinguished list of contributors, "of a higher social class than most newspaper men" as Smith said, naturally consisted largely at first of *Cornhill* authors. But the marketing effect of using such famous writers was partly neutralized by the custom of leaving all contributions, including letters, anonymous. Matthew Arnold, though, thought that this made the correspondence more effective; he complained that his letters were too easily recognizable, "so what I urge does not get the benefit of coming with the weight of impersonal newspaper authority".[2] In the early numbers, it was only Trollope's "American Letters" that were signed, and this was to show that his strongly Yankee sympathies were not necessarily shared by the editor.

The first impression on looking at these early numbers of the *Pall Mall Gazette* is of a well-produced journal printed on particularly good paper. It was serious-minded, deliberately unsensational, with brief reports of news and, as might be expected, well-written comments and essays. It was meant to complement, rather than replace, *The Times*. "We had to create", wrote Smith, "the very appetite for a good evening paper, and the process was not easy. I used to be told that a newspaper was all very well for the morning, but nobody wanted any high class reading after dinner!"

When the *Pall Mall Gazette* started, *The Times* had sixteen pages, eight of them, including of course the first, entirely advertisement. There would also be a page of law reports, one of money market and city news, and the rest home and foreign news with about a page of editorial comment and perhaps half a page of book or theatre reviews. The *Pall Mall Gazette* looked more welcoming, with eight smaller pages, and advertisements only on the back. The first page was an editorial, then would come Occasional Notes – short comments on odd news stories in a style that was highly successful and was later adopted in other papers. Two or perhaps three pages would be given to essays or reviews; reporting of news would take only two pages, made up of brief foreign notes, "Mr Reuter's telegrams", and a summary of the morning's news. It all seems very good leisurely club reading, something between present-day weeklies and a daily paper. The problems discussed are depressingly timeless – troubles in Ireland, oppression of the Poles, the government of Russia, the higher education of girls.

Nothing was said about politics in the prospectus, but generally the paper was to support Palmerston's Liberal government, while remaining "faithful to our purpose of independent criticism".[3] In fact it turned out to be a little too Liberal for Henry King, who decided, perhaps to Smith's relief, to withdraw from the whole enterprise after seeing a trial number – the *Pall Mall Gazette* therefore became Smith's own venture, not run by Smith Elder & Co.

Other unproclaimed policy decisions were that no Smith & Elder books might be reviewed in the paper and that no advertisements were to be accepted from quacks or from moneylenders. Smith says that, as an exception, they did publish a review of Theodore Martin's *Life of the Prince Consort* – only to find that Martin, not at all pleased at the independence of what had been written, thought that Smith had been "very ill-served at the *Pall Mall Gazette* office".[4] There was also, in March 1865, an article about a Smith Elder book on capital punishment, but Smith may have considered this to be more a discussion of the issue than a review of the book. Leslie Stephen wrote rather sadly to Norton in 1873, when his *Free-thinking and Plain-speaking* (published by Longman) was not getting noticed, "The *Pall Mall Gazette* is too virtuous to mention the work of a former contributor, for the proprietor, George Smith, is a gentleman."[5]

It was noble, when advertisements were in appallingly short supply, to refuse two sources on moral grounds; but Smith had seen distress caused by moneylenders, and had had hard personal experience of the false hopes raised by quacks – it was the effect on his mother of Dr Hunter's claims to cure consumption that later led Smith to encourage an attack on Hunter in the *Pall Mall Gazette*, bringing a libel action on himself in 1866. As we shall see later, Smith could cope well with libel cases.

Greenwood, writing in the 10,000th issue of the *Pall Mall Gazette* on 14 April 1897, looked back to the early days:

We did not begin with the splendid confidence which nowadays builds palaces for newspapers before they are born. We began modestly, but efficiently, with a printing-office on the then naked foreshore of the Thames where descent was made to its melancholy flats from the river end of Salisbury Street, and with editorial and publishing offices in a dwelling-house in Salisbury Street itself. It had a castaway, precarious look, the printing office, as if, washed up from Wapping or thereabouts by one tide, it would probably be carried on by the next; but it was well-appointed and perfectly comfortable, except on the rare occasions when excessive rain or spring floods compelled the printers to go in and out on each other's backs.

The launching of the *Pall Mall Gazette* had none of the wild success of the *Cornhill*. It is curious to see that there is no mention of it at all in contemporary copies of *The Times*. "The reception accorded to the new journal was", Smith wrote, "of the most chilly quality. Of the first number – as to which there was naturally some curiosity – exactly 3,897 copies were sold. In six weeks the sale had dropped to 613 copies! For the month of March the gross average amount received for advertisements was £3.4.10 per day!" Some extracts from Smith's diary show how things progressed:

6 *March 1865:* I am beginning to fear the PMG cannot succeed.
22 *March 1865:* Very low about PMG, which does not look like success.
23 *March 1865:* Rather seedy and out of spirits about PMG.
17 *April 1865:* Paper looking up a little, and I am in better spirits.
18 *May 1865:* Two extracts from PMG in Times; this gives me some hope!
5 *August 1865:* PMG published six months; sale 1,400 to 1,500. Hopeful of success before this time next year.
7 *October 1865:* PMG published eight months; sale over 2,000, and increasing regularly. Very hopeful – almost confident – of success.

Only a wealthy proprietor could have carried the paper over those difficult early days. In 1826 John Murray had given up an attempt to start a Tory paper, the *Representative*, after losing £26,000 in six months; there are no surviving figures for the *Pall Mall Gazette*'s losses, but they must have been considerable. It was only after ten months, on 9 December 1865, that a sudden increase in advertisements made an issue of the paper pay its way. But Smith was putting enormous energy, as well as money, into the *Pall Mall*, and would not accept failure. His friends were often discouraging, but his family were consistently loyal, his wife saying she would rather pawn her jewels than see the paper discontinued.

Smith used to go to the Salisbury Street office three or four times a day, and he has described times when, with an echo of his boyhood excitement at Waghorn's breathless arrival with the Indian mail, he himself became involved in getting the news into print. He saw the news of Lincoln's assassination come through on the telegraph:

> Then what may be called the newspaper instinct awoke within me! I rushed back into the editor's room with the news. It was just about one o'clock, and I asked, "Who is to write the article?" We discussed several names but the man who seemed most suitable, and at the same time available, was Fitzjames Stephen. I jumped into a cab and raced to his chamber; found he was at court and drove there. He was on his legs addressing the judge. I scribbled my news on a scrap of paper and added, "You must write the leading article." Stephen finished his address with praiseworthy brevity; I went with him into one of the waiting rooms, and finally bore the leading article back to the office.

Smith wrote of other memories which give the atmosphere of his newspaper life – there was

> the sudden and unexpected arrival one day at the crisis of the Franco–German War, of one of our two war correspondents with the German army. He came running upstairs, with every sign of fatigue and hurry. He had come straight from the spectacle of the tragedy of Sedan, and the traces of the haste of his journey were plainly upon him. He produced his account of the battle; he had wired it to us, he said, but deemed the news so important that, in addition, he had come on with the written account, and as a matter of fact had outraced the telegraph.

He had been present when Napoleon's messenger had arrived with a letter of surrender, and had dashed back by special boat and train. "The telegraphed account arrived just as we had got the whole thing in type," Smith continued, "and we had the honour and glory of being the first journal in London to publish the tale of the great battle."

Smith does not add that during that war the *Pall Mall Gazette* had been printing an impressive series of articles on the military situation, written by Engels. Engels, who had already written occasionally for the *New York Tribune* and the *Manchester Guardian*, was at that time living in England and was anxious both to earn more money and to write for an influential

English newspaper. At two and a half guineas a time, he wrote about sixty "Notes on the War", some of which were considered important enough to appear as leaders; later he reprinted them all as a book. Recommending the *Pall Mall Gazette* to Engels, Marx had told him that it was "the gentlemen's paper *par excellence* and one which sets the tone in all the clubs, including the military clubs".[6]

"Newspaper life, from the proprietor's point of view," wrote Smith,

is a sort of perpetual game of whist, against keen and clever players. It is a battle of wits to secure the earliest news of everything, and strange devices are employed to win the game. There was always the fiercest competition amongst the evening newspapers as to who should be first in the streets with the results of the Oxford and Cambridge boat-race. I determined to be first, and spared no pains to succeed. We trained two or three pigeons; I told our reporters they might lavish money in trying to keep the telegraph wire in their hands, and I confided my plans and aspirations to Mr Woodgate, who was our boating contributor, and also the coach of the Oxford boat. . . . Woodgate galloped off as soon as he saw how the race was going to end – but before its actual termination. . . . We were first in the street with the news, but the *Evening Standard* was hard on our heels, and came out within five minutes of us. This puzzled me much, for no message, as far as I could judge, had reached the *Standard's* office. . . . I used frequently to go up to the compositor's room and exchange a few words with the men, many of whom were old employees, who had been drafted from the printing-house of Smith Elder and Co; I said in the composing room one day, "I don't wish to invite anybody to betray confidence, but I should like to know how the *Standard* got out with the result of the boat-race as soon as we did. In fact I would give £5 to know.

Five pounds bought him the information that the *Standard* had prepared two sets of copies, one for Oxford and one for Cambridge, ready to be rushed out the moment the real results were known.

Once, after hearing Gladstone make an important policy speech in Parliament, Smith dashed back to the *Pall Mall Gazette* office and dictated it as well as he could from memory to eight or ten clerks, giving each, as the custom then was, a few lines, then passing on to the next. "In a few minutes," he wrote, "the boys were crying the news in the streets. I cannot help smiling yet, after so many years, as I recall the simple vanity with which I walked home that night."

[156]

Another occasion when he enjoyed playing at being a reporter was the opening of St Thomas's Hospital:

> I found a card of invitation in the editor's room, and, as I thought I should rather like to go to the ceremony, I put it in my pocket and went. On my way back I called at the *Pall Mall Gazette* office and found the sub-editor almost literally tearing his hair in despair. "We are in a nice mess," he said, "somebody has taken our card for the opening of St Thomas's Hospital and we must wait for some of the other evening papers before we can publish a line about it." I was the guilty cause of the disaster, and must do my best to repair it. "Can you write shorthand?" I asked. "Oh, yes." "Then," I said, "fire away," and I began a high-faluting account, in true reporter's English, of the scene. I pictured the sun glancing on the varied dresses of the lovely peeresses . . . I plunged into all the terms of millinery, with most audacious courage. I read the report the next morning, side by side with that of the *Morning Post*, and, with the natural partiality of a fond parent, preferred my own! The one mistake I had made was in the technical description of a lady's dress, for which I had to endure some ridicule in the family circle.

By the time Smith was cheerfully writing these reports, the *Pall Mall Gazette* was well established. The turning point had come early in 1866 when, although the circulation was slowly increasing, there seemed need for something sensational to get the paper really under way. It was, in Greenwood's words, "like a captive balloon, ready to soar, and restive against the rope that held it down".[7] The rope was cut by a series of articles on the treatment of paupers in the "casual wards" of the workhouses, written by Frederick Greenwood's brother James. Any journalist investigating such a situation today might well dress as a pauper and experience their treatment from the inside for a night – this is just what James Greenwood did, but it was a new approach to journalism then, and he was treated as a hero. There was great publicity, the articles by the "Amateur Casual" were reprinted complete in *The Times*, the editor of the *Morning Post* wrote of the venture as "an act of bravery, at, it is to be hoped, a very handsome fee, which ought to entitle him to the V.C.". More important, circulation went up by 1,500 for a time and by about 1,200 permanently, and Smith was happy.

Under Smith and Greenwood the paper's highest circulation was 9,000, and then, Smith claimed, "we had a greater influence on public opinion than any other newspaper save *The Times*''. The *Pall Mall* was influential because it was read by an influential public, although it was not a large public. The total sale of all London evening papers was only 15,000–20,000. At that time *The Times* had a circulation of about 65,000, and the *Daily Telegraph*, aiming, for the price of a penny, to ''cater for the million'', had shot up to 200,000, with the one-penny *Daily News* following at 150,000.[8]

The *Pall Mall Gazette*'s distinction lay in its comments and its literary features even more than in its reporting. Essays and reviews were produced daily on a daunting scale. A large share of this enormous output was borne by Fitzjames Stephen. He had worked for Smith on the *Cornhill*, writing an article most months in the first four years, but was now happy to move from a magazine where Smith was asking for his articles to be more ''light and amusing'', and to write instead for a paper where, in his brother Leslie's words, ''he was able to speak out with perfect freedom upon all the graver topics of the day''.[9] He became a compulsive writer as well as a busy lawyer, turning out articles before breakfast and delivering them on his way to chambers, or writing in the *Pall Mall Gazette* office itself as soon as he heard the latest news. ''To pour himself out in articles had become a kind of natural instinct,'' Leslie Stephen wrote. ''It had the charm, if I may say so, of a vice; it gave him the same pleasure that other men derive from dram drinking.''[10] His views filled so much of the *Pall Mall Gazette* in its early years that he gave an individual character to the paper; it was coloured by his fascination with problems of law and liberty, of church and state, of democracy and of state interference. The following table[11] gives an idea of his output, and of the way in which he dominated the paper:

	Articles	*Occasional Notes*	*Letters*
1865	143	103	8
1866	147	36	22
1867	194	27	9
1868	226	29	11
1869	142	5	–

When, in 1869, Fitzjames Stephen went to India, his friend Sir Henry Maine took over from him to some extent, writing two or three leaders a week. But Stephen could not bear to stop altogether. He wrote twenty articles on his outward journey and started a major series of Letters to J.S. Mill on his way back; these were later collected and published by Smith Elder as *Liberty, Equality, and Fraternity*.

This was not the only book to come to Smith through the *Pall Mall Gazette*. As with the *Cornhill*, his dual role of book publisher and newspaper proprietor boosted both sides of his business – his old authors helped him by writing for his new enterprise, while the *Pall Mall Gazette* brought him new books and new authors.

Leslie Stephen who, as editor first of the *Cornhill* and then of the *Dictionary of National Biography*, became the most important figure in Smith's later publishing life, started his connection with Smith in the second number of the *Pall Mall Gazette*. He had just made his decision to leave Cambridge and the Church, and to follow his brother into journalism and literary life in London. By that time he had written a little about Alpine climbing and not very much else, but Fitzjames introduced him to the *Saturday Review* and the *Pall Mall Gazette*. He started splendidly in the *Pall Mall* with "Sketches from Cambridge", a series of essays on Cambridge life and characters, but he never became a very active contributor – he was too much of a radical, and increasingly disapproved of the paper's politics as Frederick Greenwood led it further into conservatism. Theological matters, which he would have liked to write about, were his brother's department, and Leslie felt that he himself had to keep to the " 'padding' and other second-rate parts".[12] This was obviously unsatisfactory for him, and it is not surprising that in the following year, when he found an outlet for his anti-theological or other heavyweight essays in Froude's *Fraser*, and was contributing regularly to the *Cornhill*, he more or less gave up the *Pall Mall Gazette*.

Thackeray's friend Matthew Higgins (Jacob Omnium) joined the *Pall Mall* team from the start. Smith had a special archway cut for him over the staircase in Salisbury Street so that, with his six feet eight inches, he did not knock his hat on the way in. Trollope considered him to be the most forcible newspaper writer of his day and attributed the *Pall Mall Gazette*'s success to him, to Fitzjames Stephen, and to "the untiring energy and general ability of its proprietor".[13] Higgins's speciality was Occasional

Notes – "the best Occasional Notes", according to Smith, "that ever appeared in a newspaper." With the *Pall Mall* campaigning against the excess of royal mourning, one of these Notes suggested that the extraordinary number of memorials to Prince Albert appearing all over England could even make a new focus for country expeditions; the sarcasm was lost on the Queen, who was touched at the idea and sent a message of appreciation to Smith.

Higgins was known, too, for his skill as a letter writer. "He came into my room in *Pall Mall* one day," wrote Smith,

> and found me in the agonies of composition. "Are you writing an epic poem?" he asked. "Worse than that," I replied, "I am writing a letter to *The Times*." Higgins looked at what I had written. "Do you mind my giving you a little help?" he asked, and in a very brief time brought me a letter putting my case so clearly that, for at least twenty-four hours, all my natural conceit disappeared.

It was Higgins who wrote a series of articles in the *Pall Mall Gazette* comparing the prices of goods in various shops with the lower prices in the Civil Service Stores; when George Smith was told he could not shop in these Stores as he was not a civil servant, he sent a message that he was proprietor of the *Pall Mall Gazette* "and was at once informed 'we can refuse the *Pall Mall Gazette* nothing'."

Trollope was a regular contributor to the early *Pall Mall Gazette*. Besides his signed "American Letters", he wrote other political articles, some criticism, and the various series that were later collected and published (by Chapman and Hall) as *Hunting Sketches*, *Travelling Sketches*, and *Clergymen of the Church of England*; later, in 1880, he contributed a further series on *London Tradesmen*. But Trollope was not really happy as a journalist. When he was asked by Smith to report on the May Revivalist Meetings, he wrote protesting that he

> would not go to another to be made Editor of the *Pall Mall Gazette*! You do not know what you have asked. Go to one yourself and try. You sit for four hours and listen to six sermons. . . . I will tomorrow morning write you an article (A Zulu at a May Meeting) for which the materials arranged themselves not unhappily; but I *can do no more*. Suicide would intervene after the third or fourth.[14]

As he wrote in his *Autobiography*,

> I found myself unfit for work on a newspaper. I had not taken to it early
> enough in life to learn its ways and bear its trammels. I was fidgety when any
> word was altered in accordance with the judgement of the Editor, who, of
> course, was responsible for what appeared. I wanted to select my own subjects,
> – not to have them selected for me; to write when I pleased, – and not when it
> suited others. As a permanent member of a staff I was no use, and after two or
> three years I dropped out of the work.[15]

Trollope says that the proprietor at that time also acted as chief editor – he
is wrong about this, of course, but it does imply that Smith was seen to
take a prominent part in the day-to-day running of the paper.

Many other old friends rallied to support Smith's new enterprise. G.H.
Lewes, who had recently resigned from being consulting editor of the
Cornhill, was paid £300 to act as "adviser" in the first year; in this
capacity he went to Paris to arrange for Eugene Fourçade, editor of the
Revue des Deux Mondes, to send articles. Lewes mainly contributed
distinguished dramatic criticism – later collected as *On Actors and the Art
of Acting* – and book reviews. Darwin wrote to Hooker in 1868 that the
review of *Variation of Animals and Plants* in the *Pall Mall Gazette* "has
pleased me excessively, more perhaps than is reasonable ... it is [by] some
one who writes capitally, and who knows the subject";[16] three years later
he commented on the *Pall Mall's* "very striking articles"[17] on the *Descent
of Man*.

A romantic story followed a severe review, by Smith's friend Lord
Strangford, of a book by a Miss Beaufort. "The lady", according to
Smith, "wrote a piteous letter to the editor, who handed it to Lord
Strangford. He was rather touched by it and said, with a kind of rash
courage, that he would call on Miss Beaufort. He did so, and she became in
due course Lady Strangford."

There were contributions from Smith's women novelists. George Eliot
wrote four articles in 1865 – "A Word for the Germans", "Servants'
Logic", "Futile Falsehoods", and "Modern Housekeeping". This was the
last year of Mrs Gaskell's life, and it was all she could do to keep up the
instalments of *Wives and Daughters*, but she did help Smith by
introducing friends – Mme de Peyronnet, who, according to Smith, wrote
frequently and was "valuable as being in the secrets of the Orleanist

party"; and Miss Courtney, who "wrote clever little articles on society". Anny Thackeray produced short articles, such as "A Book of Photographs" and "A Country Sunday", for which she was paid two or three guineas, and also sent occasional letters. With her perpetual urge to help everybody, she also suggested other writers: "You don't want by any chance a young Frenchman to do anything, do you," she wrote to Smith, "he is a young doctor who had to fly M. Thiers . . . he gives French lessons to one pupil and is nice and very miserable and highly educated. . . . It has just occurred to me to tell him that you require the number of the *Pall Mall Gazette* translated into French."[18]

Other distinguished contributors included Matthew Arnold, whose *Friendship's Garland* first appeared in the *Pall Mall*, but who refrained from writing too much "because the habit of newspaper writing would soon become too fascinating and exciting";[19] George Meredith, who in 1868 was writing almost every week; Laurence Oliphant, useful for his many contacts; Ruskin, Tom Hughes, Lord Houghton, Herman Merivale, John Morley, T.H. Huxley, Richard Jefferies. It reads like a list of the leading intellectual literary figures of the period, and it was a formidable collection for a newspaper.

Many of them wrote out of personal friendship for Smith; they rallied round because the paper meant so much to him. He put enormous energy into all aspects of its production, and was even not above helping with the proof-reading. This is clear from a story he told of the Fenian troubles. There was a scare that the Fenians might try to blow up the *Pall Mall Gazette* office; a loud bang in the middle of the night made his colleagues jump out of their chairs in fright, but he was unable to jump – and gained a reputation for calm nerves – because he was firmly anchored by a large bundle of proofs.

At that time of Irish troubles, fourteen detectives were put to watch the building, and two more on the roof – so that, Smith thought, "their vigilance would be quickened by the knowledge that, if the building were blown up, they would go up higher than anybody else." Smith refused police escort for himself – Delane of *The Times* was walking to his office flanked by four detectives – but during the crisis he took to carrying a life-preserver with the cord twisted round his wrist, and a small loaded revolver. Smith's wife happened to see the police chief at the office and asked who he was: "to tell her the news about the Fenian plot was impossible; and I told her my first and last domestic fib, and said that tall and military-looking gentleman who had just gone out was an author." When Smith's daughter Dolly hugged him on his return home she felt the revolver, but she kept the secret. Smith helped his staff to stay in good spirits through the crisis. He spoke to them to warn them of the danger and reassured the wife of one newly married man, persuading her that it would be wrong and cowardly for her husband to resign. As it turned out, there was no attack, though there was a suspicion, never confirmed, that a worker had deliberately left a machine in a dangerous state – "There was a great outburst of rage in the rooms," wrote Smith, "the man was about to be lynched. I heard the tumult, hurried down, and with much trouble I succeeded in getting the accused man in a corner and stood in front of him; I said everything should be done to punish him, if he proved guilty, but I would not have him ill-used in the office."

The social side of publishing was always important to Smith, and every good venture deserved its dinners. "I have met at a *Pall Mall* dinner", Trollope wrote, "a crowd of guests who would have filled the House of Commons more respectably than I have seen it filled even on important occasions."[20] Becoming one of Smith's journalists was almost like joining a club.

By 1869 Smith, who had recently parted with the agency and banking side of Smith Elder to Henry King,[21] was looking for further activity. He had just recovered from a long illness, and he decided to put his new energy into the experiment of running the *Pall Mall Gazette* as a morning, as well as an evening, paper. Fitzjames Stephen was unfortunately away in India at this time, but his brother rallied loyally to help Smith. "We are to fight *The Times*", Leslie Stephen wrote, "and endeavour to supply a cultivated British audience with first-class literature and high principles at the low rate of two pence. If we succeed, I shall suck no little profit thereout, being one of the chosen few who are to have the privilege of enlightening the world on a large scale."[22] Smith tried, for four exhausting months, working from nine in the evening to six in the morning at the newspaper office, while running his publishing business during the day. But when this tremendous effort brought him only continual financial loss, even he gave in. He did not consider the effort to have been entirely wasted, however, as the circulation of the evening paper at the end of the four months was greater than before.

Although the literary side of the *Pall Mall Gazette* owed so much to Smith's friends and his authors, it was Greenwood who dominated the politics and it is time now to say something of him. He was the eldest of the eleven children of a carriage upholsterer, had started work as a printer's devil and then turned to journalism, becoming the first editor of Mr Beeton's *Queen*. He hoped journalism would be a stepping stone to a career as novelist and poet, and he contributed essays, poems, and a story, "Margaret Denzil's History", to the *Cornhill*. His sympathetic writing was shown in the concluding notes that he produced in the *Cornhill* for both *Denis Duval* and *Wives and Daughters*, left unfinished when their authors died.

But Greenwood's fame was to come not as a novelist but as a journalist. The inspiration for the *Pall Mall Gazette*, his greatest success, came originally from reading old copies of Canning's brilliant satirical weekly, the *Anti-Jacobin*. "Get a copy of that famous sheet", Greenwood wrote,

> with another of the 1864 or 1865 *Saturday Review*, put them together, turn their pages over, and you will recapture the idea for the original *Pall Mall*. Here is one sort of thing, and here another; make as good a combination of the two as the current supply of mind allows, throw in a scrap or so of novel feature, mix with an eye to the needs and demands of the hour, publish every day, and you will have a new thing that ought to be a power and a glory.[23]

That was the idea Greenwood took, first to the publishers of *Fraser's Magazine*, and then to Smith. It was Smith who, discussing and developing the plans, persuaded Greenwood to become the editor himself.

To start with, the partnership was entirely successful. Smith and Greenwood already moved in the same literary circles, they shared the same ambitions for the paper, and they were both liked and respected by their teams of printers and newspaper workers. The office was run by two energetic men, and although Leslie Stephen called the paper "the incarnation of Greenwood",[24] it is at first only occasionally that Greenwood's views can be distinguished from those of his proprietor. Gradually, however, Greenwood's politics became more Tory and more prominent. He came to distrust Gladstone's foreign policy, particularly towards Eastern Europe, to give strong support to Disraeli, and to turn away from the paper's original independent liberal ideals. The days when Engels could write for him seemed far away.

[164]

In 1875 Greenwood became involved in a major political issue in a surprising way. At a dinner party given by his friend Henry Oppenheim, he heard that the Khedive was ready to sell his Suez Canal shares to the French. Feeling strongly that the British government should be roused to the crisis and the opportunity, Greenwood wrote to Lord Derby that same night and followed his letter with a visit the next morning. Negotiations for the shares were begun, and Greenwood not only kept the secret throughout but even, when the deal was concluded, refused Lord Derby's offer of first publication. The announcement of the news in the *Pall Mall Gazette* makes no mention of the editor's personal involvement, and the result of his discretion is that his contribution is generally forgotten. It is not known what Smith thought of the whole affair, or how much he knew about it.

Smith was not happy with Greenwood's perpetual criticism of Gladstone. The *Pall Mall Gazette*, he wrote, "had drifted into a Conservative organ, and with a good deal of its political matter I had no sympathy". The old enthusiastic partnership with Greenwood was over and, with his energies now spread in new directions, Smith decided in 1880 to pass the management of the paper to his Liberal son-in-law, Henry Yates-Thompson, who was to make it once again a radical journal. Greenwood resigned, taking many of his staff with him, and with the backing of some members of the banking firm Antony Gibbs and Co. started the rival *St James' Gazette*. John Morley became the new editor of the *Pall Mall* and, at George Smith's particular request, Leslie Stephen once again helped for a few years by contributing book reviews and essays.

The following correspondence appeared in the *Daily Telegraph*:

3 May 1880:
Sir – I beg of you permission to explain in your pages how and why it is that I, who originated the *Pall Mall Gazette*, planned it down to little details of paper and type, and have carried it on as its editor from the day of its first appearance in 1865 down to to-day, have been forced to give up all connection with my paper. In making this explanation I allow myself to mention certain names, because they have already been published in connection with the matter.

About 10 days ago (the elections were just over) Mr Smith, the proprietor of the *Pall Mall Gazette*, informed me that he was about to assign the paper to his son-in-law, Mr Thompson. Now, I was aware of Mr Thompson as a good Manchester man and an advanced Liberal, who had once or twice tried for a seat in Parliament as representative of a northern borough. Therefore, when I was invited to meet Mr Thompson in order to talk over future arrangements, I had little doubt of the result. At this meeting Mr Thompson expressed his anxiety that I should remain at my post, if he took over the paper. I told him I was quite willing to do so on the old conditions, and if the paper was to retain its old principles. Therefore, I was cautiously informed that the principles of the *Pall Mall Gazette* must in future be those of Mr Thompson, if he had anything to do with it as proprietor. To begin with, he proposed that the paper should give a general support to the new Administration. Now at that time the Government was not yet formed; "giving a general support" to a Government is a vague expression which may mean a great deal.

So, to bring matters to a test, I advanced three questions and asked Mr Thompson to tell me how I should be expected to deal with them if he became proprietor and I consented to continue my services as editor: 1, the enfranchisement of the agricultural labourer – it must be advocated, said Mr Thompson; 2, Mr Gladstone's foreign policy, as lately proclaimed – it was to be supported; 3, the disestablishment of the English Church – it must no longer be opposed if Mr Thompson had anything to do with the *Pall Mall Gazette*. It appeared to me unnecessary to inquire any further. I was invited to remain editor of the *Pall Mall Gazette* on condition of parting with my principles, of bidding good-bye to the men who had done so much in helping me to raise the paper to its high and honourable place in journalism, and set about making the paper a turncoat to please Mr Thompson and the new Government.

I declined to do anything of the sort. And so it is that by a transaction the nature of which (though I have proprietorial rights in the paper) I am not allowed to know anything at all, I cease to be editor of the *Pall Mall Gazette*, and the men who did me the honour to associate themselves with me, they go with me, all – being men of conviction, and angry and ashamed of what has been done. But we do not propose to allow our independent little paper to be extinguished. Its spirit resides in us; and it shall soon reappear in a new shape, and "with all the latest improvements". – I am, Sir, your obedient servant,

Frederick Greenwood.

4 May 1880:
Sir – It is not my intention to enter upon a newspaper controversy with Mr Greenwood, and I will therefore only ask you to allow me to say that many of the statements of Mr Greenwood's letter, printed in the *Daily Telegraph* of to-day are inaccurate, or based upon misapprehension, – I am, Sir, your obedient servant,

George Smith.

XIV

Libels

"To most men few things are more disagreeable than litigation", George Smith wrote in the 1901 *Cornhill*,

> and from litigation of the ordinary kind I am as averse as other people. . . .
> There is only one form of litigation in which I have been engaged, and that is in
> the defence of actions for libel, and I must confess to looking back on my
> experience of the courts of law as having been interesting and even enjoyable.

In his catalogue of "lawful pleasures" Smith conveniently forgot the unhappy time he had had with poor Mrs Gaskell's *Life of Charlotte Brontë*; that trouble had been settled out of court by solicitors, and there had been no pleasure in it at all.

The first and most important court case of libel in which Smith was involved was that of Hunter v. Sharpe (Sharpe being technically the publisher of the *Pall Mall Gazette*) in 1866. Dr Hunter, whose rather dubious MD had been awarded in America when he was only twenty, advertised widely in the English press that he could cure consumption. According to Hunter, a great many people, perhaps a quarter of the population, were suffering from undiagnosed consumption; but he could treat them, by personal consultation or even by correspondence, for an initial charge of a guinea, followed by five guineas each subsequent month. Since many frightened people came to him for help at the first sign of a common cold, he had some success with his cures.

Smith became aware of Hunter, and of the false hopes and fears the advertisements raised, when his own sister died of consumption and his mother, constantly exposed to the propaganda, felt guiltily that she had not done all she should to save her.

> Hunter's plausible statements were transparent enough to me, and I felt wrathful with him for the unhappiness he caused my mother. My anger with the man was increased by my knowledge of the case of a poor girl who lived in my mother's neighbourhood in the country, and earned a scanty living as a governess. She suffered from consumption, and had sold all her small valuables in order to pay the fees of an ignorant pretender who was Dr Hunter's assistant or partner, and who had been sent down from London to treat her. The local practitioner, a perfectly competent man, assured me that nothing could have been done for the poor girl, and that the repeated visits and large fees of Hunter's assistant were a cruel imposition.[1]

So, when Hunter happened to be in the news in a police court case where he was accused of raping a patient – and acquitted – Smith arranged with Greenwood for a strong attack in the *Pall Mall Gazette*. The article,[2] written by J.M. Capes and entitled "Imposters and Dupes", condemned "advertising practices of a certain class of medical imposters and the misery they inflict upon their unhappy dupes". "No respectable physician", the article went on to say, "would thus advertise for patients. . . . The sufferance of these lures for the unwary is a thing that ought not to be longer endured." Fitzjames Stephen and Matthew Higgins, with their knowledge of the law and their skill at steering close to libel, were appalled at the draft of the article. " 'Well,' said Mr Fitzjames Stephen, 'if you are going to print *that* article you will hear of it!' 'At all events,' said Mr Higgins, 'let me take some of the worst of the libel out.' "[3] But he had not got very far with the job before it was time to go to press; Smith decided to let the article go as it stood.

In the ensuing libel action, the defence pleaded justification, and Smith spent much time and trouble collecting a team of doctors prepared to act as medical witnesses. It was a major case, lasting five days and widely reported. In his summing up the judge said that the article had been severe, but if it were true and if patients had been deliberately deluded "no language too strong could be employed; and to describe such a man as an imposter and a scoundrel was not an improper use of the English language".

But the article had contained other damaging phrases. Unwisely it had also referred to the earlier charge of rape:

> The terrifying and the plundering are, however, it appears, only one portion of the fate that may await the ladies who study the advertisements of these gentry. The charge made against Dr Hunter by the credulous Mrs Merrick sufficiently indicates this, whether he be guilty or not; and it is known to those who have given themselves the disgusting duty of inquiring into such matters, that kindred quacks (though of a more shameless kind perhaps) do unquestionably use in the basest manner the advantages given them by unfortunate women.

This devotion to disgusting duty turned the verdict into one for the plaintiff; damages one farthing.

The case had cost Smith £1,400, but although he had technically lost, it became in effect a triumph for him and for the *Pall Mall Gazette*. There were congratulations from *The Times* and other newspapers. Smith was presented with a silver vase and a salver, with a testimonial "in recognition of the important service rendered to the community by the *Pall Mall Gazette* in successfully defending the action Hunter v. Sharpe, whereby the freedom of the press was once more vindicated and the right of courageous and honest criticism affirmed". Shortly afterwards, Hunter left the country. Smith's mother was relieved and comforted.

The next *Pall Mall Gazette* libel case resulted in the same verdict and the same damages. It was brought by Hepworth Dixon, who complained that his appointment as chairman of the London Centenary Festival of Sir Walter Scott had been attacked in an Occasional Note on the grounds that he was "a man who was best known as a writer of indecent literature".

It was not an easy phrase to justify, and Smith got down to sifting through Dixon's books for obscene material. Dixon was the editor of the *Athenaeum* and the author of *New America* and of *Spiritual Wives*, where he had described an assortment of cranky communes and sects, some living in a state of "complex marriage". He claimed that writing of such things did not imply approval of them, and that he had simply been reporting. This anthropological excuse was apparently unacceptable. "What good was there", Smith's lawyer asked, "in giving the history and practices of these morbid and crazy people?" And he went on to read passages from Dixon's books, being "frequently applauded in his denunciation of the filthiness of the extracts".[4]

There is something unpleasant about such wallowing self-righteousness, and it is a relief to turn to the ludicrous stories of the next cases. In W.S. Gilbert's case against the *Pall Mall Gazette* in 1873 the problem was again prudery. The *Pall Mall* critic had objected to Gilbert's play *The Wicked World*; it was, he wrote,

> vulgar and coarse – vulgar through the air of barmaidish sentiment running through it, and coarse by the exhibition of endearments lavished on creatures in whom manner and bearing are doubtfully attractive. . . . And one line not only illustrates a dull bluntness which has marred some of Mr Gilbert's best works, but is unfit to be spoken in a theatre at all. Ethais declares that he is returning to the earth –
> "Where women are not devils – till they're dead".

In the course of the trial most of the play was read out by the officer of the court, but it was the actor Buckstone, rather than Gilbert's wit, that reduced the court to laughter; his facial expressions, and his pretence that he was too shy to reproduce his stage act in court, turned the whole trial into something of a farce. Gilbert lost his case.

The only time Smith had to pay more than a farthing damages was in a case brought in 1869 by one General George Henry De Strabolgie Neville Plantagenet Harrison. There had been an article in the *Cornhill*, "Don Ricardo",[5] which contained various odd stories from Spain, told to G.H. Baird Young by an English resident, Don Ricardo, including a story about "the notorious English swindler" General Plantagenet Harrison. The article had been published in good faith, everyone at the *Cornhill* believing the name to be entirely fictitious. Suddenly General Harrison turned up, angry because he had been branded a swindler and was therefore no longer allowed to carry on his current researches at the Public Record Office. He would not accept the offer of a letter of retraction in the next *Cornhill*, but insisted on taking the case to court. In cross-examination he admitted that he had been, like the character in the story, in trouble in Spain over a bill and had, like him, been imprisoned and expelled from Gibraltar. He emerged as an even more exotic character than the one in the story:

"You really believe, I understand, that you are the heir-general of Henry VI?"

"Yes, I do."

"And that you are rightful Duke of Lancaster, Normandy, and Aquitaine?"

"Yes, I am."

"And that your title has been recognized by the Queen under the Great Seal?"

"Yes, in a licence to Sir F. Thesiger as Queen's Counsel to plead for me."

"Her Majesty has not recognized your title in any more formal document?"

"No."

"It would be rather awkward for Her Majesty if she had, would it not?"

"Well, I don't know."

"Pray, have you asserted that you are Count of Angoulême, Flanders, Anjou, Alsace, and Champagne?"

"Yes."

"And of Kent?"

"Yes; but that was some years ago."[6]

But holding Harrison up to ridicule did not help the *Cornhill*. The judgement was that there had been defamation of character, even if it had not been intentional, and the fine was £50.

XV

Later Publishing

The *Cornhill Magazine* and the *Pall Mall Gazette* fed each other with new authors and supplied all the distinguished new names on Smith & Elder's fiction list in the last four decades of the nineteenth century, as well as Matthew Arnold, the Stephens and John Addington Symonds in non-fiction.

There was, first of all, still plenty of publishing for the Thackeray family one way and another, with constant new editions of Thackeray's novels and with the growing popularity of Anny Thackeray on her own account. It was of course natural that Anny's first efforts should have gone to the *Cornhill*. She had already had three essays printed there when she shyly asked Smith to read the manuscript of her first novel, *The Story of Elizabeth*. He accepted it – Thackeray himself was too overcome by emotion even to read the proofs – published it in five instalments giving her thirty guineas a month, and brought it out as a book in 1863. This was followed by half a dozen more novels and some collections of essays. She continued to write for the *Cornhill* all her life,* and she showered George Smith with kind ideas for other people's articles. "My poor Mr Smith," she wrote in a typical letter in 1865, "I know how you don't mind trouble

---

* After her marriage in 1877, as Anne Thackeray Ritchie.

when it is to help others out of it – please read this note from poor Mrs
Fitzroy – Would it be possible for you to give the poor soul a little
comfort? Could a scientific article be inscribed in the *Cornhill* about the
Admiral and his weather warnings?"

The idea for the Biographical Introductions to her father's collected
works, seems to have come from Anny herself. There is a letter from her to
Smith, undated, where she says:

> I have been thinking over my little dream of an Edition with notes of my
> Father's works. I brought a great parcel of his old letters down here to look
> thro' and there are so many things which would be of interest – as to when and
> how *Vanity Fair* was written for instance – as to his view of Ireland and Home
> Rule – notices of the books he is reading and so on – all this with the dates of
> where he was and where he wrote his various books and a few very little
> filigrees of mine would I think add to the interest of the books . . . . It may not
> be worth your while to reprint a new edition, with the added expense of me . . .
> but please think it over dear Mr Smith.[1]

Smith certainly welcomed the idea, and Anny started to work on it when
she had produced her own *Chapters from some Memoirs*. The edition was
advertised as "containing Additional Material and Hitherto unpublished
Letters, Sketches, and Drawings derived from the Author's Original
Manuscripts and Note-Books. And each volume will include a Memoir, in
the form of an Introduction, by Mrs Richmond Ritchie." The Introductions are the nearest thing to a biography of Thackeray that could be
allowed, since he had asked that there should be none, and they are entirely
delightful.

Smith had earlier been instrumental in saving some of the letters used
for Anny's *Memoirs* and those Introductions. Shortly after Thackeray's
death, Frederick Greenwood had a note from a Mr Julian Portch, saying
that his landlady had a collection of letters written by Thackeray to his
mother, Mrs Carmichael-Smyth, dating from his schooldays right on to
recent times. Smith had called round, and learnt that the landlady had
borrowed the letters from an upholsterer, who had found them in a drawer
of a table bought at the sale of Thackeray's goods. The upholsterer refused
to hand over the letters for Anny Thackeray, as her rightful property, even
after a solicitor's warning letter. Instead, he threatened to sell them in New
York. Smith bargained with him, managed to buy the letters, and

presented them to Anny, who immediately suggested the best thing would be to burn them so that they could not be lost again. Fortunately, Smith prevented her.

Anny Thackeray married Richmond Ritchie in 1877, and when their daughter Hester was born the following year Helen Faucit (Lady Martin), the actress George Smith had so much admired in his youth, was the godmother and Smith was the godfather. Judging by various thank-you letters that have survived, he was a very generous godfather too: "You had given baby *the piano*", Anny wrote on receiving a bowl in 1879. "What a kind but forgetful godfather to send her this golden bread and milk too. My daughter and I have nearly ruined you this year."[2] (The charge of forgetfulness came well from Anny, who was famous for it herself; she was so likely to arrive several days early for a dinner that, Smith said, there was often the double pleasure of entertaining her on both occasions.) When Hester was twelve, Anny thanked Smith for

> this great gift which I scarcely feel we ought to take only we have become so used to your kindness dear Mr Smith dear Lizzie . . . . I saw the letter and shall I confess it – I thought can it be a birthday present and a *postal* order did just cross my mind – then Hester came in beaming with her letter and when I exclaimed "Hester you are an heiress" she went on beaming and said "I don't feel different mom!"[3]

There was a tiresome coda to the Thackeray story in 1887, when Mrs Brookfield had her letters from Thackeray published in America by Scribner & Son. Smith had refused to publish such personal letters himself, and his copyright had prevented her from publishing them with anyone else in England, but once they had appeared in print Smith thought it best to bring out his own edition, giving half the profits to Anny. This edition caused an argument with Charles Brookfield in the *Standard*, and a highly critical article headed "Legality Morality and Publishing" in the *Saturday Review*,[4] which slightly implied that though the publication might be legal, it was not entirely moral: "The dates are doubtful," the article went on, "the notes confusing and not always to be found where they are most wanted; and, what is worse, an absurd and misleading index is added by the publishers . . . there is no legal cause of complaint, but it is unlucky that Mr Smith did not devote more pains to the matter." Any criticism about his treatment of Thackeray's family was particularly upsetting for Smith. He

[175]

took the attack personally, denied that the index had been added this side of the Atlantic, and insisted on a printed apology in the *Saturday*.

Smith's association with Trollope, begun with the first number of the *Cornhill*, continued for business purposes for the next ten years and for far longer as a family friendship. If *Framley Parsonage* brought distinction and popularity to the early *Cornhill*s, Smith for his part helped Trollope, not only financially but also by introducing him to literary London. After years in Ireland, Trollope was out of touch. The *Cornhill* brought him into the world of periodical writing, and no one could have been more appreciative of the social side of the *Cornhill* dinners. In his *Autobiography* he talked of the first of these dinners, where for the first time he met Thackeray, Charles Taylor, Robert Bell, G.H. Lewes, Russell (of *The Times*) and Millais – all later to become his close friends. The *Pall Mall Gazette* widened this circle further, to his great pleasure.

The success of *Framley Parsonage* led Smith and Thackeray to accept the comparatively feeble *Struggles of Brown Jones and Robinson*. This did the *Cornhill* no good but, though Smith was never Trollope's sole publisher, it kept Trollope on Smith's list, so that the reward came with *The Small House at Allington*, *The Claverings*, and *The Last Chronicle of Barset*. Besides these major works Trollope wrote occasional articles for the *Cornhill*, contributed a great deal to the *Pall Mall Gazette*, and in both places was full of ideas, introducing his brother Thomas, and through him various Italian contacts. One slightly perverse idea of Trollope's, when his reputation was at its height, was that he should publish a story anonymously so that it would stand or fall by its own merits; Smith was unwilling to experiment, and *Nina Balatka* was taken, on Trollope's terms, by Blackwood. There was no bad feeling, and Trollope continued to write for Smith. An interesting idea from Smith's side, which failed to materialize, was that Trollope should go to India in order to produce a travel book like the one he had written on the West Indies; Trollope was not over-keen – "I should certainly like to do the Indian book, but will not break my heart if the plan falls to the ground. *Per se* going to India is a bore, – but it would suit me professionally."[5]

The Smiths stayed with the Trollopes at Waltham Cross, and the Trollopes stayed with the Smiths at Brighton. In 1864 Trollope joined the distinguished group of authors whom Smith honoured with a portrait; Trollope's, like Thackeray's, was drawn by Samuel Laurence and, like Thackeray, Trollope was delighted.

Matthew Arnold was another author who entered Smith's life with the first year of the *Cornhill*. He entered as a poet, but after this first appearance he wrote for Smith only as an essayist and a critic. He became an occasional contributor to the *Pall Mall Gazette*, and his important articles from both the *Cornhill* and the *Pall Mall* were collected and reprinted by Smith & Elder. He liked writing for the *Cornhill* because, as he told his mother, "it both pays best and has much the largest circle of readers".[6] One way and another he wrote for Smith so frequently and so amiably that Smith kept a room always available for him, first at Pall Mall and then at Waterloo Place.

There are many letters from Matthew Arnold to Smith, about books, visits, plans, family matters. We find him joining Smith in the most unlikely occupations – playing billiards, for example, and planning a jaunt to the Derby. As it turned out, Smith was laid up with gout on Derby Day and he sent Yates Thompson to look after Arnold; Arnold had his pocket picked, and said sadly that G.S., as he called him, would have taken better care of him.[7]

In 1867 Arnold wrote to Smith saying he was short of money to educate his sons and asking to borrow £200:

> And why on earth should I come to you? you will say – Because you have treated my productions with a liberality the poor things were never accustomed to before, and I can offer you, by undertaking to write in no periodical but the Cornhill so long as the money is unpaid, a sort of security which is no regular security, indeed, at all, but which you may perhaps be willing to accept as one.[8]

Matthew Arnold realized only too well that his rather formidable essays were not likely to bring him a fortune. As he wrote to his mother about the *Celtic Lectures*, "George Smith well said to me, it is hardly the sort of book a British parent buys at a railway bookstall for his Jemima."[9]

One perceptive letter in this collection tried to console Smith for the failure of the morning *Pall Mall Gazette*: "Your not succeeding is due to your having succeeded so consistently before, and produced a newspaper quite unique and which the public will not abandon its preference for.''[10]

In 1876 there was a brief crisis when Macmillan, who published Arnold's poetry, outbid Smith for his prose, and Arnold considered accepting. Smith must have reacted quickly and generously, for Matthew Arnold's next letter said,

"You want to heap coals of fire on my head, but there was no need to send this cheque in order to prove that you were a liberal and generous man, for I never doubted it . . . . I certainly did not mean to withdraw my books . . . . they shall stay as they are and I accept your two letters, with their thoroughly friendly expressions, as an end of all difference between us. And I accept your kind proposals and your cheque in the same sense . . . I must really now endeavour, with time, to get all my prose books, at any rate, into your hands, or I shall have the look of playing you and Macmillan off against one another, which would be odious . . . . It now only remains to hold a feast of Concord at our joint expense at the new place in Soho.[11]

Matthew Arnold's son Dick often features in the letters. First there is friendly rivalry with Smith's eldest son – "Does George read? Dicky doesn't so I hope George doesn't'';[12] then there are schoolboy problems – "You have been very kind in listening to my anxieties about Dick, and I wrote to him much in the sense you suggested – look at his answer, which I think is satisfactory, though penitential sentiment is not exactly his forte'';[13] and again, when his son had clearly not behaved as well as he should have at Waterloo Place – "Dick has been blown up, and told he is never to sleep in Mr Payn's room again.''[14] But these were minor problems, and in 1882 we find Smith being asked to give a character reference for Dick for the civil service.

An unexplained and undated letter asked Smith, "How is the gout? and how is the cow? How could you think of buying a cow without asking me to look at her?" Smith certainly suffered increasingly from gout, but this seems to be the only reference to him as part-time farmer and cow-owner.

Matthew Arnold introduced the Humphry Wards to Smith. Humphry Ward edited *The Reign of Queen Victoria* for Smith & Elder in the year of the Golden Jubilee, and his wife, Matthew Arnold's niece, became the most important novelist in the last years of Smith's publishing career. Mrs

Humphry Ward was George Eliot's successor as a popular and formidably intellectual woman writer. She had first sent Smith & Elder a story when she was eighteen, and she had philosophically acknowledged its rejection: "*Ailie* is a juvenile production and I am not sorry you decline to publish it. Had it appeared in print I should probably have been ashamed of it by and by."[15] Matthew Arnold had told Smith that "Mary cannot write a novel. No Arnold could write one, otherwise I should have done it myself".[16] But she did write novels, starting with *Miss Bretherton*, published by Macmillan in 1884. Smith admired her writing and her intelligence, and when she brought him the first part of her next novel, *Robert Elsmere*, and asked him whether, as Macmillan thought it an unpromising theme and had turned it down, he would give her £250 for it, he accepted without even reading it and advanced £200 straight away. When it turned out that *Robert Elsmere* would fill three volumes, instead of the original estimate of two, Mrs Humphry Ward asked for, and received, a further £50;[17] in his *Recollections* Smith wrote that the extra was suggested by him and gave her "surprise and pleasure", but this must have been wishful thinking.

Robert Elsmere was a long book on a tough subject – the problems of new biblical criticism – and it was not an easy one to publish. "I well remember the depressed countenance of Mr George Smith – who was to be to me through fourteen years afterwards the kindest of publishers and friends – when I called one day in Waterloo Place, bearing a basketful of type-written sheets", Mrs Ward wrote in her *Recollections*,

> "I am afraid you have brought us a perfectly unmanageable book!" he said; and I could only mournfully agree that so it was. It was far too long, and my heart sank at the thought of all there was still to do. But how patient Mr Smith was over it! – and how generous in the matter of unlimited fresh proofs and endless corrections. I am certain that he had no belief in the book's success.

Even after Smith had persuaded her to cut it, Gladstone could say, "It is not far from twice the length of an ordinary novel; and the labour and effort of reading it all, I should say, sixfold; while one could no more stop in it than in reading Thucydides."[18]

It is astonishing how many people were happy to make the effort to read *Robert Elsmere*. Even before Gladstone's famous article "Robert Elsmere and the Battle of Belief" appeared in the May *Nineteenth Century*,[19] four editions of five hundred copies of the three volumes had sold out. Three

[179]

more three-volume editions were printed, then a six-shilling edition which sold 44,000 copies by January 1890, and a cheap edition which sold 23,000 copies at half-a-crown. These later editions brought Mrs Ward a helpful stream of royalties – nearly £3,000 by January 1889 – but the runaway sales of *Robert Elsmere* in America, just too early for the International Copyright Agreement, brought her only £100 – and that was from Lowell & Co., who had sold tens of thousands of copies. Endless pirated editions appeared, each undercutting the last, and Mrs Ward estimated that probably half a million copies were sold in America in the first year.[20] It was offered at ten cents, at four cents and, as a final indignity, the Balsam Fir Soap Company announced that "we have purchased an edition of the Hyde Park Company's *Robert Elsmere*, and also their edition of *Robert Elsmere and the Battle of Belief* . . . . These two books will be presented to each purchaser of a single cake of Balsam Fir Soap."[21]

The International Copyright Agreement became law in America in March 1891. Three months later Smith negotiated terms for Mrs Ward's next three-volume novel, *David Grieve*. "I met Frederick Macmillan in the Park this morning", he wrote to her.

> It flashed on my mind that I would sell him the American copyright of your book, and after a long talk (which made me late for breakfast) I promised him that if he made me a firm offer of seven thousand pounds for the American copyright, including Canada, before one o'clock to-day, I would accept it on your behalf. He has just called here and written the enclosed note. I am rather pleased with myself, and I hope that you will not reproach me.[22]

The book did not sell as well in America as had been hoped, and Macmillan complained to Smith that he could not afford to ride in the Park with him again; but he took the American rights of her next book, *Marcella*, with very much more success. *Marcella* was the occasion of some unusual inverted bargaining between author and publisher. Smith sent Mrs Ward an advance on royalties, and explained how much his firm expected to make from the same number of copies; Mrs Ward thought the firm would not make enough, and proposed a decrease of royalties on the first two thousand copies. "I hardly know what to say," replied Smith. "It is not often that a publisher receives such a letter from an author."[23] Next came *Bessie Costrell* and then, perhaps at the height of Mrs Ward's fame,

Sir George Tressady, for which Smith gave the enormous sum of ten thousand pounds. In 1898, still actively involved in the firm, he asked her to write Prefaces for the Haworth Edition of the Brontë novels, linking his last great woman novelist with his first.

Though Smith had such faith in Mrs Ward from the start, and though her books came to be admired by such powerful critics as Jowett, Henry James, Haldane, Huxley, and Meredith, it is strange that a hundred years later those books, not all as alarmingly long as *Robert Elsmere*, are just coming back into print after a long period when they were scarcely read. For many years Mrs Ward was remembered, if at all, only for her social work.

Two other authors who brought distinction to the house of Smith Elder and pleasure to George Smith himself in the later part of his publishing career were Robert Browning, and Queen Victoria. For Queen Victoria, the link was once again the *Pall Mall Gazette*. Arthur Helps, Clerk of the Privy Council, had contributed to the first number of the *Pall Mall*, and later transferred his essays "Friends in Council" to Smith & Elder. As a literary man in constant contact with the Queen he became in effect, as Smith said, "Her Majesty's literary adviser", and when the Queen decided to bring out *Leaves from the Journal of our Life in the Highlands*, it was Helps who suggested Smith & Elder as publishers.

"If it was an honour to publish Her Majesty's books", Smith wrote,

the distinction was not lightly earned. The office, indeed, involved an extraordinary amount of care and labour. Nearly every morning, when I arrived at my office, I found a letter marked "private and confidential", in Mr Arthur Helps' fine large handwriting. The letter almost invariably ran, "Can you come and see me for a few minutes: important." I had, of course, to go to the Privy Council Office, and hold an anxious and lengthy discussion with Mr Helps on some question – often of grammar or of literary form, in connection with Her Majesty's book. Ought a particular verb, for example, to be in the present or past tense? Mr Helps' loyal anxiety on behalf of the Queen's book dulled his sense of humour; it made him anxious to the point of distress about trifles which the Queen herself would have dismissed as indifferent.

The book was printed, in the first instance, for private circulation only, and we took unusual precautions to prevent any of the proofs going astray, and falling into unauthorized hands. The compositors employed on the book worked under lock and key, and were kept apart from other workmen. Only the exact number of sheets necessary for pulling proofs were sent into the room, and they were carefully checked on coming out. I chose men for employment on the book in whom I believed I could repose perfect confidence, and my choice was amply justified. The proprietor of a New York newspaper, with characteristic enterprise and lack of scruple, offered one of the compositors £1,000 for a set of the proofs, and offered the amount in vain! The book was finally printed for the general public, and had, I need hardly say, an enormous sale.

The 10s 6d edition of 1867 was soon followed by an edition at 2s 6d (which sold more than 103,000 copies) and a handsome illustrated edition at two guineas. A sixpenny edition was brought out in 1882. The royal connection also brought Smith the very successful *Early Years of the Prince Consort* by General George Grey, and Theodore Martin's five-volume *Life of the Prince Consort*.

The roots of Browning's association with Smith go back much further, to the days of Thomas Powell and the Museum Club. They had been friends in those days, and Browning had presented Smith with inscribed copies of his early books. In 1848, when he had settled in Italy after his marriage, Browning asked Smith to be his publisher. Unhappily, this was just the wrong moment, when Smith was struggling to keep the firm afloat after the disasters of Patrick Stewart, and he did not dare take on any major new publishing. The chance did not come again until twenty years later, when Browning quarrelled with Chapman and once more approached his old friend.

They had not, however, been totally out of touch for all those twenty years. Contact had been renewed when Browning, back in England in 1861 after his wife's death, wanted permission to reprint three of her poems that had appeared in the *Cornhill*. After that they met socially.

There was a surprising episode, which even more surprisingly Smith does not mention in his *Recollections*, when Browning seems to have been offered the editorship of the *Cornhill*. In a letter to his American friends the Storys, Browning wrote:

> Thackeray has just resigned the Editorship of the *Cornhill*. Why should I not trust you, what I know you will keep to yourselves – but what will certainly

amuse you, as nothing else I write is like to do? . . . the Editorship has, under the circumstances etc etc been offered to – *me*! I really take it as a compliment because I am, by your indulgence, a bit of a poet, if you like – but a man of the world and able editor, hardly! They count on my attracting writers, – I who could never muster *English* readers enough to pay for salt and bread! My first answer was prompt enough – that my life was done for & settled, that I could not change it & would not – but the conveyor of the message made me consider, in a flattering way, & I took the [week] to do so accordingly: I can't be sure how I shall answer – that's the end: for I have rather an impulse – first to get the salary, which Pen might find something to do with, – next to figure as a man actually capable of choosing better articles from the quantity always on hand than have illustrated the *Cornhill*, – and last, to try what the business is like. It requires *merely editing* – no line of my own writing – (*that* would be another matter). On the other hand, the little to do ought to be honestly done, might take more of my time than I choose to part with, – and what do I want with more money? I shall diplomatize accordingly – write for a full statement of what I am expected to do, if I accept, and what, and for how long, I am to receive in that case – one farthing less than Thackeray got, apart from the price of his substantive articles I shall not take, of course: and if I don't like the terms, the publishers have my bow, I have my little piece of satisfied conceit, and *you* have what is amusing you dear three, I engage!"[24]

By his next letter to the Storys, the idea has collapsed:

You surely never thought for a moment that I meant to accept Thackeray's glories whether discarded by him or subtracted by the Firm? I was simply amused at the notion of their coming to me – and a little flattered: I at once, however, told the messenger that there was no chance of my accepting – but he bade me think it over for a week: I coasted the week out, & then wrote that I had no sort of inclination to do anything of the kind, but that it was due to the politeness of the Publishers to give every attention to their proposal, & if, therefore, they would put it into black & white, stating explicitly what they wanted of me & what they would give me in return, my answer should soon follow. Since then, – silence! – as I expected: tho', from something I heard, they seem to have wanted the thing more than one would have fancied possible. All's as well with me now as it ever can be, and, as you say, what has Editorship to do with me?[25]

So, who was the "messenger"? There are no clues. Perhaps, if there was no offer forthcoming in black and white, it was only an unofficial approach, someone's over-enthusiastic private enterprise.

In a letter to Isabella Blagden in 1864, two years before his quarrel with Chapman, Browning wrote, "I saw Geo: Smith yesterday; – don't know his wife, who seems a very nice person; I like him, however, – his generous ways and unpretentiousness."[26] There are letters to Smith about dinners at Greenwich, and Fridays at Hampstead, and one telling Smith of Browning's Fellowship at Balliol so that the *Pall Mall Gazette* could be first with the news. It was natural that when Browning did break with Chapman he should once again turn to Smith, and this time Smith was delighted to be able to respond. On 11 November 1867 Browning wrote to him[27] asking whether he would undertake a new edition, in six volumes, of his collected works. Smith offered him five times as much as Chapman had previously given (so he must have offered £600), and Browning was happy. "You need no telling that your offer is a most liberal one which absolutely contents me," he wrote, "but I need some reflecting on the probability that you understand business, and will not harm yourself by your generosity."[28] Browning need not have worried, for this was the start of a change in his popularity and fortune. Such was the speed of publishing in those days that less than two months after the suggestion was first made, Browning was admiring the look of the book and its printing. Then came his major new work, *The Ring and the Book*, which, at Smith's suggestion, was brought out in four volumes at monthly intervals; it was a triumphant success, beyond anything Browning had published before, having a second edition the following year and greatly increasing the sale of Browning's earlier works which, together with his wife's, were now all transferred to Smith & Elder.

For the rest of Browning's life Smith remained his publisher. He guided him away from libel over *Red Cotton Nightcap Country*, he bought *Hervé Riel* for £100 for the *Cornhill* so that Browning could give the money to the sufferers in the siege of Paris, he reissued his old works and brought out his new. They now had a very good business and personal relationship. Browning gave poetry readings in Smith's house, and Smith helped him in all the ways he so much enjoyed helping his famous authors – in house-hunting for example, or in arranging for the transport of Pen Browning's paintings from Belgium and even lending a house for their exhibition. He bought, for a hundred guineas, Pen's portrait of his father. "Browning trusted me absolutely," Smith wrote. "I was deeply touched when his son related that, on his death-bed, his father told him that if he was ever in any difficulty he was to go to me and act exactly on my advice; and that all matters of business in regard to his works were to be left absolutely in my hands.''

When Browning died, on 12 December 1889 in Italy, the news reached Smith by telegram just after midnight. Feeling too disturbed to sleep, and perhaps also stirred by memories of his days as a newspaper proprietor, Smith searched out Buckle, the editor of *The Times*, so that the news appeared in *The Times* that morning. It was Smith who made all the arrangements for the funeral in Westminster Abbey, and he himself was one of the pall-bearers. The Smiths kept up their friendship with Browning's sister and with his son, visiting them whenever they went to Italy.

Adding to the great variety of books published by Smith & Elder in this period – novels, books of Indian interest, theology, essays, biography – there is an interesting new emphasis on medical literature, under the guidance of Ernest Hart, editor of the *British Medical Journal*. It was not entirely a new departure – *Gardner's Household Medicine and Sick Room Guide* went pottering on with ever newer editions through the second half of the century – but in 1872, at the sale of stock of a firm of medical publishers, Smith bought the publishing rights in Quain and Wilson's *Anatomical Plates*, Ellis and Ford's *Illustrations of Dissections*, and Ellis's *Demonstrations in Anatomy*. There were seventeen new medical books the following year, and forty-three by 1891. Hart also suggested and edited two new weekly journals – which both became monthlies after about four years – the *London Medical Record*, valued for its reports of foreign medical practice, and the *Sanitary Record*. Socially, Smith found that his medical authors added a new pleasure and interest, and he used to invite them to whist parties on Saturday evenings at his rooms in Waterloo Place. Ernest Hart himself – Jewish doctor, journalist, sanitary reformer, and collector of Japanese art – must have been the most colourful of them all and, as we shall see, he became by chance an important figure in Smith's life.

[185]

XVI

Sickness and Wealth

The publishing history has brought us nearly to the end of the century, but we must turn back to 1868 to see the changes in Smith's own life which had been going on in the background. He was then, at the age of forty-four, extremely prosperous and well established in Victorian intellectual society: he kept a carriage, rented a box at the opera, had a wide circle of friends, and sent his sons to Harrow. He was also extremely hard-working; his business was too large and too varied to be managed by himself alone, but he was not happy working in partnership with a brother-in-law with whom he was scarcely on speaking terms. Smith admitted that he did not easily share responsibility – "partnerships have their disadvantages as well as their advantages", he wrote; "I had been always accustomed to determine matters without reference to any other judgement than my own; to be, in a word, the 'captain of my own quarterdeck' and had the fault of being not too patient with opinions that differed from my own."

The solution, when in 1868 the arrangement with Henry King was due for renewal, was to split the business. A new firm, Henry S. King & Co., took over the agency and banking business and continued to run it from the old premises in Cornhill and Pall Mall. George Smith himself, with many of his old staff, moved the publishing business of Smith Elder & Co., including the *Cornhill Magazine* and the *Pall Mall Gazette*, to a very handsome house at 15 Waterloo Place. He looked forward to a happy and less strenuous life.

Things did not work out as planned. Recalling those times, Smith wrote:

> As soon as the pressure of work was lifted off my life – like Charles Dickens' famous cab-horse which having been taken out of the shafts, straightway collapsed – I immediately fell ill. My nervous collapse was complete and most distressing. For two years or more I may say I hardly had a night's rest. My nerves were so thoroughly wrecked that I could not sit patiently through my meals, and had to get up and walk about in another room. I lost my power of sustained thought. My courage went. I was whipped with vain and shapeless fears.

In fact it was a little less than two years, but it was a deeply depressing time. He remembered taking "gallons of chloral", and feeling that he had wrecked his fortunes and had no right to look his children in the face. His wife, who had earlier had to put up with his long hours of overwork, now patiently looked after him, took him away for rests in Yorkshire, in Scotland, and on the Continent, and gradually nursed him back to health. One night in Yorkshire he dined with W.E. Forster, the great educational reformer, in such a weak state that he felt intoxicated after one glass of sherry and had no memory of any subsequent conversation; meeting Forster later, he was startled to be greeted with, "Well, Smith, I suppose you saw I adopted those suggestions of yours about the Education Bill." When their travels took them to Florence, the Smiths were looked after with great kindness and understanding by the Thomas Trollopes.

As his strength returned, Smith felt the need for a fuller life. First he tried the exhausting experiment of bringing out a morning edition of the *Pall Mall Gazette*. When that failed he branched out in an entirely new direction which brought him much pleasure over the next eight years – he became a ship-owner. Working in partnership with Arthur Bilbrough, he spent the mornings at the shipping office in Fenchurch Street and the afternoons at Waterloo Place. He enjoyed meeting the sea captains and hearing their stories, and the business itself appealed to him, with its scope for enterprise and its need for quick decisions. Once more there is an echo of Waghorn, and a new outlet for Smith's experiences in worldwide trade. Smith and Bilbrough bought a commanding interest in thirteen or fourteen ships and built a large cargo boat which, to the disgust of its captain, Smith named "Old Kensington" in honour of Anny Thackeray's novel; the "Old Kensington" brought the largest cargo of wool that had ever been carried from Melbourne.

Smith tells a strange story of the contracts offered to ship-owners a little over a hundred years ago. The French government, he said, wanted ships

> to dispatch a large body of convicts – the product of the recently suppressed Commune – to New Caledonia, and our firm had a chance of getting the job. Bilbrough had already filled some sheets of paper with calculations. He proposed with his usual energy that we should start for Paris that evening. We went, and passed several days in negotiations. Whether we should have secured the contract I cannot tell; but we abandoned the attempt directly we learnt what the plans of the French government were. The general arrangements for the unfortunate convicts were harsh in every detail to the point of inhumanity. But one feature of the arrangements was quite too much for me. The French officials required that, athwart the compartment prepared for the convicts, should be iron plates extending from the keel to the deck, perforated with loopholes for light cannon, or for rifle fire. On any disturbance arising amongst the convicts the guards were to instantly fire through these loopholes, and to maintain their fire till every convict was shot down . . . . The contract was large and profitable; some eighteen or nineteen ships would have been required. But neither Bilbrough nor I could tolerate the idea of our vessels being turned into slaughter-ships, and we withdrew from the negotiations.

On his way back from that trip to Paris, Smith realized that his passport had been sent on to London packed in his baggage. Unwilling to be delayed or to risk missing the dinner party he knew his wife was preparing, he showed himself fully restored to a youthful vigour by choosing a suitable place and time to slip down a greasy pole from the dock to the deck, giving a little French boy five francs to keep quiet, and then quickly hiding his messy coat in a cabin.

The shipping business was profitable until steam ships increasingly took over from sail. Then, in 1879, Smith sold his partnership in Smith Bilbrough & Co., keeping, for sentimental reasons, only a share in "Old Kensington".

There were various other unexpected commercial enterprises, mostly, but not all, successful. Smith turned down a suggestion from his friends Arthur Helps and Theodore Martin that he should join them in a scheme for a pottery, but with other friends, Sir Henry Thompson and Tom Hughes, he was for some years involved in the Aylesbury Dairy Co. The Dairy did well with its literary directors, and in 1880 Matthew Arnold recorded going to a dinner given by the Company, "whose business has flourished wonderfully",[1] to celebrate its success. On the whole, Tom Hughes was known for generosity and good intentions rather than for business success; he was, in Leslie Stephen's phrase, "a most excellent fellow with muddled brains."[2] Smith tells how, when Hughes's idealistic settlement at Rugby, Tennessee, ran into financial chaos, he came to the rescue, helped Hughes sort out the problems, and lent him money. Smith also describes the different ways in which he and Hughes would go to an evening in a working men's club, a description which throws light on both their characters – "Hughes's method was 'Let us take off our coats and smoke a pipe in our shirt sleeves!' He aimed, in a word, to come down to the manners of his company . . . . When I had to preside at any meeting of that kind, or to attend one, I always put on my best frock coat and provided myself with a cigar instead of a pipe."

The spectacular Apollinaris deal, which brought Smith one and a half million pounds from a capital outlay of £3,000, a transaction which Smith claimed was a record in its day, arose almost by chance. Since it was so wildly successful, and since it had such great results for English literature – financing the *Dictionary of National Biography* – it is worth giving Smith's full account.

On a hot evening in 1872 when Smith was dining with Ernest Hart, he asked for some soda or Seltzer water; Hart offered him some Apollinaris.

I had never heard the name before, but the stone bottle was brought and I found the water very palatable.

A few days afterwards I accidentally met Hart in Pall Mall. The weather was still of a thirsty character, and I inquired "where he got the water with the long name which he had given me at his house, I should like to get some". I found that the porter of a little club, to which Hart belonged, imported it for some of the members, and he undertook to tell the man to send me a hamper. A few days later I heard from Hart that the water was sent to an agent in the city whose name he gave me. I procured a few hampers, and we drank the water for some months with general approval. At a dinner party one night it happened to

[190]

have been highly commended: at breakfast the next morning, while my wife and I were talking idly together, I said, half jestingly, "People seem to take to that Apollinaris water. I think I will go over to Germany and buy the spring." My wife laughed and said, "I think you have enough irons in the fire already." In a sense that was quite true. I was a newspaper proprietor; I was a ship-owner; I was a publisher; I was an underwriter at Lloyds; and my part in these vocations was very active and strenuous.

The matter rested for a few days until I happened to be dining at Hampstead with a Mr Steinkopff, a German, a merchant on a modest scale, who had bought from me a house at Hampstead. After dinner I asked him if he had ever heard of Apollinaris water. "Oh, yes," he replied, "it is a good deal drunk on the Rhine." No one else at the table had heard the name before, and eyebrows were elevated in doubt when I said I thought it would be a nice little speculation to buy the spring. At this Steinkopff himself laughed. Next morning however he called at my office in the city and asked me if I was serious in what I had said about the Apollinaris spring. He was going to Frankfurt the next day; should he stop at Remagen on the way and see the owners of the spring? I said there could be no harm in that if he did not mind the trouble, and it was understood that we might go into the matter together.

When Steinkopff returned he told me that the owners of the spring were willing to negotiate for its sale, and that the basis of the negotiation must be that the spring was worth £100,000. He added that it could, no doubt, be bought for half that sum. (It was sold in 1898 to the Apollinaris and Johannes Co., for £600,000.) I told Steinkopff it was out of the question to pay a very large sum for the spring. My idea had been that it could be bought for about £10,000; if this was impossible the idea must be abandoned, or the matter approached on a quite different basis. Could he get the owner of the spring to come to London? This was arranged; Mr Anton Kreuzberg came to England and we had a meeting at Mr Steinkopff's office.

After a preliminary and general talk I asked him what sale the water had in England? Kreuzberg said, with some pride, that last year they sold nearly 200,000 bottles. Would he sell me, I asked, 10,000,000 bottles, to be delivered at the rate of not less than a million bottles annually, and give me, as part of the arrangement, the entire monopoly of the English market? Kreuzberg was staggered at the proposal; he asked for time to meditate, and we arranged for a meeting the following day. Mr Steinkopff, too, was alarmed at the amount involved; I told him that if he did not like to take the risk, or counted the scale of the affair too great, I would take the transaction in hand myself.

The meeting was duly held the next day; Kreuzberg had risen to the level of my proposals and accepted them. Steinkopff's apprehensions were satisfied by

[191]

a provision that we should be free to abandon the contract at any time on paying a fine of two or three thousand pounds.

The water was largely advertised; it caught the popular palate, the demand for it grew fast and we had sold more than a million bottles before the end of the year.

In order to avoid a technical partnership, which might involve and perplex many interests, a limited liability company was formed, the shares being equally divided between Steinkopff and myself, a few shares being held by our clerks in order to comply with the requirements of the act as to the number of shareholders.

I had insisted on Hart being offered one-third share of the venture, but he did not see his way to provide his proportion of the capital of the Company (£20,000) in the event of its being called up. I was still wishful that he should have a salary as "scientific adviser" to the Company, and a small percentage of the profits after a certain dividend had been paid. As a matter of fact his literary gifts were more serviceable to us than his scientific attainments. He was chiefly useful in the business of concocting advertisements, and storing them with happy phrases, such as "The Queen of Table-Waters".

The business was new; it grew fast, and ran into great figures; the parties with whom we were dealing were foreigners and at a distance, and naturally, many unforeseen difficulties arose, many details not provided for in our original agreement had to be settled. I went personally to Remagen in order to settle many of these questions with the proprietors of the spring.

My knowledge of German was scanty, or even non-existent, and I took my eldest daughter, Dolly, with me as interpreter. I was always – happily for myself – able to see the humorous side of business affairs – and we passed a rather amusing week of negotiations at Remagen.

I had begun to forecast the probable area of the English demand for the water and framed my proposals on a large scale. A million bottles per annum was, I felt sure, a quite inadequate supply, and the term of ten years too brief. But when I proposed that the limit of the annual supply should be five or six million bottles, the row of listening Kreuzbergs fairly lost their heads. They became so excited that they could do no more business that day. They must calm themselves, they declared, by going off immediately for a long drive. We went with them. Two carriages were ordered from the hotel, and we had a charming drive to Altenahr, where a good deal of Rheinwein was consumed to aid the cooling process.

Ultimately we concluded an arrangement for the extension of our contract to fifty years, with certain powers of supervision as to bottling etc. which were very advantageous. The Kreuzbergs were cautious people, and probably felt they were wading in waters too deep for them. They pressed us to undertake to provide bottles for ourselves; they were afraid of fixing a price for the water which included bottles. The price of bottles, they reflected, might rise, and this, considering the stupendous quantities that had to be provided, would be fatal. We cheerfully consented to take that risk. The very scale of the quantities required, we knew, made it pretty certain that the cost would not be raised but lowered. This proved to be the case. The price of bottles fell, and under this head alone we secured an incidental profit of £30,000 per annum.

The scale to which the sale of Apollinaris water grew made many improvements in the method of handling it both necessary and possible. At first we were accustomed to pack the bottles of water in hampers, send them to Rotterdam, and trans-ship them thence to London. This meant handling them many times, and the breakages were enormous. It occurred to me that we might send small vessels up the Rhine direct, and put the bottles on board at Remagen, "binned", so to speak, in the holds of the vessels, with the contrivance of a spring to keep them steady. I endeavoured to charter a vessel to Remagen and back, but ship-masters are creatures of habit. This was a new route; it was supposed to be impossible to go up the Rhine and down again in any reasonable time, and I could secure no charter. I at last engaged a vessel at so much a week, and was much laughed at. I was asked whether I expected her back in six months or in nine months. But the plan succeeded; we reduced the breakages by an enormous percentage, and the new plan certainly saved the Company some thousands of pounds per annum.

Mr Steinkopff devised a system for checking the breakages. The system was most elaborate, and its working occupied the time of a small staff of clerks. Each bottle was followed and recorded through all its transit, from the time it left the factory until it reached our wharf in the Thames. All the men employed in handling the bottles received a bonus on the reduction of breakages. Here again, on what seemed a trivial detail, we made economies which ran into thousands yearly.

Apollinaris water was sold in England, America, Europe, India and the colonies. Care was taken over all details of marketing. Not only were the advertising slogans written by Ernest Hart, but George du Maurier was commissioned to design the bottle label. His first design, with a delightful but mildly indecent nymph rising from a fountain, was rejected by the board in favour of "a spring bubbling up among some reeds and a lovely evening sky"; he was sorry to abandon his "Venus Apollinaris". Table waters appeal to an upper-class market, and here the "Queen of Table

[193]

Waters" was clearly successful. It was advertised as suitable for "Good-wood Races, Volunteer Fêtes, Garden Parties etc.", and "Apollinaris and Champagne" were suggested for "Balls, Dinners, Suppers and Festivities". Anny Thackeray, visiting the Misses Gaskell in 1891, wrote home to her husband: "Meta met me at the station in a beautiful brougham. Pheasant, jelly, Apollinaris for dinner, champagne on the side table. It is very funny of what consequence one feels when one is paying a visit. The best of everything is not too good for one."[3]

It is time to say something about George Smith's family, and the way their lives reflected his ever-rising position in society. His eldest daughter Dolly (Elizabeth) took part in the Apollinaris story, as we have seen, as an accomplished interpreter. In 1877 her portrait by Helen Allingham was exhibited at the Academy under the title "Spring Days". The following year she married Henry Yates Thompson and was again drawn, this time by du Maurier as a wedding present. Trollope sent Dolly a charming letter of advice on her engagement:

> Of course I need not tell you of all the duties of your coming life. Your mother will have done that. How you must find out what he likes best to eat, – and never let him have it lest it should disagree. How you must remember always to sit up for him if he should ever go to the club. How you should always have your own way about anything inside the house because you are a woman, and take care that he never has his outside the house because he might go astray as a man. You have to be responsible for his morals, his dress, and his tempers. All this I am sure you will remember and not think that as a bride you are merely to have a good time of it.[4]

Yates Thompson is described in the *Dictionary of National Biography* simply as a book collector; having inherited books and manuscripts from his grandfather Joseph Brooks Yates, he built up a finer and famous collection of illuminated manuscripts, never keeping more than a hundred but always ready to change them for examples of yet higher quality. He and Dolly had no children and used their considerable wealth phil-anthropically, giving great manuscripts to the British Museum and the Fitzwilliam Museum, endowing parks and hospitals and adding an art school to Harrow, a library to Newnham College, and three rooms to

[194]

Dulwich Art Gallery. Two years after the wedding Smith handed over the *Pall Mall Gazette* to him and he kept it until 1892, when he sold it to William Waldorf Astor. Much earlier, in 1866, Yates Thompson had made an interesting proposal – he had offered to endow a lectureship at Cambridge for a visiting American, to be chosen by Harvard, to teach "the History, Literature, and Institutions of the United States of America"; almost unbelievably, Cambridge rejected the offer for fear of Unitarian influence from Harvard. As Leslie Stephen wrote to Lowell,

> Directly I went into the Senate House yesterday I saw at a glance that we were done for. The district round Cambridge is generally supplied with parsons from the University, who can be brought up when the Church is in danger. Beings whom I recognized at once by their rustic appearance, ancient and shiny silk gowns, elaborate white ties and shabby hats instead of college caps, were swarming all around me . . . . They began by bemoaning themselves about democracy without much effect, when one of them luckily discovered for the first time that you were Socinians, and that effectually did the business. Every intelligent man in the place voted for the professorship, including even Kingsley, who was very energetic about it, though he has been unsound upon America generally; but when once the Church is having its foundations sapped, and that by an American democrat, it would be easier to argue with a herd of swine than British parsons.[5]

The motion was defeated by 110 votes to 82, and it was not until 1944 that a visiting American professorship was established in Cambridge.

The Smiths had two other daughters and two sons. Each of their sons in turn spent nine years as a partner in Smith & Elder, but neither of them seems to have had his heart in the business. George Murray Smith, who married Lord Belper's youngest daughter, left the firm in 1890 to settle in the country and become chairman of the Midland Railway; Alexander Murray Smith, who married the daughter of Dr Bradley, Dean of Westminster, left the firm to spend his time on social work. The middle daughter, Ethel, never married and lived with her parents until their deaths, devoting her life to theirs in the manner traditional for unmarried Victorian daughters. The youngest, Isabel, married the barrister Reginald Smith in 1893. The following year he took silk, left the Bar, and joined Smith & Elder. In 1899, when Alexander Murray Smith retired, Reginald Smith became head of the firm, a more true successor to George Smith

[195]

than either of his sons. As Leonard Huxley, who became Reginald Smith's literary adviser in 1901, wrote,

> From the first Reginald Smith was in close sympathy with his father-in-law. Without equalling the older man's speculative dash, he shared his ideal of the publisher – in literature a trustee of the public, in business the actual partner and trustee of the author . . . . The possession of independent means enabled both men to show more concern for good literature than for mere profit-making.[6]

Reginald Smith also gave much time to his work for Poplar Hospital.

There was a strong tradition of social work in George Smith's family. After the death of his mother in 1878 and of his elder sister two years later, George was anxious to find worthwhile work to occupy his surviving sister. Possibly through Ernest Hart, who had become Henrietta Barnett's brother-in-law, he knew Henrietta and Samuel Barnett and introduced his sister Ethel to them. They were beginning to be well known for their work among the poor of Whitechapel, and Ethel Smith joined the band of devoted ladies who became rent collectors for houses that were run to provide accommodation at reasonable cost. Going on her rounds with her one day, George was shocked at the conditions he saw. He was moved, by a mixture of compassion and an urge for efficiency, to show that he could build a block of homes that were both better and cheaper, and still make a respectable profit. Using the same argument that Ruskin had earlier used to Octavia Hill, George Smith claimed that if he could show that building decent homes for the poor could be done on a business basis, bringing a return of five per cent, other people would follow his example. Smith's block for forty families in fact brought a return of only three per cent but this, Smith said, was because his standards of comfort and sanitation were high; there were window-boxes, a place for washing clothes and hanging them out on the roof, and "I thought it was impossible that the class of people for whom I was catering could lodge under one roof, and could maintain a high standard of cleanliness and health, unless each household were made a unit, and each family held responsible for its own tiny cluster of rooms."

Ethel Smith collected the rents and looked after the tenants' problems until her marriage, and George's interest still continued after that. All the tenants were invited to Christmas parties at Toynbee Hall and to country outings at the Smith house at Weybridge – the type of outing advocated by Henrietta Barnett in the *Cornhill* in 1881 in her article "At Home to the Poor".

Smith's views on charity had a Victorian severity. Rent had to be paid without fail, "for a too easy charity has a very enervating moral effect", though in cases of genuine hardship, Smith says, his manager " 'happened to know a friend' to whom she could represent the condition of affairs, and who provided whatever sum was necessary". Even so, he went on to write of a penniless old lady, unable to work any longer, who, before the days of old age pensions or national assistance, had nowhere to go but the workhouse; he was gentle in persuading her that she must go, but had no doubts about turning her out of her home. "It is odd," he commented, "to note the dread and hate the poor cherish for the workhouse."

One small contribution to his tenants' welfare met with unexpected opposition and had to be abandoned – he tried buying coal wholesale and reselling it without profit; his tenants were suspicious and thought this unfair to the local coal-dealer, although they had earlier complained of the poor quality and short weight of the dealer's goods.

XVII

The Dictionary of
National Biography

The social work described in the previous chapter was in keeping with the conventional liberal conscience of the late nineteenth century. But Smith's literary empire-building also led him to use his wealth in a more original way. While Germany, Austria and Belgium were starting to produce National Biographies through their state-aided National Academies, it gave Smith enormous pleasure that he could organize a British *Dictionary of National Biography* through his own friends and his own fortune.

On 23 December 1882 the *Athenaeum* printed an announcement, signed by Leslie Stephen, that there was to be a new *Biographica Britannica*. Lists of names to be included would, Stephen said, be published so that readers could point out errors and omissions, make suggestions, and volunteer themselves as contributors; a specimen "life" would be available. In the event, lists of 900 to 1,000 names, the proposed subjects for two volumes, appeared twice a year and the whole literary world was thus invited to enrol in the project. The *Dictionary of National Biography*, 29,120 lives written by 653 different people, was a triumph of Victorian amateurs, organized by the business ability of George Smith, with the literary and historical judgement of his editors Leslie Stephen and Sidney Lee.

The history of earlier attempts at national biography is littered with oddities and failures. The *Biographica Britannica* itself, which had appeared in seven volumes from 1747 to 1763 had, Sidney Lee pointed out, been the first Dictionary which aimed to cover all people of note, not, like *Athenae Oxoniensis* or *Foxe's Book of Martyrs*, just to record a particular class or sect. Lee[1] saluted it as a pioneer, but criticized it for capricious selection of names and length of lives, and for showing patriotic and class prejudices; besides that, too much of the good information was packed into unreadable footnotes. Still, as Lee admitted, unlike some of its successors it did reach the letter Z. The first attempt at a second edition got as far as F. In 1814 Alexander Chalmers achieved a 32-volume *Biographical Dictionary*, largely drawn from the old *Biographica Britannica* updated by obituary notices from the *Gentleman's Magazine*. Thirty years later the Society for the Diffusion of Useful Knowledge decided to tackle universal as well as national biography, with the result that seven volumes were needed for the letter A, and there the project stuck. Rose's *Biographical Dictionary*, still rather lacking in planning, used six volumes for A, B and C and packed the rest into a further six. John Murray considered taking over the problem and got as far as working on a list of names beginning with A, but decided it would be financially impossible. So, with plenty of past experiments to point out the dangers, and with continental National Biographies progressing under their state support, the idea was very much in the air and presented just the sort of challenge George Smith was willing to accept.

The *Dictionary* dominated the last nineteen years of George Smith's life. It was planned for two years before the first volume appeared on 1 January 1885; the sixty-third and final volume appeared in midsummer 1900, less than a year before Smith's death. Smith's own contribution was three-fold: the whole undertaking depended on his initiative and organization, it was backed by his money, and it was his idea that Leslie Stephen should be the editor.

Smith, planning on a characteristically grand scale, originally wanted to produce a *Dictionary of Universal Biography*. Fortunately Stephen soon persuaded him that this was impossibly ambitious. Limiting the project to national biography made it manageable, "national" being defined as inhabitants of the British Isles and the Colonies, whatever their origin – thus the entries range between the un-British names of Abbadie and Zuylestein.

Smith took constant interest in details of the *Dictionary*, even after he had practically retired from all other activities in the firm. It was run by a small staff with marvellous efficiency; every quarter, as planned, never a day late, a volume of 400–500 pages was produced – a contrast to the continental Dictionaries, which were appearing irregularly and over a far longer period. "To secure such unfailing punctuality", Smith wrote when it was all complete,

> needed sleepless vigilance, perfect organization, and, if I may use the word, a despotic will . . . . I have had my own anxious moments, of course, in the history of the book. Sometimes – say about 4 o'clock in the morning – I would wake and perplex myself with fears that, from a literary point of view, the work might fail. I was haunted by a dread of inaccuracies. But, on the whole, the work has been very well done and I am very proud of it. I venture to say that no other book involving the same amount of labour and anxiety has ever been published. Nobody who has not been behind the scenes, and witnessed the difficulties we have had to meet, can appreciate the real quality of the work. We have taken infinite pains, we have never grudged toil or expense. We have, of course, met with much generous help. Every eminent name in English literature has been, more or less, at our service, and the authorities of the British Museum have helped us in every possible way. There has been notably too a very fine spirit amongst the contributors, a loyalty to the interests of the Dictionary, a zeal to maintain its standard, a generous willingness to take infinite pains in its service. I suppose the sense that they were taking part in a great enterprise acted as some sort of an inspiration. They knew, too, that the Dictionary was not undertaken for commercial ends, nor designed to fill its originator's pockets. They were serving literature when writing for it.

The offices were rooms at no. 14 Waterloo Place, connected to Smith & Elder in no. 15 by a speaking tube.

> The small back room of the flat was the editor's sanctum. The large front room looking into Waterloo Place was the workshop; several large tables, many ink-pots, piles of proofs and manuscripts on chairs and tables, a little pyramid of Stephen's pipes at one end of the chimney piece, a little pyramid of Lee's pipes at the other end. The narrow side room opening out of it held on its shelves a fine assortment of reference books, sets of the *Gentleman's Magazine* and of *Notes and Queries*, Wood, Le Neve, and other biographical collections.[2]

The staff consisted of editor, sub-editor – later with an additional sub-editor – a compiler of lists of names, and a clerk in charge. The system as described by Leslie Stephen in 1884 was that he read and corrected all the manuscripts, Lee read the proofs as they came from the authors, and he himself then read the revises or the corrected proofs. The printers were Spottiswoode & Co., whose proof-reader, Frederick Adams, also corrected the proofs of the entire *Dictionary*. In 1888 Smith modernized the organization by employing a typist – "I do not care to see the young lady beforehand," Stephen wrote to him, "I do not think that we shall be able to give her much to do beyond typewriting . . . . I fancy that our typewriter will want some grooming. It may be a little rusty and the blacking has to be done. But I suppose your young lady is up to that – Is she to be in the next room?"[3]

The financial responsibility for the *Dictionary* rested with Smith himself, not with his firm. He was not, as Murray had been, inhibited by lack of money. Although he had made no public announcement that the *Dictionary* was intended as his gift to the nation, it became generally known that this was so; he fully expected to lose at least £50,000 on his investment of £100,000, and in fact lost considerably more without complaint. His endless enthusiasm made his family laugh at him – "When my children want to protest, say against the price I am about to pay for a horse, or any other extravagance, they don't say 'Remember *us*, Papa', but 'Remember the Dictionary'." He offered Stephen more pay for the *Dictionary* than for the *Cornhill* but Stephen refused, saying that the work was worth doing for its own sake and that after his *Cornhill* record he did not want to run Smith into further losses; if it should turn out a success he might ask for more pay or more help later. But though the *Dictionary* was welcomed and praised there was no sign of financial success; in 1887 Smith decided to raise the price from 12/6 to 15/- a volume, since the sales had been disappointing and the first nine volumes had lost over £9,000.

"Mr Stephen's qualifications as editor were manifold", Smith wrote.

He was a scholar, a student, a master of clear and exact English. He was an old and trusted friend, and there existed such perfect confidence between us that no scrap of formal agreement was required to define the terms on which he accepted even a task so serious as the editorship of the Dictionary of National Biography! Mr Leslie Stephen naturally hesitated a little before committing himself to an undertaking which must absorb him completely, and stretch through years. But he had faith in me, and the conception of the work kindled him. He took almost, if not quite, as keen an interest in it as I did myself.

The scope and shape of the *Dictionary* were the joint responsibility of Leslie Stephen and George Smith. They have both written of the importance of including minor as well as major names. Stephen quoted Cowper's comment on the *Biographica Britannica*:

> A fond attempt to give a deathless lot
> To names ignoble, born to be forgot.

All the same, he defended the policy of covering not just the great and the good but malefactors as well as benefactors, and also

> the second-rate people – the people whose lives have to be reconstructed from obituary notices, or from references in memoirs and collections of letters; or sought in prefaces to posthumous works; or sometimes painfully dug out of collections of manuscripts, and who really become generally accessible through the dictionary alone.[4]

As Smith put it, "The value of such a dictionary lies not so much in its account of the few great and rare men of the race, for enough ink is shed on them elsewhere, but in the fact that it saves the memories of an enormous number of useful and noble citizens from perishing."

Once the question of the range of articles had been settled, there was still the problem of relative lengths. "Our plan of employing specialists," Smith wrote,

> whilst it ensured each article being written with the amplest knowledge, rather increased our difficulties at this point. A specialist is always tempted to over-estimate the importance of his own particular department. An enthusiastic angler, for example, writing on, say, Izaac Walton, would naturally think his subject was of greater importance, and deserved greater space, than say Shakespeare or Newton. Each expert, in a word, cherishes the conviction that his own subjects are the most important ones in the whole volume, and he spreads himself out accordingly. It needed the cool and balanced judgement of the editor to adjust the relative scale of the articles, and the process was not always either easy or pleasant. Sometimes, again, human nature – the human

nature of affectionate surviving relatives – quarrelled with the scale of particular biographies.

Theodore Martin's life of the Prince Consort brought its own special problem of that sort. Smith tells how, once the life had been approved by the Queen, they felt unable to cut and alter it; the article was then criticized in *The Times* for its length. Martin happened to tell Smith at that time that he felt some of the *Dictionary* lives were too long – Smith agreed with him and referred him to *The Times* review.

Stephen's "clear and exact English" set the style of the *Dictionary*. His article on Addison, "a model of terseness and balance" as Smith called it, was the one sent to each contributor as a pattern. Smith, rather long-winded in his own writing, could appreciate conciseness in others. As Canon Ainger said in a well-known remark at a *Dictionary* dinner, the motto was "no flowers, by request".

The biographies were inevitably of varying merit because, as Stephen admitted, he had to employ "a number of second-rate (or tenth-rate) authors".[5] He explained how he had to struggle to cut away the fat:

> I used rigidly to excise the sentence, "Nothing is known of his birth or parentage", which tended to appear in half the lives, because where nothing is known it seems simpler that nothing should be said; and yet a man might have to consult a whole series of books before discovering even that negative fact . . . . [The biographer's problem is] to condense without squeezing out the real interest . . . he is not to pronounce a panegyric upon heroism, but he ought so to arrange his narrative that the reader may be irresistibly led to say bravo![6]

Stephen himself was one of the most prolific contributors, with 378 articles, including some of the longest (the first Duke of Marlborough, Scott, Byron, Swift). Professor Laughton, who wrote about all the naval people, contributed roughly the same amount but in a greater number of shorter articles. They were beaten only by Sidney Lee (870 articles, totalling, 1,370 pages, to their 1,000), who also wrote the longest article of all, forty-nine pages on Shakespeare – a record he himself was to beat in the Second Supplement with the 110 pages on Queen Victoria.

Leslie Stephen was the sole editor for the first twenty-one volumes, a third of the whole. For the next five volumes he worked in association with Sidney Lee until, for the sake of his health, Stephen had to give up the editorship altogether and Lee took over, carrying right on until 1916, four years after the publication of the Second Supplement. For a worrying nature like Stephen's, the *Dictionary* was a constant strain. His whole family were only too aware of the extent of the strain, from his wife who was afraid it was making him seriously ill, to his small son Thoby, not yet five, who, Stephen wrote to Charles Norton,

> produced a box the other day, which he called his "contradictionary box", and gave as a reason for the name that it was full (as indeed it was) of rubbish. What muddled notions had got into his little noddle I cannot imagine; but there were gleams of epigrammatic satire, as it seemed to me.[7]

Virginia believed volumes of the *Dictionary* had crushed and cramped Adrian and herself in the womb[8] – an image which needs considerable poetic licence, since she was born in 1882, when the plan had hardly begun.

At the end of 1886 Stephen was ordered two months' rest, and was sent to the Alps to recover his strength. In January 1888 he was writing to Norton that the "damned thing goes on like a diabolical piece of machinery, always gaping for more copy, and I fancy at times that I shall be dragged into it, and crushed out into slips".[9] Shortly afterwards he had a fit, and was warned that his brain must rest; his response was a gallant pretence that the *Dictionary* was no worry at all, he could cope perfectly well without in any way wearing himself out. His wife Julia was not convinced, and feared he would collapse completely. Smith was in a difficult position. If, as Julia wanted, he suggested to Stephen that he should retire, it would be taken as criticism and Stephen would be upset; it needed tact to make the decision come from Stephen himself, encouraged by his wife and his doctors. Gradually Stephen came to accept first that he could no longer be in sole charge, and then, in spite of his loyalty to the *Dictionary* and to Smith, that he must give up altogether.

Lee had been introduced to the *Dictionary* by Stephen, on Furnivall's recommendation, as a bright young man just down from Oxford who had already, as an undergraduate, published two articles on Shakespeare. The *Dictionary* became the main work of Lee's life. He was scholarly, exact, conscientious, and brought with him a much-needed atmosphere of calm and confidence. After he had served his apprenticeship under Stephen he felt fully ready to become editor himself, and worked in a happy

[205]

partnership with Smith to the end. Smith and Lee between them managed not only to maintain the high standard set by the first volumes but, it is generally considered, even to improve it now that the organization was well established, teething troubles were over, and historical scholarship was helped and encouraged by the earlier volumes themselves.

The first supplementary volumes, bringing the list of biographies to the end of the century, were planned in Smith's lifetime. They appeared in October 1901 and Sidney Lee's memoir of George Smith was added, together with the Watts portrait, to the 22-volume thin-paper reprint of 1908–9. Smith had also planned the epitome, "purely as a matter of business; I have no sentiment about it". He made a rule that none of the biographies was to be published separately, though occasionally – notably with Lee's lives of Shakespeare and of Queen Victoria – they formed the basis of future books.

The *Dictionary*, of course, generated dinners. There were dinners given by Smith for the contributors, dinners given by the contributors for Smith, and grand dinners to celebrate the completion in 1900 – a small party attended by the Prince of Wales, and a great banquet given by the Lord Mayor at the Mansion House. These celebrations were to have been followed by some public honour for Smith, but the proposal came too late. So he never achieved knighthood, but he did have great pleasure, in 1895, in an honorary MA from Oxford. Stephen was knighted in the Coronation honours in 1902, and Lee in 1911.

As the *Dictionary* was his own property, George Smith left it in his will to his wife in the hope that the work would always be kept up to date. With the help of her son-in-law, Elizabeth Smith saw that this tradition was started by bringing out the Second Supplement in 1912. In 1917, after Reginald Smith's death, the family decided that the *Dictionary* should be offered to the University of Oxford, on the honourable understanding that the work would be carried on by the Clarendon Press. As Reginald Smith's widow wrote to Sidney Lee, "Oxford University is the right place for the greatest achievement of my father's life and we all regard the Dictionary of National Biography with pride."

It was in the summer of 1899 that W.H. Fitchett, already a *Cornhill* author, arrived in England from Australia. Within twenty-four hours, he tells us in "How I came to know the Cornhill",[10] he was in Waterloo Place being overwhelmed by the breadth and charm of Smith's literary memories. Full of hero-worship, Fitchett encouraged Smith to assemble those memories, taking them down himself by dictation so that they could later be organized in a book. But time was short and only four articles were ready for publication in Smith's lifetime. In January 1901, after six years of some tiresome but unspecified illness, Smith had an operation, performed as was the custom of the day, in his own home in Park Lane. He seemed to be on the way to recovery, but died on 6 April, at the age of seventy-seven, while convalescing near Weybridge. He had kept his liveliness, his interest in publishing and his full mental faculties to the end; only six weeks earlier he had written to *The Times* announcing a reorganization of the Supplement to the *Dictionary*, so that it should include a biography of Queen Victoria.

As we have seen, when George Smith was on the brink of success Charlotte Brontë had written about him to Smith Williams: "I am sure he possesses a fine nature, and I trust the selfishness of the world, and the hard habits of business, though they may and must modify his disposition, will never quite spoil it." In fact, it does not seem that he ever was greatly changed or spoiled. The faults that show from time to time – the occasional high-handedness or intolerance, the hard bargaining when dealing with fellow-businessmen – are perhaps aspects of ambition, necessary for someone who is building his own empire. They are there throughout Smith's career, from his turbulent schooldays and his impatience with the slow-moving Alexander Elder, to his dealings with Thackeray's other publishers, his pantomime party at Covent Garden, or his quarrel with Greenwood. But though Charlotte Brontë may have been worried, and though Thackeray had commented on Smith's determination to have his own way, Smith did not let his faults get in the way of friendship. For his authors and his friends he had infinite kindness, patience and generosity.

Memorials were an essential part of the success story for Victorians. Smith's friends put a tablet in St Paul's Cathedral in memory of the man "to whom English literature owes the *Dictionary of National Biography* and whose warmth of heart endeared him to men of letters of his time." But more important than the tablet, Smith's memorial lies in the *Dictionary* itself, now a hundred years old and still appearing every ten years as he would have wished.

Notes

Chapter II: Early Days with Smith & Elder

1 For much information on Waghorn I am indebted to two pamphlets issued by the Postal History Society: *Care of Mr Waghorn*, by Marjorie Sankey, 1964, and *The Overland Mail*, by J.K. Sidebottom, 1948.

Chapter III: Publishing Under Alexander Elder

1 E.T. Cook, *Ruskin* (George Allen, 1911), vol. I, p.137.

Chapter IV: George Smith Takes Over the Publishing

1 Letter from Horne to Leigh Hunt, 3 June 1843, quoted in Ann Blainey, *The Farthing Poet* (Longman, 1968).
2 Quoted in Cyril Pearl, *Always Morning* (F.W. Cheshire [Melbourne], 1960), p.83.
3 Ibid., p.85.
4 Ibid., p.69.
5 *The Farthing Poet*, p.246.
6 Letter dated 3 July 1846 K. Tillotson (ed.), *Letters of Charles Dickens*, vol. 4 (Oxford University Press, 1977).
7 *The Times*, 10 Jan. 1849.
8 See articles by Wilfred Partington in *The Dickensian*, 1947 and 1948, "Should a Biographer Tell?".
9 Letter to John Ingram, 1886 (Thomas Wise (ed.), *Browning Letters*, Murray, 1933, p. 258).
10 Letter to F.J. Furnival, 1883, ibid., p.224–5.
11 Letter to Walter Slater, 1886, ibid., p.257.

Chapter V: A Crisis in the Firm

1 Letter to Ellen Nussey, 2 June 1851 (T.J. Wise and J.A Symington, *The Brontës: Their Lives, Friendships and Correspondence*, Oxford, Shakespeare Head Press, 1932, vol.iii, pp.240-1). Winifred Gérin speculates (*Charlotte Brontë*, Oxford University Press, 1967, p.483) that this letter might refer to George submitting to his mother's wishes and abandoning dreams of marriage with Charlotte Brontë; since he had in fact been through an economic crisis, and probably never had such dreams, that interpretation is unlikely to be right.

Chapter VI: Charlotte Brontë

1 Letter to Smith Williams, 22 June 1848 (Wise & Symington ii, p.225).
2 Letter to Miss Wooler, 7 Dec. 1852 (W & S iv, p.23).
3 Letter to Smith Elder & Co., 10 Dec. 1847 (W & S ii, p.159).
4 Letter to Smith Williams, 10 Nov. 1847 (W & S ii. p.154).
5 Letter to Smith Williams, Dec. 1847 (W & S ii, p.165).
6 Letter to Smith Williams, 28 Jan. 1848 (W & S ii, pp.183-4).
7 George Smith, *Recollections*, and *Cornhill Magazine* 1900.
8 Letter to Mary Taylor, 4 Sept. 1848 (W & S ii, pp. 250-4).
9 Letter to Smith Williams, 22 Nov. 1848 (W & S ii, p.287).
10 Letter to Smith Williams, 1 Feb. 1849 (W & S ii, pp.305-6).
11 Letter to Smith Williams, 2 April 1849 (W & S ii, pp.319-20).
12 Letter to Smith Williams, 31 Aug. 1849 (W & S iii, p.15).
13 Letter to Ellen Nussey, 4 Dec. 1849 (W & S iii, p.52).
14 *Villette*, ch. VII, and letter to Ellen Nussey 4 Dec. 1849.
15 *Villette*, ch. XX.
16 Letter to Ellen Nussey, 9 Dec. 1849 (W & S iii, p.55).
17 Hemlow, *History of Fanny Burney* (Oxford, 1958), p.128.
18 Letter to Patrick Brontë, 4 Dec. 1849 (W & S iii, p.54).
19 Letter to Ellen Nussey, 18 Dec. 1849 (W & S iii, p.60).
20 Letter to Mrs Smith, 17 Dec. 1849 (W & S iii, p.58).
21 Letter to George Smith, 17 Dec. 1849 (W & S iii, pp.58-9).
22 Letter to Mrs Smith, 9 Jan. 1850 (W & S iii, p.65).
23 Letter to George Smith, 15 Jan. 1850 (W & S iii, pp.67-8).
24 Letter to Ellen Nussey, 16 Feb. 1850 (W & S iii, p.77).

25 Letter to Smith Williams, 22 Feb. 1850 (W & S iii, pp.79–80).
26 Letter to Smith Williams, 25 April 1850 (W & S iii, p.103).
27 Letter to George Smith, 18 April 1850 (W & S iii, pp. 101–2).
28 Letter to Mrs Smith, 25 May 1850 (W & S iii, p.113).
29 Letter to Ellen Nussey, 3 June 1850 (W & S iii, p.115).
30 Letter to Mrs Smith, 28 June 1850 (W & S iii, p.122).
31 *Cornhill Magazine*, Dec. 1900.
32 Robertson Scott, *Story of the Pall Mall Gazette* (Oxford University Press, 1950, p.55).
33 Letter to Frances Wightman, 21 Dec 1850 (G.W.E. Russell (ed.), *Letters of Matthew Arnold*, Macmillan, 1901).
34 Letter to Mrs Humphry Ward, 18 Aug. 1898 (Janet Trevelyan, *Life of Mrs Humphry Ward*, Constable, 1923, p.166).
35 Letter to George Smith, 15 Sept. 1851 (Parsonage Museum, Haworth).
36 Letter to Ellen Nussey, 21 June 1850 (W & S iii, pp.120–1).
37 Letter to Ellen Nussey, 8 Jan. 1851 (W & S iii, p.197).
38 Letter to Ellen Nussey, 20 Jan. 1851 (W & S iii, pp. 201–2).
39 *Villette*, ch. XIX.
40 *Transactions of the Brontë Society*, 1909.
41 *Villette*, ch. XXVI.
42 Letter to George Smith, 3 Nov. 1852 (W & S iv, p.16).
43 Letter to Ellen Nussey, 12 June 1850 (W & S iv, p.118).
44 Anne Thackeray-Ritchie, *Chapters From Some Memoirs* (Macmillan, 1894), p.60.
45 George Smith, *Recollections*.
46 Letter to Smith Williams, 20 July 1850 (W & S iii, p.125).
47 Letter to Smith Williams, 5 Sept. 1850 (W & S iii, pp.155–6).
48 Letter to George Smith, 5 Aug. 1850 (W & S iii, pp.131–2).
49 Letter to George Smith, 27 July 1850 (W & S iii, p.127).
50 Letter to George Smith, 18 Sept. 1850 (W & S iii, pp. 158–60).
51 Letter to George Smith, 31 Oct. 1850 (W & S iii, pp.175–7).
52 Letter to Ellen Nussey, 20 Jan. 1851 (W & S iii, pp.201–2).
53 Letter to George Smith, 31 March 1851 (W & S iii, pp.216–7).
54 Letter to George Smith, 19 April 1851 (W & S iii, pp. 227–8).
55 Letter to George Smith, 11 March 1851 (W & S iii, pp.210–11).
56 Letter to Ellen Nussey, 2 June 1851 (W & S iii, p.241).

57 Letter to Ellen Nussey, 23 April 1851 (W & S iii, pp.228–9).

58 Letter to George Smith, 2 July 1851 (W & S iii, pp.258–9).

59 From text of Dr Browne's report on G.S., at Parsonage Museum, Haworth.

60 Letter to George Smith, 8 July 1851 (W & S iii, p.261).

61 Letter to George Smith, 22 Sept. 1851 (W & S iii, p.279).

62 Letter to George Smith, 7 Nov. 1851 (W & S iii, p.286).

63 Letter to George Smith, Nov. 1851 (W & S iii, p.292).

64 Letter to Ellen Nussey, 1 July 1852 (W & S iii, p.341).

65 Letter to George Smith, 30 Oct. 1852 (W & S iv, pp.13–14).

66 Letter to George Smith, 3 Nov. 1852 (W & S iv, pp.16–17).

67 Letter to Mrs Smith, 25 Nov. 1852 (W & S iv, pp.21–2).

68 Letter to Ellen Nussey, 9 Dec. 1852 (W & S iv, p.24).

69 Letter to Ellen Nussey, 9 Dec. 1852 (W & S iv, p.24).

70 Letter to Ellen Nussey, 11 Jan. 1853 (W & S iv, p.33).

71 *Cornhill Magazine*, Dec. 1900.

72 Letter to George Smith, 16 Feb. 1853 (W & S iv, p.46).

73 Letter to George Smith, 26 Feb. 1853 (W & S iv, pp.47–8).

74 Letter to George Smith, 26 March 1853 (W & S iv, pp.55–6).

75 Letter to Smith Williams, 6 Dec. 1853 (W & S iv, p.100).

76 Undated letter from Mrs Smith, in Parsonage Museum, Haworth.

77 Letter to George Smith, 25 April 1854 (W & S iv, pp.118–9).

Chapter VII: Marriage

1 Sidney Lee, *Memoir of George Smith*, in *DNB* Supplement 1909.

2 Letter, 1882, in National Library of Scotland.

3 Letter to Elizabeth Smith, 1859 (J.A.V. Chapple and Arthur Pollard (eds.), *The Letters of Mrs Gaskell*, Manchester University Press, 1966, p.560).

4 Letter to George Smith, Feb. 1862, in National Library of Scotland.

5 *Some Thoughts on Charlotte Brontë*: Centenary Memorial, Brontë Society, 1917.

6 Hester Ritchie (ed.), *Letters of Anne Thackeray Ritchie* (Murray, 1924).

7 Letter from G.H. Lewes to George Smith, 17 Feb. 1864, in John Murray Archives.

8 See ch.XI, pp.130–1.
9 Letter, 13 April 1901, in National Library of Scotland.
10 Kegan Paul, *Memories* (Routledge & Kegan Paul, 1971).

Chapter VIII: Mrs Gaskell

All Mrs Gaskell's letters quoted in this chapter are from *The Letters of Mrs Gaskell*, ed. J.A.V. Chapple and Arthur Pollard, Manchester University Press, 1966.

1 Letter to George Smith, 31 May 1855.
2 Letter to George Smith, 4 June 1855.
3 Letter from Patrick Brontë, 16 June 1855 (W & S iv, pp.190–1).
4 Letter to George Smith, 18 June 1855.
5 Letter to Marianne Gaskell, 27 July 1855.
6 Letter to Ellen Nussey, 24 July 1855.
7 Letter to Ellen Nussey, 3 Nov. 1855.
8 Letter to George Smith, 26 Dec. 1856.
9 Letter to George Smith, 20 Dec. 1856.
10 Letter to Ellen Nussey, 9 July 1856.
11 *Villette*, ch. XVII.
12 Letter to George Smith, 30 Sept, 1856.
13 Letter to George Smith, 2 Oct. 1856.
14 Letter to George Smith, 29 Dec. 1856.
15 Ibid.
16 Lock and Dixon, *A Man of Sorrow* (Thomas Nelson, 1965), p.504.
17 Letter to Storys, Sept. 1857.
18 *The Times*, 26 May 1857.
19 Letter to George Smith, Aug. 1857.
20 Letter to Ellen Nussey, 16 June 1857.
21 Letter to George Smith, 17 March 1858.
22 Letter to George Smith, 27 Dec. 1859.
23 Elizabeth Haldane, *Mrs Gaskell & Her Friends* (Hodder & Stoughton, 1930), p.206.
24 Letter to George Smith, 23 Aug. 1865.
25 Letter to Smith Williams, 1 Feb. 1862.
26 Letter to George Smith, 4 Aug. 1851 (W & S iii, p.266).
27 Letter to Marianne Gaskell, 1 June 1863.

28 Letter to George Smith, 2 June 1859.
29 Letter to George Smith, 29 June 1859.
30 Letter to George Smith, 23 Dec. 1859.
31 Letter to George Smith, 18 March 1862.
32 Letter to George Smith, 3 May 1864.
33 Letter to Marianne Gaskell, 2 Sept. 1865.
34 Leonard Huxley, *The House of Smith Elder* (privately printed, 1923).
35 Letter to George Smith, 12 Oct. 1865.

Chapter IX: Ruskin

1 Undated letter from Ruskin to George Smith in John Murray Archives.
2 Letter from J.J. Ruskin, 5 Aug. 1863, (National Library of Scotland).
3 George Smith, *Recollections*.
4 Quoted in E.T. Cook, *Ruskin* (George Allen, 1911).
5 George Smith, *Recollections*.
6 E.T. Cook, *Ruskin* (George Allen, 1911).
7 Letter from J.J. Ruskin, 9 Oct. 1860, in John Murray Archives.
8 Correspondence in John Murray Archives.
9 John Murray Archives.
10 John Murray Archives.

Chapter XI: Thackeray and the Cornhill Magazine

1 Gordon Ray, *Thackeray, The Age of Wisdom* (Oxford University Press, 1958, p.222).
2 Anne Thackeray Ritchie, *Chapters From Some Memoirs* (Macmillan, 1894), p.130.
3 Quoted in Gordon Ray, *Thackeray, The Age of Wisdom*, p.222.
4 Letter to Thackeray (National Library of Scotland).
5 Letter to Smith (National Library of Scotland).
6 Letter to Smith (National Library of Scotland).
7 *Cornhill*, Jan. 1910.
8 Letter to Smith, 7 Sept. 1859 (Gordon Ray (ed.), *Letters & Private Papers of W.M. Thackeray*, Oxford University Press, 1946, vol. iv, p.149).
9 Letter to Charles Lever, 27 June 1859 (ibid., iv, p.144).
10 *Cornhill*, July 1896.

11 Trollope, *Autobiography*, ch. VIII.
12 Letter to Smith, 5 Dec. 1859 (National Library of Scotland).
13 Biographical Introduction to *Philip*.
14 J.T. Fields, *Yesterdays with Authors* (Boston, 1900, facsimile reprinted AMS Press, NY, 1970).
15 Trollope, *Autobiography*, ch. VIII.
16 Letter to Smith, 23 Dec. 1859 (Chapple and Pollard).
17 Letter to Smith, 14 March 1860 (National Library of Scotland).
18 Letter to Smith, 1862 (National Library of Scotland).
19 Letter to Smith, 1860 (National Library of Scotland).
20 Letter to Smith, 1860 (National Library of Scotland).
21 Letter to Smith, 12 Feb. 1860 (Michael Sadleir, *Trollope*, ch. V, Constable, 1927; Oxford Paperback, 1961).
22 Letter to Smith (John Murray Archives).
23 George Smith, *Recollections*.
24 Letter to Smith, June 1860 (Ray (ed.) *Letters of W.M.T.*, iv, pp.189–90).
25 Letter to Smith (National Library of Scotland).
26 Letter to Thackeray, 2 May 1861 (National Library of Scotland).
27 *Roundabout Paper* No.5.
28 Letters to Smith, March 1862 (Ray (ed.) *Letters of W.M.T.*, iv, pp.256–7).
29 *Cornhill*, April 1862.
30 Letter to Smith, 18 July 1863 (National Library of Scotland).
31 Letter to Smith, 1 July 1862 (Ray (ed.) *Letters of W.M.T.*, iv, pp.269–70).
32 Letter to Smith, 17 Dec 1863 (ibid., p.295).
33 See Chapter XV, "Later Publishing", p.175.
34 Letter to Smith, Aug. 1864.
35 25 Jan. 1864 (John Murray Archives).
36 Correspondence, August 1864 (John Murray Archives).
37 John Murray Archives.
38 John Murray Archives.
39 28 Feb. 1865 (John Murray Archives).
40 5 April 1865 (John Murray Archives).

Chapter XII: The Cornhill after Thackeray

1 John Murray Archives.
2 G.H. Lewes, *Journal* 27 Feb. 1862 (Gordon Haight, *George Eliot*, Oxford University Press, 1968).
3 G.H. Lewes, *Journal*, 17 May 1862, ibid.
4 19 May 1862 (Gordon Haight (ed.), *The George Eliot Letters*, Oxford University Press, 1954-6, vol. iv, pp.34-5).
5 20 May 1862, ibid., pp.35-6.
6 Haight, *George Eliot*, ch. XI.
7 Haight (ed.) *George Eliot Letters*, iv, p.38.
8 Ibid.
9 Undated letter in John Murray Archives.
10 Letter to Smith, 25 Sept. 1880 (John Murray Archives).
11 George Smith, *Recollections*.
12 Letter to Smith, 6 Aug. 1864 (John Murray Archives).
13 25 Oct. 1864.
14 *Pall Mall Gazette*, 1868.
15 Letter to Smith, 2 Jan. 1866 (National Library of Scotland).
16 F.W. Maitland, *Life of Leslie Stephen*, (Duckworth, 1906), p.257.
17 Ibid., p.258.
18 *Cornhill*, Jan. 1910.
19 *Manchester Guardian*, 23 Feb. 1904.
20 Maitland, p.268.
21 Dec. 1872 (Maitland, pp.270-1).
22 Letter to Hardy (Maitland, p.274).
23 Maitland, p.276.
24 Letter to Smith, 23 Sept. 1880 (National Library of Scotland).
25 3 Dec. 1876 (Maitland, p.295).
26 Maitland, p.369.
27 31 Oct. 1882 (Maitland, pp.353-4).
28 In 1864.
29 *Murray's* 1891, *Longman's* 1905, *Temple Bar* 1906, *Macmillan's* 1907.

Chapter XIII: The Pall Mall Gazette

For information about the *Pall Mall Gazette* in general, and about

Frederick Greenwood in particular, I am indebted to J.W. Robertson Scott, *The Story of The Pall Mall Gazette* (Oxford University Press, 1950).

1 Kennedy Jones on *Evening News* in *Fleet Street & Downing Street* (Hutchinson, 1919).
2 Letter to his mother, 3 Feb. 1866 (G.W.E. Russell, (ed.), *Letters of Matthew Arnold*, Macmillan, 1901).
3 George Smith, *Recollections*.
4 Ibid.
5 F.W. Maitland, *Life of Leslie Stephen* (Duckworth, 1906), p.238.
6 Marx to Engels, 3 Aug 1870.
7 10,000th issue of the *Pall Mall Gazette*, 14 April 1897.
8 *History of The Times*.
9 Leslie Stephen, *Life of Fitzjames Stephen* (Smith & Elder, 1895), p.214.
10 Ibid., p.241.
11 Ibid., pp.213–14, note.
12 Letter to Oliver Wendell Holmes, 8 Nov. 1866 (Maitland, pp.182–3).
13 Trollope, *Autobiography*, ch. XI.
14 Letter to Smith, 1865, quoted in Michael Sadleir, *Trollope*, ch. VIII.
15 Trollope, *Autobiography*, ch. XI.
16 Darwin to Hooker, 10 Feb. 1868 (Francis Darwin (ed.), *Life & Letters of Charles Darwin*, Murray, 1887, vol. iii, p.76).
17 Darwin to Wallace (ibid., iii, p.138).
18 Undated letter to Smith, in possession of Belinda Norman-Butler.
19 Letter to his mother, 3 Feb. 1866 (G.E.W. Russell (ed.) *Arnold Letters*).
20 Trollope, *Autobiography*, ch. XI.
21 See ch. XVI, p.187.
22 Letter to Oliver Wendell Holmes, 23 Dec. 1869 (Maitland, pp.214–15).
23 10,000th issue of the *Pall Mall Gazette*, 14 April 1897.
24 Letter to Charles Norton, 28 April 1880 (Maitland, p.340).

Chapter XIV: Libels

1 *Cornhill*, Feb. 1901: George Smith, "Lawful Pleasures".

2 *Pall Mall Gazette*, 10 Nov. 1865.
3 *Cornhill*, Feb. 1901: George Smith, "Lawful Pleasures".
4 *The Times*, Nov, 1872.
5 *Cornhill*, April 1868.
6 *The Times*, June 1869.

Chapter XV: Later Publishing

1 Letter, circa 1890, in possession of Belinda Norman-Butler.
2 Letter in possession of Belinda Norman-Butler.
3 Letter, 19 June 1890, in possession of Belinda Norman-Butler.
4 15 Oct. 1887.
5 Letter, 3 July 1860 (Michael Sadleir, *Trollope*, ch.VI).
6 Letter to his mother, 16 June 1863 (G.W.E. Russell (ed.), *Letters of Matthew Arnold*, Macmillan, 1901).
7 George Smith, *Recollections*.
8 Letter, 1 March 1867 (National Library of Scotland).
9 Letter, 10 Feb. 1867 (G.W.E. Russell (ed.), *Letters of Matthew Arnold*, Macmillan, 1901).
10 Letter, 5 May 1870 (National Library of Scotland).
11 Letter, 29 Jan. 1876 (National Library of Scotland).
12 Undated letter in National Library of Scotland.
13 Undated letter in National Library of Scotland.
14 Undated letter in National Library of Scotland.
15 Letter, 1 Oct. 1869 (Janet Trevelyan, *Life of Mrs Humphry Ward*, Constable, 1923, p.25).
16 George Smith, *Recollections*.
17 Letter, 11 May 1886 (John Murray Archives).
18 Letter to Lord Acton (Janet Trevelyan, *Life of Mrs Humphry Ward*, p.56).
19 *Nineteenth Century*, May 1888.
20 Mrs Humphry Ward, *Recollections* (Collins, 1918) p.252.
21 Janet Trevelyan, *Mrs Humphry Ward*, p.75.
22 Ibid., p.97.
23 Ibid., p.109.
24 Letter, 19 March 1862 (Gertrude Reese Hudson (ed.), *Browning to his American Friends*, Bowes & Bowes, 1965).

25 Letter, 10 April 1862, ibid.
26 Letter, 19 Oct. 1864 (*Browning Letters*, Thomas Wise (ed.), Murray, 1933, p.82).
27 Letter in John Murray Archives.
28 Letter, 10 Dec. 1867 (John Murray Archives).

Chapter XVI: Sickness and Wealth

1 Letter to his Son, 3 Dec. 1880 (G.W.E. Russell (ed.), *Letters of Matthew Arnold*, Macmillan, 1901).
2 Leslie Stephen, *Mausoleum Book*, (Oxford University Press, 1977).
3 Nov. 1891 (*Letters of Anne Thackeray Ritchie*, Murray, 1924).
4 13 March 1878 (National Library of Scotland).
5 F.W. Maitland, *Life of Leslie Stephen*, (Duckworth, 1906), p.177.
6 *Dictionary of National Biography*.

Chapter XVII: The Dictionary of National Biography

1 *Cornhill*, March 1896: "National Biography".
2 C.H. Firth, *Memoir of Sidney Lee* in *Dictionary of National Biography*, 1912–21.
3 Letter in National Library of Scotland.
4 Leslie Stephen, *Studies of a Biographer*, vol.i (Duckworth, 1898).
5 Letter, 21 Sept. 1884, in National Library of Scotland.
6 Leslie Stephen, *Studies of a Biographer*, vol. i. (Duckworth, 1898).
7 23 Aug. 1885 (F.W. Maitland, *Life of Leslie Stephen*, (Duckworth, 1906), p.387).
8 Quentin Bell, *Virginia Woolf*, vol. i, (Hogarth Press, 1973).
9 11 Jan. 1888 (Maitland, p.394).
10 *Cornhill*, Jan. 1910.

Bibliography

1 *Manuscript Sources*
  Smith, George, *Recollections of a Long and Busy Life*, on loan to
    National Library of Scotland
  Smith Elder Archives, in the National Library of Scotland
  John Murray Archives
  Archives in the Parsonage Museum, Haworth
  Huxley, Leonard, *History of the House of Smith Elder*, privately printed
    1923

2 *Published Works*
  Blainey, Ann, *The Farthing Poet*, Longman 1968
  Brontë, Charlotte, *Villette*
  Brontë Society, *Transactions*
  Chapple, J.A.V. and Pollard, Arthur (eds.), *Letters of Mrs Gaskell*,
    Manchester University Press 1966
  Cook, E.T., *Ruskin*, George Allen 1911
  Cornhill Magazine
  Dickensian, The, 1947 and 1948
  Dictionary of National Biography
  Fields, J.T., *Yesterdays with Authors*, Boston 1900, Facsimile reprinted
    ANS Press N.Y. 1970
  Gaskell, Mrs, *Life of Charlotte Brontë*
  Gérin, Winifred, *Charlotte Brontë*, Oxford University Press 1967
  — *Mrs Gaskell*, Oxford University Press 1976
  — *Anne Thackeray Ritchie* Oxford University Press 1981
  Haight, Gordon, *George Eliot*, Oxford University Press 1968
  — (ed.), *The George Eliot Letters*, Oxford University Press 1954–6
  Haldane, Elizabeth, *Mrs Gaskell and Her Friends*, Hodder and
    Stoughton 1930

Hudson, Gertrude Reese, (ed.), *Browning to his American Friends*, Bowes and Bowes 1965

Kegan Paul, C. *Memories*, Routledge and Kegan Paul 1971

Lock, J. and Dixon, W.T., *A Man of Sorrow*, Thomas Nelson 1965

Maitland, F.W., *Life of Leslie Stephen*, Duckworth 1906

Pall Mall Gazette

Pearl, Cyril, *Always Morning*, F.W. Cheshire (Melbourne) 1960

Ray, Gordon, *Thackeray: The Age of Wisdom*, Oxford University Press 1958

— (ed.), *Letters and Private Papers of W.M. Thackeray*, Oxford University Press 1946

Ritchie, Hester (ed.), *Letters of Anne Thackeray Ritchie*, Murray 1924

Russell, G.W.E. (ed.), *Letters of Matthew Arnold*, Macmillan 1901

Sadleir, Michael, *Trollope*, Constable 1927; Oxford Paperback 1961

Sankey, Marjorie, *Care of Mr Waghorn*, Postal History Society 1964

Scott, Robertson, *Story of the Pall Mall Gazette*, Oxford University Press 1950

Sidebottom, J.K., *The Overland Mail*, Postal History Society 1948

Stephen, Leslie, *Life of Fitzjames Stephen*, Smith Elder 1895

— *Studies of a Biographer*, Duckworth 1898

— *Mausoleum Book*, Oxford University Press 1977

Thackeray Ritchie, Anne, *Chapters from Some Memoirs*, Macmillan 1894

Tillotson, K. (ed.), *Letters of Charles Dickens*, Oxford University Press 1977

Trevelyan, Janet, *Life of Mrs Humphry Ward*, Constable 1923

Trollope, Anthony, *Autobiography*

Ward, Mrs Humphry, *Recollections*, Collins 1918

Wise, Thomas, (ed.), *Letters of Robert Browning*, Murray 1933

Wise, T.J. and Symington, J.A., (eds.), *The Brontës: Their Lives, Friendships and Correspondence*, Oxford, Shakespeare Head Press 1932

Index

Blackwood's Magazine, 140
Blagden, Isabella, 184
Blakeway, Elizabeth (later Mrs
George Smith), 77–85, 101,
126, 129, 146, 162, 175, 191,
206
Blanc, Dr, 80
Bowring, Sir John, 125
Bradley, Dr (Dean of
Westminster), 195
British Medical Journal, 185
Brontë, Anne, 53, 54, 81, 90
Brontë, Branwell, 54, 89, 90
Brontë, Charlotte, 13, 31, 47,
49–75, 118, 120, 127–8, 207;
Gaskell *Life*, 87–93
Brontë, Emily, 54, 85
Brontë, Patrick, 60, 88, 90, 91
Brontë Society *Transactions*, 61,
64
Brookfield, Charles, 175
Brookfield, Mrs, 67, 134, 175
Brother Jacob (Eliot), 139, 140
Brown, Dr (phrenologist), 62,
70–71, 73
Browning, Elizabeth Barrett, 37,
85, 127, 184
Browning, Robert, 40, 43, 46, 82,
85, 181, 182–5
Burgoyne, General Sir John, 125
Burton, Frederick, 83–4
Byron Gallery, The, 27

Cameron, Julia, 83
Capes, J.M., 168

Carmichael-Smyth, Mrs, 134,
136, 174
Celtic Lectures (Arnold), 177
Chalmers, Alexander, 200
Chambers' Journal, 147
Chapman, Edward, 89, 99, 119,
134–6
Chapman, Thomas, 41
Chapters from Some Memoirs
(Anny Thackeray), 83, 136
Christmas Books (William
Makepeace Thackeray), 118,
121, 135
Chronicles of London Bridge, 27
Claverings, The (Trollope), 142,
144, 176
*Clergymen of the Church of
England* (Trollope), 160
Clive, Mrs Archer, 125
Cloister and the Hearth, The
(Reade), 81
Coast Scenery (Stanfield), 27
Cole, Henry, 134
Collins, Wilkie, 79, 98, 142–3
Cook, Dutton, 137, 143
Cook, Edward, 145
Coral Reefs (Darwin), 29
Cornhill Gallery, The, 128
Cornhill Magazine, 13, 38, 81,
82, 84, 97, 98, 99, 101, 102,
103, 113, 115, 119, 120,
121–48, 152, 154, 159, 167,
170, 171, 173, 176, 177,
182–3, 187, 197, 202, 206
Courtney, Miss, 162
"Cousin Phillis" (Gaskell), 29
Cousin Stella, 95